# Excusing Sinners and Blaming God

# Princeton Theological Monograph Series

K. C. Hanson, Charles M. Collier, D. Christopher Spinks,
and Robin A. Parry, Series Editors

# Excusing Sinners and Blaming God

*A Calvinist Assessment of Determinism, Moral
Responsibility, and Divine Involvement in Evil*

Guillaume Bignon

foreword by

Paul Helm

☞PICKWICK *Publications* · Eugene, Oregon

EXCUSING SINNERS AND BLAMING GOD
A Calvinist Assessment of Determinism, Moral Responsibility, and Divine
Involvement in Evil

Pickwick Publications
An Imprint of Wipf and Stock Publishers
199 W. 8th Ave., Suite 3
Eugene, OR 97401

www.wipfandstock.com

PAPERBACK ISBN: 978-1-5326-1865-9
HARDCOVER ISBN: 978-1-4982-4441-1
EBOOK ISBN: 978-1-4982-4440-4

*Cataloguing-in-Publication data:*

Names: Bignon, Guillaume | Helm, Paul, foreword

Title: Excusing sinners and blaming God : a Calvinist assessment of determinism, moral responsibility, and divine involvement in evil / Guillaume Bignon.

Description: Eugene, OR: Pickwick Publications, 2018 | Series: Princeton Theo-
logical Monograph Series | Includes bibliographical references.

Identifiers: ISBN 978-1-5326-1865-9 (paperback) | ISBN 978-1-4982-4441-1
(hardcover) | ISBN 978-1-4982-4440-4 (ebook)

Subjects: LCSH: Freewill and determinism—Religious aspects | Calvinism |
Freewill and determinism—Philosophical aspects | Providence and the govern-
ment of God | Responsibility

Classification: BL51 G845 2018 (print) | BL51 (ebook)

Permission has been granted by the editor of *Philosophia Christi* to use parts of
"The Distasteful Conditional Analysis: On Compatibilism and the Not-so-Wretch-
ed Counterfactual Ability to Do Otherwise" (*Philosophia Christi* 18.2). Parts of
this book are based on this essay in *PC*. More info can be found about *Philosophia
Christi* at www.epsociety.org.

Manufactured in the U.S.A.                                    11/27/17

To my lovely wife Katherine,
selfless enabler of this work, and *femme extraordinaire*.

# Contents

# Foreword

THIS IS NOT THEOLOGICAL WORK but it is nonetheless concerned with the advocacy and defense of Reformed religion. In Guillaume's estimate, that religion is committed to compatibilism. Here compatibilism is given a thorough defense. I'd say, as thorough a defense as you'll find. So the book can be thought of as a work of apologetics. It is concerned to offer sustained defenses against crucial objections to compatibilism, that determinism destroys human moral responsibility, and ensures that God is the author of sin. The objection goes, on compatibilism God would not be merely the decreer of sin, he is himself a sinner. The book is rammed full of arguments about such charges, providing arguments for compatibilism, arguments against libertarianism, arguments on God and evil.

Does determinism undermine free will, turning men and women into puppets or automata without them realizing it? Guillaume offers new arguments brought by contemporary analytic philosophers as well as new versions of older ones. Particularly significant are those in which libertarians beg the question without realizing it, because they work with an indeterministic view of agency as the norm, arguing as if compatibilists are all the time inconsistent libertarians.

Guillaume has a voracious appetite for hunting down objections to compatibilism wherever he can, and delights in spotting weaknesses in the formulation of an argument, then reformulating it into the strongest version he can think of, in order to make the objection he is considering as pointed and clear as a form as he can. He has not hidden from any objection he has come across. His is a frank and open treatment. He takes on all the objections to compatibilism he can find, except the objection that compatibilism is not libertarianism, in defense of Calvinism. Even if the reader does not like the sound of Calvinism, much less a defense of Calvinism, he or she will find Guillaume's arguments engaging.

And if the reader espouses Calvinism, then the arguments afford him or her with conceptual fortification. Calvinism is a historically-based phenomenon, but the arguments considered by Guillaume are contemporary arguments against compatibilism. Guillaume thus takes the view that compatibilism is intrinsic to Calvinism, and much of the book is taken up with establishing this connection.

Guillaume faces these objections to compatibilism (and hence to Calvinism) head on. He provides exhaustive sequences of these. So for example, he considers variants of the objection that compatibilism is a form of manipulation or coercion and so inconsistent with one of Calvinism's tenets, that human beings are responsible for their actions. And on responsibility he has a searching account of the conditions for responsibility in indeterminism, and in the case of compatibilism. Especially interesting, I think, is his discussion of divine permission, and his treatment of analogical language, and the closing discussion of middle knowledge.

Guillaume's style is bold, clear, and direct. He takes pains to keep arguments from ambiguity and fudge. The careful reader will be impressed by his thoroughness. He is also painstaking. He does not leave an argument before it is considered in various versions. He applies these standards to those arguments that he champions, as well as to those he explains and defends.

It is to be hoped also that many who are compatibilists but who are not Calvinists will take up this book. If they will do so, they will find many of Guillaume's discussions strengthening their understanding of their own positions.

With his careful and energetic attention to sound arguments Guillaume is not a typical French philosopher, perhaps, but he here makes a sterling contribution to the defense of compatibilism that will be of interest both to analytic philosophers, and to theologians. I commend the book to Calvinists and non-Calvinistic compatibilists alike, and of course to indeterminists of any color.

Paul Helm

Emeritus Professor, University of London.

# Acknowledgments

IN BOOK-WRITING NO LESS than in human redemption, all the praise belongs to God—especially on the theological view defended here—but it so happens that God saw fit to use the following secondary causes, who accordingly deserve all my gratitude.

I wish to thank Paul Helm, whose thoughtful feedback and friendly exchanges have greatly encouraged me to "solve puzzles" and ask the right questions.

I thank the following reviewers for their helpful remarks on earlier drafts of the work: James N. Anderson, Thomas Atkinson, W. Paul Franks, Daniel J. Hill, Paul Manata, Paul Rezkalla, and David Wood.

Parts of this work and papers on related issues were presented, and received helpful feedback from participants at the following conferences: the annual meeting of the Evangelical Theological Society in Baltimore, MD in 2013, the eastern meeting of the Society of Christian Philosophers in Niagara Falls, NY in 2014, the annual meeting of the Evangelical Theological Society and that of the Evangelical Philosophical society in San Diego, CA in 2014. I particularly thank John D. Laing and James N. Anderson for including my paper on divine permission language as part of the consultation on Molinism in San Diego, and James N. Anderson for his invaluable constructive feedback on that material.

Glen M. Shellrude and Louis A. DeCaro Jr. deserve my thanks for their thoughtful influence on my theological formation, their contagious passion for theology and the scriptures, and their personal encouragements, ultimately inspiring me to pursue doctoral work.

I also thank Robert M. Baxter and Vincent Salonia, for playing crucial parts in turning this French atheist into a Christian scholar.

Finally, all my thanks and love belong to my wife Katherine Elizabeth Bignon, who has lovingly shared my burden through seminary and doctoral work, encouraging and affirming me at every turn and filling my life with joy and adorable children. This academic accomplishment is hers in every respect.

# Introduction, definitions, and methodology

"Is there unrighteousness in God?"
—Romans 9:14

"Why does he still find fault? For who can resist his will?"
—Romans 9:19

## Then and now—encountering the objections to Calvinism

ON THE HEELS OF what is perhaps the strongest, most perspicuous scriptural teaching on the matter of God's sovereign choice of election, Paul in Romans 9 felt the need to address two objections; two potential problems that he anticipated could be found troublesome by the reader of his bold truth claims. One is the worry that such a high degree of divine providence could nullify human moral responsibility: if God is in providential control of human affairs to such a degree as Paul asserted, how are humans morally responsible for their sins? If humans cannot "resist his will," how can he hold them to be at "fault" and blame them for anything that they choose and do? The other objection, penned five verses earlier, asserted that God's very righteousness hangs on the balance against such a view of providence. One may wonder indeed: if God were to unilaterally decree the outcome of human choices, including their sins and unrepentant unbelief, then would there not be "unrighteousness in God"?

A number of Calvinist theologians have found the anticipation of these two objections remarkable.[1] The reason for this is simple: named after the sixteenth-century French reformer John Calvin, Calvinists are those

---

1. "These are the very objections which today, on first thought, spring into men's minds, in opposition to the Calvinist doctrine of Predestination; but they have not even the least plausibility when directed against the Arminian doctrine. A doctrine which does not afford the least grounds for these objections cannot have been the one that the Apostle taught." Boettner, *Doctrine of Predestination*, 253.

theologians in the so-called "Reformed" tradition, who, together with the Westminster Confession of Faith, affirm that God providentially ordains everything that comes to pass:

> God, the great creator of all things doth uphold, direct, dispose, and govern all creatures, actions, and things, from the greatest even to the least, by his most wise and holy providence, according to his infallible foreknowledge, and the free and immutable counsel of his own will, to the praise of the glory of his wisdom, power, justice, goodness, and mercy.[2]

One might call this thesis theological determinism.[3] If this doctrine is true, then Paul's anticipated objections are precisely those we will expect to be brought forward by opponents of the doctrine. These objections will have some significant degree of plausibility and it will make sense for Paul to anticipate them. Notice that even the Westminster Confession anticipates these two exact objections, in the very sentence whereby it famously affirms God's decree of all things:

> God from all eternity, did, by the most wise and holy counsel of His own will, freely, and unchangeably ordain whatsoever comes to pass; yet so, as thereby *neither is God the author of sin, nor is violence offered to the will of the creatures*; nor is the liberty or contingency of second causes taken away, but rather established.[4]

Conversely, if Calvinism were *not* true and human free will were such that God does *not* determine its outcome—that is the so-called "libertarian" view of free will[5]—then not only would these objections lose much if not all of their intuitiveness and it would become harder to see why Paul would anticipate them when they lack even superficial plausibility, but also we would expect him to provide a wholly different answer than the one he in fact offers: "who are you O man, to answer back to God?" Paul scolds the questioner for his impertinent indiscretion, rather than cater to the objection with a proper refutation. But if human beings were equipped with such an indeterminist, libertarian free will, the answer to the no-longer rhetorical

---

2. Westminster Confession of Faith, 5.

3. For precise definitions of the concepts and a brief word on whether Calvinism does in fact commit one to determinism, see the next section on definitions and methodological concerns.

4. Westminster Confession of Faith, 3.1.

5. "Libertarian free will" and "libertarianism" will be more precisely defined in the next section on definitions and methodological concerns.

question "who can resist his will?" would have been utterly trivial: "every-body." By definition, if human free will is such that God does not determine the outcomes of a person's choices, that person is able to freely choose otherwise than what God would have him choose;[6] he is able to freely choose otherwise than God "wills" in this world. In this case, objecting that "an inability to resist God's will is morally problematic" is no objection at all.

Of course, Calvinists must not go as far as to grant that the objections are *justified* against Calvinism. It still remains that, whichever theological view Paul adopts, it is being *opposed* by the objector, and given Christianity, the truth certainly lies in Paul's camp. On the other hand, given the truth of determinism, these objections have a certain "bite" to them, which explains well the need for Paul's interruption, and therefore serves as confirmation of the Calvinist interpretation of Paul's teaching. Plausibly, the presence of these objections cannot stand as the premise of an irrefutable deductive argument for Calvinism, but more modestly, it can be conceded that their presence is much more easily explained by a Calvinist reading of the text, and hence they serve as positive evidence in support of Calvinism.

It is additionally remarkable that these two objections—Calvinism destroys moral responsibility ("why does he still find fault?") and Calvinism makes God evil or the author of sin ("is there unrighteousness in God?")—remain to this day the most important arguments championed in the theological and philosophical literature by critics of Calvinism; it is not infrequent even to find the two offered in the same sentence.[7] There is accordingly a certain irony in this: the very objections voiced against Calvinism serve as one more piece of evidence in its favor.

This being said however, one may still wonder whether the two arguments, if unsound, can receive a better rational refutation than Paul's scolding. Can we offer a philosophically satisfying rebuttal? I think that we can (and probably should!). Yet in doing so, are we trying to be smarter

6. Much will be said about the "ability to do otherwise" in chapter 5, on the so-called "principle of alternate possibilities."

7. Norman Geisler writes: "Not only does extreme Calvinism tend to undermine personal responsibility, it also logically lays the blame squarely on God for the origin of evil." Geisler, *Chosen But Free*, 162; Roger Olson similarly writes: "First, if sinners cannot do otherwise, how are they responsible? Second, if God renders sin certain, how is he not stained by it?" Roger E. Olson, "Responses to Bruce A. Ware," in *Perspectives on the Doctrine of God*, 135; William Lane Craig says that the determinist view of free will "seems to lead inescapably to making God the author of sin and to a denial of human freedom and responsibility in general." Craig, *Divine Foreknowledge and Human Freedom*, 272–73; and Clark Pinnock writes that Calvinist views "eliminate human freedom and take away human responsibility; they make God the author of sin." Clark H. Pinnock, "Room for Us," 217–18.

than God? I think not. Paul's slap on the hand is called for by the sinful motives that are assumed to be present in the questioner. Paul rebukes the reader who would use divine providence as an excuse for his sin and an escape from judgment. But however uninformed, passionate Calvinist new converts may feel about the matter, not all objectors to Calvinism are evil sinners, out to explain away their guilt, and blame God for their sin.

In any case, whether or not Paul's imaginary interlocutor's arguments are precisely those of modern-day critics, it remains that the latter are still offered against Calvinism today, and call for refutations by Calvinist philosophers. This constitutes the burden of the present work.

## A minimal dose of definitions and methodological concerns

Before engaging these two grand arguments against Calvinism, a few important terms need to be defined in order to properly discuss the matter at hand. Unfortunately, some of the concepts behind these terms are sometimes as easy to grasp intuitively, as they are difficult to define precisely— and to the satisfaction of all who engage in this debate. While it might be upsetting to encounter controversy already in definitions, one needn't resolve all the disputes ahead of time. At present, I will just point out some of these disagreements as I provide the general understanding of the terms, and will delay any comments on the particulars until they come to matter for any later argument I make. Minimally, the following concepts deserve mention, and some clarification.

*Determinism.* The main idea behind determinism is that everything that comes to pass is *determined*, or *necessitated* by prior conditions,[8] natural or supernatural. The concept is meaningful whether theism or atheism is true, as these prior determining factors could consist in divine providential activity, or, (say if God does not exist) merely natural laws.

If a determination by the laws of nature is in view, then determinism is purely *natural*, it is a *physical* determinism, and can be defined as the thesis that, at any instant, the state of the universe and the laws of nature entail that there is only one physically possible future. Note however that this purely physical description need not be atheistic. If this sort of determinism obtained, it could simply be the means by which God providentially

---

8. The conditions that are in view could either be temporally prior, or logically prior, thus leaving room for things like backwards causation or the possibility of a timeless God causing things to occur in time.

determined all things: actualizing initial states of affairs, and putting in place laws of nature from which all subsequent natural events follow necessarily according to his design.[9]

If God does exist, however, physical determinism is not the *only* way determinism could obtain. One could still affirm that God determined all things while not doing so through physical means alone. Clearly that is the case if God ever acts supernaturally, performing miracles such as raising people from the dead or splitting the red sea. But a determinist may also affirm this distinction between physical and non-physical means of determination in the area of human free will. On that view, for all the laws of nature entail, the future would not be physically determined, but it could still be determined by God's providential decree and the full scope of his supernatural activity, whatever shape one thinks it may take.[10] Whether God determines all things through physical determinism or through directly supernatural means, both views can be described as "theological determinism": God providentially determines everything that comes to pass, including human choices.

Whether they are theological or atheistic, natural (and physical) or supernatural, all these views count as "determinism" and will be referred to as such in the present work, as they are all targets of the two grand arguments reviewed therein: they are all suspected to exclude human moral responsibility, and—obviously only the ones that posit God's existence—are alleged to improperly involve God in evil.

With respect to the definition of physical determinism just offered, it is worth pointing out that the notion of "law of nature" is itself controversial. I make no attempt to offer a formal definition of the phrase, as the idea is intuitive enough, and the reader is free to read into it his favorite understanding of the concept, since no argument of mine will hang or fall with the specifics. Peter van Inwagen himself is able to write his classic work *An Essay on Free Will*, discussing at length the consequences of determinism, while voicing the same ignorance I just confessed: "Finally, I need the notion of a *law of nature*. I have no idea how to explain this term, much less define it."[11]

Similarly, I have carefully avoided any mention of the word "cause." Determinism is sometimes described as the thesis that every event has

9. As Thomas Flint puts it, "If physical determinism is true, it will presumably be seen by the theist as merely the means by which God determines all events, including free human actions." Flint, "Two Accounts," 172.

10. For explicit developments of such views, see McCann, *Creation*, and Crabtree, *Most Real Being*.

11. Peter van Inwagen, *Essay*, 60.

"sufficient causes," or on theism, that all events are "caused" by God. There is nothing wrong in employing these terms if they are clear for those who use them, but I for one find them usually unhelpful and so as much as I can, I shall follow Peter van Inwagen once more, who thinks that causation is "a morass in which I for one refuse to set foot. Or not unless I am pushed."[12] Accordingly, if the word "causal" is used at all, as in the phrase "causal determinism," it shall not mean anything more than "determinism" *simpliciter*, as understood in the presently offered definition.

*Indeterminism* is simply the denial of determinism; it is the thesis that not everything that happens is determined as described above. On this view, some events are fully *indeterminist*, they are *not* necessitated by prior determining factors—be they natural laws, divine providence, or anything of the sort.

*Calvinism.* While the thesis of determinism is of great interest to theists and atheists alike, the present work is particularly concerned with its *theistic* expression, and aims to uphold the coherence of a certain theological viewpoint known as *Calvinism*. In this context, the word does not refer to all the doctrinal views held by John Calvin the French reformer—matters such as ecclesiology or the sacraments are not in view. Instead, in the present context, *Calvinism* is employed to describe a particular understanding of divine providence over human free will, and it is usually understood to refer to either one of two different though related theses: *Calvinist soteriology*, and *Calvinist determinism*.[13] Calvinist soteriology is a set of theological doctrines about the state of fallen humanity and the means by which God sovereignly saves sinners: these are the so-called "five points" of Calvinism, conveniently listed under the acronym TULIP: Total Depravity, Unconditional Election, Limited Atonement, Irresistible Grace, and Perseverance of the Saints. These need not be defined here, as they are not the primary focus of this work, whose main concern is to defend the coherence of *Calvinist determinism*, in the face of its two most important objections. *Calvinist determinism* is here understood as the thesis that God exists and that theological determinism is true, as defined above and affirmed for example by the Westminster Confession: God sovereignly determines everything that comes to pass, including human choices. At this point, some who identify themselves as Calvinists (maybe for their affirmation of Calvinist soteriology) may

12. Ibid., 65.

13. These helpful distinctions are made by Daniel Johnson in Johnson, "Map of the Territory," 20–24.

question whether this view in fact commits them to determinism: do the five points of Calvinism or the Westminster Confession necessitate the thesis of theological determinism? I assert that they do, but the point need not be demonstrated here. Those who disagree with the inference[14] should simply see the present work as answering the *conditional* question: *if* Calvinism required theological determinism, *would* it be so bad? *Would* it exclude moral responsibility and improperly involve God in evil? These questions are valuable even if Calvinism does not equate determinism. But as for the use of the phrase in the present work, it will be so as a matter of definition: theological determinism will be referred to as "the Calvinist view," or simply "Calvinism." With this understanding in mind, I must finally point out that the term "Calvinist" could even theoretically be employed meaningfully in superficially anachronistic sentences such as "Saint Augustine was a Calvinist." This isn't affirming the absurdity that Augustine had read John Calvin, but rather that he espoused broadly the same view of divine providence, referred to in this work as "Calvinism."

*Moral responsibility.* A person is *morally responsible* for a given action if and only if that action is morally significant—it involves either good or bad, right or wrong—and the person may be rightly praised or blamed for it. In other words, to say that a person is morally responsible is to say that he is *praiseworthy* or *blameworthy*, that he *deserves* praise or blame for his morally significant actions—the right and the wrong.[15]

*Compatibilism* and *Incompatibilism*. *Compatibilism* is the thesis that determinism is compatible with moral responsibility. Note that compatibilism in itself says nothing about the *truth* of either determinism or moral responsibility. It only says that both *could* be true together; that they are compossible. More often than not, philosophers who affirm compatibilism do so because they do maintain the truth of the two theses, and if both are true then surely they are compatible, but theoretically, one could be a compatibilist and yet reject determinism, or moral responsibility, or both.

*Incompatibilism* is the denial of compatibilism; it is the thesis that determinism is incompatible with moral responsibility: on this view, if moral agents

14. See for example Crisp, *Deviant Calvinism*.

15. Kevin Timpe further unpacks the concept of moral responsibility in terms of "reactive attitudes," "ledger," and "accountability," all of which capture correct aspects of moral responsibility. Nothing of importance in the coming debate hangs on which of these descriptions is preferred. See Timpe, *Sourcehood*, 6–8.

are determined, they cannot be praised or blamed for anything that they choose and do.

*Free will.* To say of a person that he has *free will* is to say that he has the power or ability to make morally responsible choices, to perform morally responsible actions. When such a person makes use of his free will, we will say that he makes a *free choice*, or performs a *free action*, and we shall take it to entail that he can be morally responsible for them. It doesn't necessarily mean that he in fact *is* morally responsible for them, because besides having free will, there are other necessary conditions for moral responsibility, most notably epistemic elements such as the need to know some of the relevant facts about one's actions.[16] It is important to acknowledge that these additional conditions for moral responsibility exist, but since the focus of the present work is mostly the "freedom" condition for moral responsibility (sometimes called the "control" condition for moral responsibility[17]), one need not pin down the exhaustive list of other necessary conditions, which jointly secure moral responsibility. We shall instead concern ourselves with a more modest study of the one specific ingredient of moral responsibility that is the need to have free will.

On an important note, this definition of free will says nothing about the free choices being determined or not. As I shall very soon complain,[18] it is not unusual for philosophers or theologians to read "free will" and just assume indeterminism, and that may or may not follow—depending on the truth of compatibilism or incompatibilism—but as far as the mere phrase "free will" is concerned, it *can* be used by determinists and indeterminists alike, to refer to what *they* take to be morally responsible choices and actions.

A last important distinction must be drawn with respect to free actions: there is a difference between a *directly free* action, and an *indirectly free* action. When a morally significant action is performed straightforwardly out of an agent's free will, we speak of the action as being *directly free*, and the agent is morally responsible for it, because he freely chose it. But there is another type of action for which agents may be morally responsible: those that aren't performed out of a free choice, but that still result inevitably from an *earlier* choice that was made freely. For example, the drunk driver who earlier in the evening freely chose to drink and drive may later be held morally responsible for a crash, even though *on the moment of the accident,* the

16. This is the reason given by Laura Ekstrom for why she disagrees with Susan Wolf and Paul Benson when they posit the equivalence between "free act" and "morally responsible act." Ekstrom, *Free Will*, 19n12.

17. Kevin Timpe, *Philosophical Theology*, 7.

18. See chapter 1.

alcohol had incapacitated him and removed his free choice about whether to crash or not. We will then say that the action was *indirectly free*, and the agent is responsible, because even though he wasn't free on that moment, his inability was brought about by an earlier free decision of his. This is an important distinction, which will come to matter in the discussion of one of my coming arguments,[19] and it will be properly acknowledged at that point. Until then, whenever I speak of an agent making a "free" choice or performing a "free" action, it will be supposed to mean "directly free."

*Libertarianism* and *libertarian free will*. The standard definition of *libertarianism* in the literature is usually stated as follows: "Libertarianism is the thesis that freedom is incompatible with determinism, plus the claim that at least some of our actions are free, and so determinism is false."[20] Accordingly, *libertarian free will* is the ability to make free choices that are not determined by prior conditions. It is the sort of free will which persons must have if incompatibilism is true: it is a free will that is not determinist, and it is the sort of free will that Calvinists (as I have defined the terms above) must reject. This said, I do have a minor personal complaint to voice. I personally find the typical definition of libertarianism unhelpful in one respect, because it entails that a libertarian is necessarily an incompatibilist, and thus it conflates two theses that are relatively independent. One could affirm that free will choices are made indeterministically, without having to add that this indeterminism is *necessary* for moral responsibility. It is perfectly coherent to maintain that free choices are in fact indeterminist, but that if, contrary to fact, they *were* determined, they still *could* be morally responsible. But according to the standard definition, such a person wouldn't be a libertarian. Nevertheless, these are the standard definitions, so it is best to abide by them, and I shall not depart from the usual meaning of the terms: libertarianism will be understood to mean that free choices are indeterminist, *and* that indeterminism is necessary for moral responsibility.

Finally, I shall note that "libertarian free will" is often expressed in terms of an "ability to do otherwise," or ability to actualize an "alternate possibility." An agent with libertarian free will is not determined to choose one way or another; all antecedent conditions being just as they are at the moment of choice, the person has the ability to choose one way or another. And when he has chosen one option, it is said that all things being equal, he "could have done otherwise." While a large majority of libertarian philosophers affirm this understanding of libertarian free will and even see it

19. See chapter 6, where I introduce and discuss a principle named $PAP_{Past}$.
20. Perszyk, "Introduction," 4.

as absolutely essential to the notion,[21] some others have reservations about the concept of an "ability to do otherwise," and do not see it as a necessary ingredient of libertarianism.[22] I will postpone any comments on the controversy until it comes to matter for an argument of mine.

*Arminianism.* Finally, just as Calvinism was the theological name for the philosophical doctrine of theological determinism, we shall use the word *Arminianism* as the theological name for the philosophical doctrine of theological indeterminism. Named after the Dutch theologian Jacob Arminius, who in the late sixteenth century took issue with the standard Reformed view and criticized its theological determinism, *Arminians* will be understood in this work to refer to all theologians who affirm libertarian free will. This conveniently loose usage entails that "Arminians" are all the non-Calvinist theologians: they are those who affirm that free will is libertarian, regardless of their view on the separate question of divine foreknowledge. Without entering into unnecessary details, we can note that on this question of foreknowledge, some of them affirm that God has no foreknowledge of future free choices—the so-called "open theists." Some others affirm that God has a so-called "simple foreknowledge" of future tense statements about what humans *will* freely choose (they are sometimes called "classical Arminians"), and some others affirm that God also has a so-called "middle knowledge" of subjunctive conditional statements about what humans *would* freely do in any hypothetical set of circumstances—they are the so-called "Molinists." These qualifications matter little at the moment; it is only important to note that in the present work, all these theologians will simply be referred to as "Arminian," for their common affirmation of libertarianism.

Finally, just as I imagined there might be some who identify as "Calvinists" though they reject determinism, there might also be some who—for some reason—identify as "Arminians" though they affirm determinism. For these unusual determinists (if such people even exist), all I can do is apologize for still calling them Calvinists against their wills, and I shall simply point out that though we disagree on whether their professed "Arminianism" is compatible with determinism, they should welcome my study of whether their professed determinism is compatible with moral responsibility and with divine righteousness. They are thus not excluded from

21. Thomas Flint: "For the heart and soul of libertarianism is the conviction that what an agent does freely is genuinely up to the agent to do freely and refrain from doing freely; no external circumstance, no other agent, does or even can determine what I do freely." Flint, "Two Accounts," 174. Equally strong statements are found in Plantinga, *God, Freedom, and Evil*, 29; Rowe, *Can God Be Free?*, 6 and Hasker, *Providence*, 125–26.

22. See my discussion of so-called "Frankfurt libertarians" in chapter 6.

the present discussion, although I will take it as a matter of definition that Calvinists are determinists, and Arminians are indeterminists—they affirm libertarian free will.

Now that key terms have been defined, let me say a word about methodology. The burden of the present work is to assess the merits of the two main criticisms of Calvinist determinism: that it excludes moral responsibility and that it improperly involves God in evil. This will be conducted by evaluating various arguments whose conclusion is the truth of either of these propositions. For the sake of exhaustiveness, these arguments will be either taken from the literature, or anticipations of what one *could* possibly argue. Assuming that all the arguments thereby surveyed are successfully shown to fail, the goal of this work will be met, and a merely negative refutation of invalid arguments is certainly helpful in itself, but whenever possible, we will try to go beyond this. Whatever the case may be in sports, at least in philosophy, the best defense is offense, and an unconvinced philosopher who merely defensively brands one charge after another of circular reasoning can in time be rightly suspected of rabid skepticism. Furthermore, to show that an argument is unsound is not to establish that its conclusion is *false*, only that it is—as of yet—unjustified. Being mindful of this, whenever possible, I shall do more than voicing skepticism about the premises (and conclusion) of an unsound argument, and will additionally offer positive arguments of my own, to prove its thesis false. This will make for a comprehensive case in favor of the compatibility of Calvinist determinism with human moral responsibility and with divine righteousness.

With these goals clearly set before us, the two grand arguments can now be engaged: does Calvinism exclude moral responsibility, and does it improperly involve God in evil? Does it justify "excusing sinners and blaming God"?

# PART I

# Calvinism and
# Moral Responsibility

THE FIRST OF THESE two grand arguments to be reviewed is the claim that Calvinism is incompatible with moral responsibility. Though the argument can take a number of shapes, it is at bottom a deductive one of the sort:

1. If Calvinism is true, people are never morally responsible for their choices and actions.

2. At least some people, at some time, are morally responsible for some of their choices or actions.

   *Therefore*

3. Calvinism is false.

The argument is logically valid, so that if both premises are true, the conclusion follows, and Calvinism stands refuted. One way to avoid the conclusion would be to reject premise (2); indeed, the denial of moral responsibility is a route taken by the so-called "hard determinists,"[23] but I take it that premise (2) is a firm commitment of orthodox Christianity, so I will not (and Calvinists should not) employ that way out of the argument. No Calvinist committed to the truth of scripture should reject the belief that (at least some) people are morally responsible for (at least some of) their sins.[24] Thus, all the focus of the present work with respect to this argument will reside on premise (1). Is it the case that Calvinism entails the impossibility of moral responsibility? Let us note that the feature of Calvinism

---

23. See Pereboom, *Living*.

24. The contention is symmetrical with respect to blameworthiness or praiseworthiness, both of which I maintain humans possess. Sin is used here for the simple reason that the Bible is more vocal about humans being sinful than it is about their praiseworthiness.

that allegedly excludes moral responsibility is its theological determinism. Premise (1) can thus be split into two steps as follows:

1a  If Calvinism is true, then determinism is true.

1b  If determinism is true, then people are never morally responsible for their choices and actions.

2   At least some people, at some time, are morally responsible for some of their choices or actions.

*Therefore*

3a  Determinism is false. (Follows from (1b) and (2))

*Therefore*

3b  Calvinism is false. (Follows from (1a) and (3a))

The logical validity is still unobjectionable. This refined analysis now theoretically permits a Calvinist to evade the force of the argument by rejecting (1a) in asserting that determinism is not essential to Calvinism. But as was supposed as a matter of definition, whether it be physical determinism or theological determinism, a Calvinist must affirm some form of determinism, which means that premise (1a) is unobjectionable, because it does not specify which variety of determinism is in view. Given this, all the debate now lies on whether premise (1b) is true.

Premise (1b) is the infamous thesis of *incompatibilism*. It is the claim that determinism is incompatible with moral responsibility. Accordingly, the discussion of the present anti-Calvinist grand argument calls for the resolution of the so-called "compatibility question," a long-standing controversy in the history of metaphysics: is determinism incompatible with moral responsibility? Yet as we endeavor to do so, we must be careful to approach it in its proper dialectical context: that of an *objection* to Calvinism. Premise (1b) as we encounter it is a premise in an argument against Calvinism. In order for this objection to fail, it is therefore not necessary at this point for Calvinists to prove the premise false (that is, to prove compatibilism). The burden of proof is squarely on the shoulders of the non-Calvinist objector presently making the argument. It may be useful for Calvinists to prove the premise false (and we will surely assess whether this can be done), but it is not necessary in order for the argument to be shown to fail. The modest task of the Calvinist facing this argument is to review all the arguments that non-Calvinists have to offer in support of premise (1b), and show that they have no purchase on him. To this review we now turn.

# I

# Free will, pets, and puppets

## The "no free will / no choice" argument

WHAT THEN CAN BE said in support of incompatibilism? A first attempt at
supporting the thesis would be to say that if determinism is true, then humans "do not have free will"; they do not "make their own choices." As Hugh
McCann puts it, "people unspoiled by philosophy are often inclined to believe that if determinism is true, we never 'really' get to decide anything."[1]
And how could we be morally responsible without a choice and without free
will? If anything is ever ground for excusing a failure, it is surely the absence
of free choice. As to the Calvinist rejection of "free will," there is even decent
ground in the writings of the reformers to document the charge: all one
needs to do is to pick up Martin Luther's *Bondage of the Will* to know how
he felt about "free will," that "empty term whose reality is lost."[2] But surely,
if humans have no free will, they are not morally responsible; how could
they be?

Framed this badly, however, the incompatibilist contention is easily
put to rest by exposing a handful of equivocations. By the above claims, the
objector must mean something like the following:

4. If determinism is true, then humans make no choice.

5. If humans make no choice, then they are not morally responsible.

   *Therefore*

6. Determinism is incompatible with moral responsibility.

Or

7. If determinism is true, then humans have no free will.

8. If humans have no free will, then they are not morally responsible.

   *Therefore*

1. McCann, *Works of Agency*, 145.
2. Luther, *Bondage of the Will*, 148.

6. Determinism is incompatible with moral responsibility.

To serve as a cogent argument against Calvinism, these claims must show that "free will" or "choice," *as they are necessarily rejected by Calvinists*, are in fact necessary for moral responsibility. But both of these expressions are still equivocating with respect to the metaphysical assumptions that they package. If by "choice" in premises (4) and (5) the objector means "libertarian free choice" and by "free will" in premises (7) and (8) he means "libertarian free will," then sure enough Calvinists reject both of these items, but will in turn demand a non-question-begging reason why *those* are necessary for moral responsibility. Why should the Calvinist believe premises (5) and (8) on their libertarian reading?

If on the other hand the alleged requirements of "choice" and "free will" for moral responsibility do not encapsulate any libertarian assumption, then their incompatibility with determinism as asserted by premises (4) and (7) is at least far from certain if not demonstrably false. Calvinist philosophers are (or at any rate, I am) happy to affirm that absent any libertarian assumptions, "choice" and "free will" are necessary for moral responsibility, in the modest sense that "free choice" or "free will" simply describe a choice that features all the items on the list of necessary conditions (with respect to freedom) for moral responsibility, a list to which indeterminism has not been shown to belong.[3] As a matter of fact, with this language in view, the very meaning of the phrase "having free will," if left unqualified with respect to its compatibilist or incompatibilist pretentions, is understood in the present work to be equivalent to "having the sort of control over one's will, that allows one to be morally responsible."[4] So to claim that determinism excludes moral responsibility because it excludes free will is on the present view equivalent to saying that determinism excludes moral responsibility because it excludes moral responsibility. It is obviously not evidential progress and until this understanding of "free will" is shown to be forbidden, the Calvinist can and should go on affirming that on determinism, humans still have free will, are making choices, and are morally responsible for them.

Whenever the scriptures indicate that humans have a choice to make in "choosing" to repent and believe in Jesus, none can jump to conclusions and find in this any support for an Arminian/libertarian view. Scripture instructs humans to *choose* life (Deut 30:19), *choose* whom they will serve (Josh 24:15), *choose* good and refuse evil (Isa 7:15). Calvinists dare not explain away these expressions. Of course we choose. We have a will. We make

3. More will be said later on about what may belong in that list on a compatibilist view.

4. See my definition of "free will" in the introduction.

choices. The Calvinist's contention is simply that these human choices, while freely and responsibly made, are determinist, and hence compatibilism obtains. If an argument can be made that the very language of choice and free will are forbidden a Calvinist, it has not been encountered so far; but let us proceed.

## The "pets and puppets" argument

The above critique is sometimes phrased in more colorful terms, as incompatibilists contend that if human beings are determined, their choices amount to those of pets, or puppets. A collection of injurious metaphors can be found in Arminian literature: "smoothly operated puppet,"[5] "a marionette show"[6] of "contracted performers,"[7] "falling dominos,"[8] "dancing mannequins,"[9] ventriloquist dummies,[10] robots,[11] toys,[12] and "pawns in God's hands."[13] The complaint is clear: if free will is determined, "We are just playing out the puppet show that God has decreed."[14] The creative metaphors all press a similar objection, but despite their clearly felt, unifying theme, it is in fact not obvious what to make of this material, because Arminian theologians rarely explain the charge, much less substantiate it.

On the one hand, if incompatibilists mean to argue "Puppets are determined; humans are determined; therefore humans are puppets," it is not hard to point out the logical fallacy of the undistributed middle: just because two things have one part in common, it does not follow that they have everything in common. And at any rate, surely incompatibilists don't mean to argue that on determinism, humans really *are* pets or puppets. Unfortunately, the same problem goes with the less obviously invalid formulation: "Puppets are determined; Puppets are not morally responsible; humans are determined; therefore humans are not morally responsible," which still commits the fallacy of the undistributed middle: from the determinism of

5. Forlines, *Classical Arminianism*, 48.
6. Pinnock, "Room for Us," 215.
7. Sanders, *God Who Risks*, 223.
8. Moreland and Craig, *Philosophical Foundations*, 273.
9. Sanders, *God Who Risks*, 223.
10. Ibid., 227.
11. Ibid.
12. MacDonald, "Spirit of Grace," 81.
13. Olson, *Arminian Theology*, 65.
14. Lemke, "Critique of Irresistible Grace," 154.

puppets and their lacking moral responsibility, it does not follow that determined humans are not morally responsible.

A more convincing reading of the objection, then, would instead understand it to be a claim that determined human choices are *analogous* to those of pets and puppets. Hugh McCann develops the charge a step further than Arminian theologians usually do: "If the relationship between God's will and ours took this form, the spontaneity of free will would be gone; we would have every right to feel we were mere puppets, and God the puppeteer."[15] So far this only restates the allegation, but he proceeds to explain it as follows:

> If, say, human decision and willing were nothing but the causal product of an agent's strongest motive—we would not really *be* persons or agents. We would be reduced to the same status as our house pets: admirable in many ways, perhaps, but utterly bereft of the dignity of a *moral* being.
>
> Why . . . should we hold a killer morally responsible for the death of his victim on the ground that had he willed otherwise that death would not have occurred, when all along there was no hope whatever that he *would* so will? How is this kind of behavior any more responsible than that of a vicious dog—which, surely, would not have mauled the postman had it not been so motivated? If there is a relevant difference here, compatibilism does not seem to point to it; and if no such difference can be found, then the man is no more responsible than the dog.[16]

This is helpful. It confirms that what the argument at hand alleges is the existence of an analogous feature between determined human choices and those of pets. The claim being made is that whatever annuls the moral responsibility for the dog is also found in determined human choices, and should annul moral responsibility in that case as well. The common denominator would be determinism, the reason why both exclude moral responsibility. But, as McCann objects, if on the other hand indeterminist, libertarian free will is not what marks humans out, then there remains no "relevant difference" explaining why humans are morally responsible and pets and puppets are not; "no such difference can be found."

The problem with this argument is that such difference is in fact very easily found. What exactly would be needed to refute the charge? To make this requirement clear, let us state the argument by analogy in a more rigorous syllogistic form. The argument becomes:

15. McCann, *Creation*, 94.
16. Ibid., 94–95.

9. Actions performed by pets and puppets have a certain property that excludes moral responsibility.

10. If actions performed by pets and puppets have a property that excludes moral responsibility, then that property is also predicated of actions performed by humans on determinism.

*Therefore*

11. Actions performed by humans on determinism have a property that excludes moral responsibility.

*which is to say*

6. Determinism is incompatible with moral responsibility.

It is thus premise (10) that must be rejected. First of all, compatibilists can point out that it is question-begging. Why think that if actions performed by pets and puppets are not morally responsible, neither are actions performed by humans on determinism? Why think that actions of pets and puppets are in fact analogous to human choices and actions on determinism in that way? We are not told. But more importantly, premise (10) is demonstrated false by easily finding a property, which: 1. is featured by pets and puppets, 2. excludes moral responsibility in their case, and 3. is not featured by humans, supposed on compatibilism to make determinist free choices.

The property of "lacking self-consciousness" fits that description exactly. Self-consciousness is quite plausibly necessary for moral responsibility, possessed by human beings (determined or not), and lacked by pets and puppets. *That* is the reason why pets and puppets are not morally responsible: they lack this necessary condition, the self-conscious awareness of what they are doing[17]—the second "*sapiens*" in *homo sapiens sapiens*—and that is the reason why they cannot serve to support incompatibilism. They lack libertarian free will all right, but in the absence of self-consciousness, pets and puppets could not have free will as understood by compatibilists either, and so of course they lack moral responsibility, but nothing of interest follows that could support the thesis of incompatibilism. Calvinists are happy to agree that self-conscious free will is necessary for moral responsibility; they just disagree with incompatibilists on whether free will is determinist or libertarian, and hence, colorful illustrations of dogs and puppets do little to arbitrate the debate.

17. If someone were to disagree, and contend instead that some advanced animals *do* reach the heights of being self-conscious, my response would then be that such self-conscious animals *would* likely be morally responsible, and hence, although determined humans would now be analogous to them, it would no longer serve to exclude human responsibility on determinism.

Finally, one may object that my reading of the "pets and puppets" argument is *still* too strong. There are technically two different ways to press the argument by analogy: a stronger claim, and a weaker claim, which would differ as follows:

*Stronger claim*: "there exists no relevant difference between pets (or puppets) and determined humans."

*Weaker claim*: "there exists one relevant similarity between pets (or puppets) and determined humans."

Since premise (10) affirmed that *any* property of pets and puppets that excludes moral responsibility is also found in determined humans, it was clearly pressing the stronger claim, whereas technically, all the objector needs to claim is that *at least one* property of pets and puppets excludes moral responsibility and is found in determined humans. That weaker claim is much harder to refute, because finding a relevant difference (as I claim to have done above) would no longer suffice, I would instead need to show that there is *no* relevant similarity: I would need to show that *all* the properties of pets and puppets which exclude moral responsibility are absent from determined human free choices, and that is much harder to prove. So what can be said in response? Very simply, the problem with the weaker claim is that it is much too weak to get the argument off the ground. Since we are not told *what* that alleged relevant similarity is, but only *that* there must be one somewhere, the claim has absolutely no purchase on the compatibilist; it straightforwardly begs the question, and compatibilists have no reason to accept it. Admittedly, that claim is now very hard to *refute*, but it is just as hard to accept on faith! And that is why proponents of the argument by analogy tend to do as McCann did above: press the stronger claim instead, *challenging* the compatibilist to find a relevant difference, and alleging that "no such difference can be found." But in this case, I *did* offer such a relevant difference, and hence premise (10) was shown false, so that the "pets and puppets" argument by analogy, whether it presses the stronger claim or the weaker one, is unsuccessful.

*2*

# The coercion argument

## Does determinism entail coercion?

A BETTER ARGUMENT MAY be thought to advance the incompatibilist thesis a bit further, by objecting that determinism thwarts moral responsibility as God is *coercing* human choices. The allegation here is that a Calvinist God who decrees our every choice would be forcing us to choose and act as we do; God would be exercising *coercion* on us, the very force that removes moral responsibility as is so clearly witnessed when it occurs among us humans. A person who is coerced into doing something that he would not have done otherwise can point to the fact in order to be excused: it was not his choice; it was imposed on him; it was coerced. The incompatibilist may argue something like this:

12. If determinism is true, then all human choices are coerced.

13. If a person's choice is coerced, then that person cannot be morally responsible for it.

   *Therefore*

14. If determinism is true, then no person can be morally responsible for any of his choices.

   *Which is to say*

6. Determinism is incompatible with moral responsibility.

In response, the Calvinist must obviously reject premise (12), and maintain that determinism does not in fact entail any sort of coercion; but to properly assess the merits of the allegation, attention must first be paid to the meaning of the word at the center of the charge: "coercion." What does coercion mean, and what sort of condition would be both necessary and sufficient to feature coercion? These questions are important for assessing the objection at hand. Unfortunately, like many concepts in metaphysics, coercion is as controversial and difficult to thoroughly analyze philosophically as it is easy to recognize intuitively (at least in some clear cases). As a modest starting point, then, a conveniently simple picture can be painted: one may define coercion as being the act of persuading an unwilling person to do something, by use of force or threats. One should further note that the coerced action could consist in either *doing* something or *saying* something. Under these headings respectively, it is proper to say that:

15. Hostages were coerced into staying in the bank by the robbers.

Or that:

16. The confession of a suspect was coerced by torture.

The former are performing an action and the latter is merely voicing information, but there is no morally significant difference between the two actions: both are cases of coercion, for persuading previously unwilling persons to *do* something (action or speech) by the use of force or threats.

Real difficulty arises however when two complications enter the picture: first, "threats" are themselves a difficult concept to pin down, and second, not even all successful threats are instances of coercion.[1] But let us prudently sidestep these difficulties for the moment, and uphold the obvious point that premise (13) is true: using this initial, intuitive (albeit incomplete) understanding of coercion, it is clear enough that coercion removes moral responsibility. Consider (15) and (16). If one of the hostages ends up missing his daughter's piano recital during that afternoon, thereby, say, breaking his promise to be there for it, his upset wife cannot hold him responsible and blame him for his failure to make good on his promise, for he was coerced to stay in the bank against his will. Similarly, if the suspect's

---

1. These two complex matters are discussed and partially resolved in Frankfurt, "Coercion and Moral Responsibility," 26–46. Regarding the first one, Frankfurt notes that threats are bi-conditional proposals to bring about a state of affairs if a person performs an action, and to not bring it about if the person does not perform the action. The difficulty is that simple *offers* are also such bi-conditional proposals, so that threats must be distinguished from offers by another criterion. To that effect, Frankfurt discusses the plausible suggestion that "a threat holds out to its recipient the danger of incurring a penalty, while an offer holds out to him the possibility of gaining a benefit" (p.28). A complex discussion follows of how to measure whether certain consequences amount to benefits or penalties, and while Frankfurt's suggestions seem convincing enough, it is not necessary for the evaluation of the present argument to interact with his complex proposals. As to the second matter, the question of when successful threats do amount to coercion, Frankfurt considers various conditions, showing one after another how they fail to suffice for coercion, as they each can be featured in a situation which still does not amount to coercion. This leaves us with a list of probably necessary conditions, but no great certainty that their conjunction amounts to a sufficient condition. Here again, a full evaluation of Frankfurt's proposal is not necessary for the proper evaluation of the incompatibilist argument at hand.

confession turned out to be a false confession, he could hardly be morally responsible for "lying" if torture made it so that his confession was coerced, and forced out of him under duress against his will. It is thus understood that true coercion excludes moral responsibility; there is no use contesting this point. Hence, the question at hand will be whether theistic determinism entails a sort of coercion that excludes moral responsibility for human choices.

Does it, then? Is a determinist choice necessarily coerced? It is hard to see why it would be. On the theistic compatibilist account, all human choices are determined by God's providential decree, but on the pain of begging the question, incompatibilists cannot assume that the only way to operate such an efficacious decree is to use force or threats. Neither of these need be involved in the compatibilist story of how God providentially determines the outcomes of human choices, or at any rate, such coercion need not be involved in *all* determinist human choices—contrary to what the incompatibilist objector would have to assume in premise (12). On theistic compatibilism, in usual cases of human free choices, God does not determine the actions of humans *against* their wills, but *through* their wills. God usually employs neither threats nor physical force, but rather, he providentially influences human hearts to willingly accomplish his purposes in all things. Of course, incompatibilists very well may disagree with this story, but it coherently excludes divine *coercion* for human choices freely made in the compatibilist sense. So premise (12) is more than unproven, it is demonstrably false, because one cannot have coercion without threats or force. At this point, the fully specified criterion of what is *sufficient* for coercion has yet to be offered, but whatever *else* may be needed to secure coercion beyond mere threats, we know that threats or force are nonetheless *necessary*. And since threats and force are absent from the coherent compatibilist account of a normal free choice, it is false that determinism entails coercion.

## Does our incomplete grasp of coercion afford an incompatibilism of the gaps?

The above conclusion is a partial victory that deserves proper celebration, but compatibilists may not be out of the woods just yet, because as long as the fully specified criterion of what is sufficient for coercion is out missing, one may fear that a commitment to compatibilism perhaps prevents the successful identification of such a criterion. If determinism isn't sufficient for coercion, then maybe there is nothing else that will work to sufficiently entail coercion. As long as we have this gap in our knowledge of coercion, it could be that this gap is filled with incompatibilist commitments. In other words, our objector would claim that "featuring determined-ness" is the only valid reason why a given instance of threats ever does amount to a coercion that excludes moral responsibility (since we saw that threats alone are not sufficient for true coercion). The charge would be that when assessing whether or not an action was coerced, the only successful way to conclude that coercion took place would be to point out that the action was determined; determinedness would be the only true measure of coercion. But if that's the case, and we as compatibilists maintain that determinism does not entail coercion, then maybe it prevents us from ever successfully identifying coercion. Maybe there is nothing else that we can identify, that will suffice to conclude that any action ever truly is coerced, short of de-terminedness. And since obviously there is such a thing as coercion in this world, it would mean that compatibilism is an impossible commitment. So what is a compatibilist to respond?

The first thing to point out is that these conjectures are, if not false, at least unsupported. Speculation about missing knowledge of what may or may not be a problematic shortcoming of compatibilism is not an argument against compatibilism. If the criterion for a successful identification of coercion is in fact truly missing in this knowledge gap, then it is missing for everyone, and no one may assume without an argument that, when found, it will undermine compatibilism and support incompatibilism.

And secondly, on the positive side, there are three options for compatibilists to refute the charge. The first would be to fill that knowledge gap: produce this golden list of conditions that are jointly sufficient for coercion and do not include determinism. This might be feasible, but it remains a rather difficult task, whereas two other, easier responses should singlehand-edly settle the matter, in the facts that: 1. the logic of the charge is actually invalid so that even if true, nothing follows about compatibilism; and 2. even incompatibilists themselves cannot endorse and coherently uphold this objection.

The shared premise for these two responses is the fact that if the present charge were correct, then it would follow that coercion entails de-terminedness.[2] Indeed, if determinedness entails coercion and allegedly

2. Notice that I here spoke of "determinedness" rather than "determinism." Both of these refer to the same metaphysical concept of determination, but "determinism" is the view that *all* choices are thus determined. Instead, "determinedness" in the pres-ent argument, only referred to the single specific choice under consideration, as one can coherently believe that coercion entails *determinedness* (in which case all coerced choices are determined), and yet that *determinism* is false as long as some other, non-coerced choices are indeterminist.

nothing short of determinedness suffices for coercion, then it means that it takes determinedness to have coercion. It means that determinedness is *necessary* for coercion. But nothing in compatibilism requires that this be false. Let us suppose that coercion entails determinedness; compatibilists could easily respond that determinedness is only one of several items in the list of what is jointly sufficient for coercion, and hence does not in itself suffice for coercion, so that we would have "coercion entails determinedness," and "coercion excludes moral responsibility," from which it would not for a moment follow that "determinedness excludes moral responsibility." If A $\Rightarrow$ B and A $\Rightarrow$ C, it doesn't follow that B $\Rightarrow$ C. Therefore, even if it turned out to be true that coercion entails determinedness, it wouldn't follow that compatibilism is false.

But secondly, is that premise even tenable for our incompatibilist objectors? It is likely not. What this charge is pressing is that coercion entails determinedness. It means that our objector must maintain that there is no coercion without determinedness. But isn't this too strong a commitment, even for a libertarian incompatibilist? On a libertarian reading of coercion, the person who is coerced by force or threats may be constrained in his accessible options and thereby lack access to "reasonable" or "attractive" alternatives,[3] but why think he has *no* alternative? He still presumably uses his indeterminist, libertarian free will to *either* submit to the threat *or* resist it and pay the unreasonably high penalty. Coercion removes his moral responsibility (because the penalty *is* unreasonably high), but presumably does not alter the metaphysical fabric of the allegedly indeterminist human will with which he picks the reasonable way out. So incompatibilists too, will need to work on providing a sufficient condition for threats to entail coercion, and it will not (for it apparently cannot) hang on mere determinism. Consequently, as long as this is the case, compatibilists will probably be happy to accept any reasonable account that libertarians may produce. Determinism being out of the picture, nothing is likely to be disputed between compatibilists and incompatibilists on this question. Coercion may still not be fully analyzed, gaps in our knowledge may still remain, but it has now been shown that determinism is neither necessary nor sufficient for coercion.

---

3. More will be said in chapter 5 on the issue of access to alternate possibilities and its relationship to moral responsibility.

## Is determinism analogous to coercion?

But finally, maybe we have been too strict in our reading of the objection in either direction. Maybe the incompatibilist does not mean to say that determinism actually *entails* (nor *is entailed by*) universal coercion. And perhaps there is a similar, more modest, objection located in its neighborhood that still demands an answer. A more promising formulation of the charge could be that determined choices and coerced choices are *analogous*. It could be that there is something *about* determinism that is *shared* with plain old coercion, and which in both cases excludes moral responsibility; a problematic feature of both determinism and coercion that is simply highlighted for determinists by raising the ugly specter of coercion.

On that reading of the coercion objection, what compatibilists need to do is ask exactly what features coercion and determinism may have in common, and present a coherent account of why, in spite of these commonalities, the former excludes moral responsibility while the latter does not. This compatibilist answer will once again expose the so-called fallacy of the undistributed middle: just because two things have one part in common does not mean that they have everything in common. In our case, it must clearly be granted that determinism and coercion do have some things in common. For example, they share a certain sort of irresistibility: just as the coercive policeman obtains what he wants without the contrary will of the criminal standing in his way, the Calvinist God obtains what he wants without the contrary wills of sinful humans standing in the way of his decrees.[4] Other decent candidates for the analogous feature may be the fact that in neither case is it "ultimately" or "absolutely" up to the person what he does, or again that the person "lacks the ability to do otherwise." These objections must (and will later on) be reviewed in their own right, but it becomes clear that they are no longer about coercion proper, and hence make way for the two following compatibilist responses. First, if it is no longer *in virtue of* involving coercion that the determinist account is said to exclude moral responsibility, we need to hear an argument for why it would. What justification is there for thinking that determinism is analogous to coercion? Why should we think that a feature of coercion that excludes moral responsibility is necessarily present (with the same effect) in determinism also? And secondly, the charge can actually be proven false. To do so, let us here again phrase the present argument as a deductive syllogism:

---

4. In particular, this is so when the decree in question is God's graceful choice to regenerate a rebellious sinner by means of his so-called "irresistible grace."

17. Choices made under coercion have a property that excludes moral responsibility.

18. If choices made under coercion have a property that excludes moral responsibility, then that property is also possessed by any choices made on determinism.

*Therefore*

19. Choices made on determinism have a property that excludes moral responsibility.

*Which is to say*

6. Determinism is incompatible with moral responsibility.

This careful statement of the argument makes it clear that premise (18) is the problem. We can better appreciate its question-begging nature: the incompatibilist has yet to prove that any property of coerced choices that excludes moral responsibility necessarily carries over to determined choices. But more importantly, this premise is more than unproven, it is false, and to show it, all compatibilists need to do is to identify a property, which: 1. is featured in cases of coercion, 2. excludes moral responsibility, and 3. is not featured by compatibilist, determinist human free choices. Such a property has in fact already been identified above: "the use of force or threats." The three above conditions for a successful defeater are fulfilled: coercion by definition employs force or threats; the use of force or threats (at a level of intensity that amounts to coercion) does exclude moral responsibility, and normal cases of determinist, compatibilist free choices feature neither force nor threats. Consequently, compatibilists possess a perfectly coherent account of why coercion excludes moral responsibility while determinism does not: the dis-analogous feature between coercion and determinist divine decrees is the use of force or threats, or lack thereof.

Of course one may object again (as was discussed in the "pets and puppets" argument) that my formulation of the argument by analogy is too strong. With its premise (18), it presses the stronger claim that "there exists no relevant difference between coercion and determinism," whereas all the objector technically needs to press is the weaker claim that "there exists one relevant similarity between coercion and determinism." But what I said in the case of pets and puppets applies here to coercion: without telling us *what* the alleged relevant similarity is, the weaker claim is too weak to get the argument off the ground without begging the question. That is why proponents of the argument must naturally turn to the stronger claim, against which I just offered a rebutting defeater by providing a relevant difference.

Therefore, the incompatibilist argument on divine coercion (even by mere analogy) is shown to fail, and we must proceed in our search for a successful incompatibilist argument.

## Repetition, exhaustiveness, and the danger of the mutatis mutandis shortcut

Besides pets, puppets, and coercion, there are a few additional, comparable conditions, which probably annul or undermine moral responsibility regardless of one's view on the compatibility question: various kinds of manipulation (such as hypnosis and brain control) or mental illnesses (such as perhaps severe cases of autism, schizophrenia, and other psychiatric disorders). All of these may be—or are in fact—similarly suggested by incompatibilists to provide grounds for a rejection of compatibilism.

Having provided a thorough refutation of the already somewhat overlapping "pets and puppets" argument and "coercion" argument, it has become apparent that many of these incompatibilist objections exhibit direct parallels and their invalid reasoning features strictly identical errors. Accordingly, their compatibilist refutations must feature a good deal of repetition, as these objections all share much of the same logical core, only declined a bit differently in each case. Given the likely repetitions, then, it is tempting to forego their full refutation, rest on the strength of the above responses, and gladly announce that all the other similar arguments fail in the same manner, as my above counterarguments apply to them *mutatis mutandis*.

Nevertheless, this temptation must be resisted. For all their similarities, some of these incompatibilist contentions do feature unique aspects (albeit small and secondary), which I believe call for special comments. In order to leave no stone unturned, these conditions must be investigated in their own right, and incompatibilist contentions refuted, running the risk of repetition, but hopefully securing exhaustiveness. The first candidate on that list is "manipulation," to which we now turn.

3

# The manipulation argument

SEVERAL FAMOUS MANIPULATION ARGUMENTS are on offer in the incompatibilist literature and need to be addressed specifically in this work. They will be in the course of this chapter, but in order to properly analyze what manipulation is, and to progressively build a coherent response, I will begin as I did for the coercion argument, with a review of simpler (perhaps more naïve) formulations of the argument, before refining the charge, and eventually interacting with the sophisticated formulations of the argument by such proponents as Derk Pereboom, Alfred Mele, Robert Kane, and Katherin Rogers. For now, let's begin by assessing whether determinism simply *entails* manipulation.

## Does determinism entail manipulation?

Similarly to the other claims mentioned above, the manipulation argument asserts that determinist decrees on the part of God amount to manipulation, leading to an exclusion of moral responsibility. The initial argument has the following form:

20. If determinism is true, then all human choices are "manipulated."

21. If a person's choice is "manipulated," then that person cannot be morally responsible for it.

    *Therefore*

14. If determinism is true, then no person can be morally responsible for any of his choices.

    *Which is to say*

6. Determinism is incompatible with moral responsibility.

As was the case with "coercion," it is not entirely clear what is meant by "manipulation" if left unqualified, so the analysis must be pushed a bit further. There are two such things in human experience that we ordinarily

call "manipulation" and which I see are good candidates for an explanation of why an agent cannot be held morally responsible.[1] I shall call them
"influencing manipulation," and "overriding manipulation." The former,
"influencing manipulation," happens when a person[2] attempts to bring
about a choice or action by another agent, by cleverly, unfairly, or unscru-
pulously influencing the agent. It can take the form of subliminal messages,
emotional blackmail, misinformation, or any such manipulating practice,[3]
as long as they are coming at the agent from the outside, to be processed as
input by his cognitive faculties, conscious or subconscious. In contrast, the
latter kind, which I called "overriding manipulation," involves a full bypass
of the agent's will, by directly handling the agent's inner, decision-making
faculties. These could be brought about by means of hypnosis, drugs, love
potions, or direct physical handling of the agent's brain activity, to bring
about a certain outcome.

Having distinguished between these two sorts of manipulation, let us
now raise first the question of whether premise (21) is true. Does either kind
of manipulation actually exclude moral responsibility?

On the "overriding" reading of manipulation, I think premise (21) is
rather obviously true. An agent who undergoes this kind of outright bypass-
ing of the will cannot be held morally responsible. He cannot be said to
"own" the decision that was forced upon him in this fashion. The compatibilist response to the manipulation argument so understood will thus have
to be a rejection of premise (20), which I shall offer in a moment.

But what should we think about the "influencing" reading of manipulation? Here, the matter is more complex, and it is not as easy to assess
whether the agent is in fact responsible. Personally, I tend to be skeptical that
mere influencing manipulation can remove the moral responsibility of the
manipulated party. I accept that such practices are usually morally wrong,
that they are indeed leading the manipulated person to do something that

1. I do not at all pretend that these are the only two possible understandings of
"manipulation." I realize the word can be used with a variety of meanings, but the ones I
identify here are the only two that are relevant to considerations of moral responsibility.
That one can speak of a chiropractor "manipulating" a spine, a chef "manipulating" his
cooking knife or a computer software "manipulating" data, has little relevance to the
question of whether determinist divine decrees amount to a manipulation that excludes
moral responsibility.

2. Or perhaps it could be a group of persons.

3. Allen Wood, following Marcia Baron, helpfully classifies these practices under
three headings: 1. Deception (lying, misleading, encouraging false assumptions, foster-
ing self-deception, etc.), 2. Pressuring (offering the wrong sort of reason, threats that
fall short of coercion, etc.), and 3. Appeals to emotions, needs, or character flaws. See
Wood, "Coercion, Manipulation, Exploitation," 31–32, 35.

he possibly or even probably would not have done in the absence of these manipulative practices, but if he does it, it seems to me he is still in control of what he chooses in the situation, even if it's a situation he would have preferred not to be in. Joe Campbell illustrates this point:

> Suppose that some radical rightwing nuts found out that Bill Clinton had a fondness for girls from Texas with big hair. Given this, they decided to manipulate him into having an affair with Monica Lewinsky. That alone wouldn't show that Clinton's actions were unfree. Nor would it show that he was not blameworthy for his actions.[4]

That seems right to me. But let's suppose I am wrong. Let's suppose that influencing manipulation at times *does* reach the height of removing the moral responsibility of a manipulated person. In that case, whether the person who undergoes these influences can be morally excused for caving in will then be a matter of degree: the degree of intensity of the emotional attacks and the degree of wrongness of the action that results. In other words, how much have these influences buffeted the agent, and how much of them is it reasonable to expect a person to absorb before they waver through what can properly be described as no fault of their own? To this question, of course, I do not have an answer; I only know that *if* influencing manipulation ever removes moral responsibility, there must be a threshold somewhere, because it is quite obvious that homeopathic doses of mild annoyances do not justify murder, even if one concedes that, on the opposite end of the spectrum, we shouldn't blame a person for failing to contain some degree of anger if they have been consistently and heavily harassed for years. Somewhere in the middle must lie the supposed threshold. Given this, for the argument at hand, we are left with two cases in which premise (21) is claimed to be true, that is, two cases wherein manipulation is said to exclude moral responsibility. They are cases of 1. "overriding manipulation," and 2. "influencing manipulation" where the intensity of the manipulation is high enough and the wrongness of the act low enough that the agent could be excused. In both these cases, manipulation is said to exclude moral responsibility. As I mentioned, I think premise (21) is true only in cases of overriding manipulation, but let's grant to the incompatibilist that premise (21) is true in both cases. The compatibilist must then turn his guns upon premise (20).

Premise (20) asserts that determinism entails manipulation in such fashion. So, does it? Here again it is hard to see why it would. Why would determinism necessarily entail manipulation? Many of the same responses

4. Campbell, *Free Will*, 69.

to the coercion argument apply here. On the theistic compatibilist account, all human choices are determined by God's providential decree, but on the pain of begging the question, incompatibilists cannot assume that the only way to operate such an efficacious decree is to use "manipulation" *proper*, whether it be influencing or overriding. Neither of these need be involved in the compatibilist story of how God providentially determines the outcomes of human choices, or at any rate, such manipulation need not be involved in *all* determinist human choices—contrary to what the incompatibilist objector would have to uphold in premise (20). On theistic compatibilism, God providentially works in human hearts thereby ensuring that his purposes are willingly accomplished in all things, but in usual cases of normal free choices, God uses none of the manipulating mechanisms described above to do so: he does not harass, blackmail, misinform, hypnotize, drug, or brain-short-circuit us. The normal mechanism used by God on Calvinism to bring about human free choices lacks the features that are necessary for "influencing manipulation," so it follows that determinism does not entail "influencing manipulation." Premise (20) is thus false on the "influencing" reading of manipulation.

When it comes to "overriding manipulation," however, the refutation may be less clear-cut, but a similar contention must be made: the compatibilist account of a free choice need not involve any of the mechanisms that have been admitted or shown to entail "overriding manipulation." This is a more modest claim: it is not a direct refutation; it is merely a demand for positive arguments, with the accusation that incompatibilist objectors are still begging the question on this point. This is still a serious problem for the incompatibilist objector, but there lies a difference between the manipulation and the coercion arguments. Whereas compatibilists could refute premise (12) on the basis that there existed features necessary for coercion which are absent from the compatibilist account of free choice (namely the use of threats or force), in the case of "overriding manipulation," there is no such feature. There is no feature absent from the compatibilist account and which our incompatibilist objectors are committed to seeing as necessary for manipulation. Hence, premise (20) cannot be directly *refuted* by compatibilists, and all that is available for us to do is respond that we disagree, that we think it is false, and that it has not been proven by incompatibilists on whose shoulders the burden of proof still lies. I think one can no more prove directly that determinism entails "overriding manipulation" than that it does not (outside of independent arguments for why compatibilism itself is true, of course[5]). Consequently, the ambitious syllogism offered above

---

5. In that case, the proof would go like this: if determinism entails overriding

must fail, and the best hope of the incompatibilist will again have to be the claim that maybe determinism and "overriding manipulation" are *analogous*, so that compatibilists are engaging in special pleading when rejecting moral responsibility on the basis of the latter and upholding it in the face of the former. I will review this claim in a moment, but let us first address a worry similar to the one which arose with coercion: does our incomplete grasp of influencing manipulation afford an incompatibilism of the gaps? Is determinism the only possible reason why outside influences ever amount to "influencing manipulation" to a degree that excludes moral responsibility?

## Does our incomplete grasp of "influencing manipulation" afford an incompatibilism of the gaps?

Just as we were missing a sufficient criterion to declare that a given course of action amounts to coercion, I have now pointed out that we might also be missing a sufficient criterion to declare that a given course of action amounts to "influencing manipulation" to the degree that suffices to exclude moral responsibility. This might be another "gap" in our knowledge, which may (for all we know) contain an incompatibilist commitment. By affirming that determinism does not entail manipulation, compatibilists might be unable to specify what *does* amount to manipulation. Maybe no such sufficient criterion can be offered short of determinedness.

Of course, if, as I suspect, influencing manipulation *doesn't* remove moral responsibility, then there is no argument here. Incompatibilist commitments will not be found in a list of conditions for influencing manipulation to remove moral responsibility, if there is no such list of sufficient conditions. But let us once more suppose that I am wrong, and see if the charge can be answered on other grounds. As it turns out, this charge admits the same answer I offered in the case of coercion: the first thing to point out is that these conjectures are, if not false, at least unsupported. Speculation about missing knowledge of what may or may not be a problematic shortcoming of compatibilism is not an argument against compatibilism. If the criterion for a successful identification of influencing manipulation is in fact truly missing, then it is missing for everyone, and incompatibilists cannot assume without an argument that, when found in the gap, it will undermine compatibilism and support incompatibilism.

As to the positive side, there are three options for compatibilists to refute the charge. First, one could fill in the gap. One could find and offer

---

manipulation, then compatibilism is false, but compatibilism is independently known to be true, therefore determinism does not entail overriding manipulation.

this sought-after criterion, which suffices to identify cases when influencing manipulation removes moral responsibility, but this is rather difficult
(especially since I think it doesn't exist), and the two other responses should
settle the matter in that: 1. the logic of the charge is invalid so that even
if true, nothing follows about compatibilism; and 2. even incompatibilists
themselves cannot endorse and coherently uphold this objection.

The shared premise for these two responses is the fact that if the present charge were correct, then it would follow that influencing manipulation entails determinedness. Indeed, if determinedness entails influencing
manipulation and allegedly nothing short of determinedness suffices for
influencing manipulation, then it means that it takes determinedness to
have influencing manipulation. It means that determinedness is *necessary*
for influencing manipulation. But nothing in compatibilism requires that
this be false. Let us suppose that influencing manipulation entails determinedness; compatibilists could easily respond that determinedness is only
one of several items in the list of what is jointly sufficient for influencing
manipulation, and hence does not in itself suffice for influencing manipulation, so that we would have "influencing manipulation (at the proper level
of intensity) entails determinedness," and "influencing manipulation (at the
proper level of intensity) excludes moral responsibility," from which it does
not for a moment follow that "determinedness excludes moral responsibility." If A ⇒ B and A ⇒ C, it doesn't follow that B ⇒ C. Therefore even if it
turned out to be true that influencing manipulation entails determinedness,
it wouldn't follow that compatibilism is false.

But secondly, that premise is not even tenable for our incompatibilist objectors. Even if incompatibilism and indeterminism are true, there
presumably are folks who undergo influencing manipulation, and yet still
employ their indeterminist will to voluntarily (even if rather reluctantly)
succumb to the manipulation rather than resist it. Since the agent is not in
this case directly caused by its manipulator but only indirectly influenced,
there can be such a situation apart from determinedness, which shows that
determinedness is not necessary for influencing manipulation, and hence
that a sufficient criterion for influencing manipulation could be found apart
from determinedness.

## Is determinism analogous to manipulation?

Having rejected the claims that determinism is necessary or sufficient for
manipulation, we now come to what is the most serious issue pressed by
incompatibilists with respect to manipulation: if manipulation excludes

moral responsibility, then how is it that determinism does not? What is the relevant difference, they ask? The incompatibilist claim at hand is that determinism and manipulation are *analogous*; they are relevantly similar, so that if one excludes moral responsibility (which manipulation does[6]), then allegedly the other one should too. Incompatibilists argue that in the recipe for manipulation, the ingredient that makes it unsuitable for moral responsibility is also found in determinism, wherein it should have the same effect.

On a side note, one should remark that this argument could now be pressed by incompatibilists on theistic *or atheistic* views alike. The earlier claim that determinism *entails* manipulation was only meaningful on theism, because presumably God would be the one doing the manipulation, and it made little sense to imagine the universe would: mindless universes don't typically engage in manipulation. But here, one need not believe in God to allege that manipulation and determinism share a relevant property, and hence the charge is of interest to all compatibilists and incompatibilists, theists and atheists alike.

In response to this claim, first, we must here again simply point out that if determinism neither entails nor is entailed by manipulation, then it is no longer *in virtue of* involving manipulation, that determinism allegedly excludes moral responsibility, and hence we must be looking for yet another incompatibilist argument, as manipulation *proper* is no longer the issue. To do so, the incompatibilist objector is invited to identify what the relevant similarity is. What is that common ingredient; that shared property which determinism and manipulation allegedly have in common, and which excludes moral responsibility? The incompatibilist cannot respond that it is their determinism (given of course a determinist understanding of "overriding manipulation" on his part), since that would presuppose that determinism excludes moral responsibility, circularly arguing for incompatibilism on the basis that incompatibilism is true. But until that relevantly shared property can be offered (and its relevance properly argued) by incompatibilists,

---

6. A theoretically available option for compatibilists is to offer the so-called "hard-line" response to the manipulation argument: responding that manipulation does *not* exclude moral responsibility. This response works just fine when all we consider are the cases of mild influencing manipulation wherein it is reasonable to maintain moral responsibility for the manipulated party, but as we have seen, these are not the only cases of manipulation, so that the hard-line response is not always available. There are at least *some* cases in which manipulation clearly excludes moral responsibility, and hence, assuming that those are the ones presently pressed against compatibilism, I here marshal the so-called "soft-line" response instead, the claim that this sort of manipulation does exclude moral responsibility, but that determinism does not, as it is dis-analogous to these cases of manipulation.

the claim that determinism and manipulation are analogous must remain question-begging.

Secondly, to go beyond a charge of begging the question and on to a positive refutation, let us phrase the incompatibilist argument in its rigorous syllogistic form:

22. Choices made under manipulation have a property that excludes moral responsibility.

23. If choices made under manipulation have a property that excludes moral responsibility, then that property is also possessed by all choices on determinism.

*Therefore*

19. Choices made on determinism have a property that excludes moral responsibility.

*Which is to say*

6. Determinism is incompatible with moral responsibility.

The gain in clarity allows us to phrase our two-fold response that premise (23) is still question-begging, and that it is in fact demonstrably false. Before I establish that, let me repeat briefly the remark I made in the case of the "pets and puppets" argument and the "coercion" argument. We can differentiate between the stronger claim that "there exists no relevant difference between manipulation and determinism," and the weaker claim that "there exists one relevant similarity between manipulation and determinism." Just as I did in the previous arguments, premise (23) is here again presupposing the stronger claim, because the weaker claim is too obviously question-begging. Let me now show that premise (23), pressing the weaker claim, is still question-begging, and demonstrably false.

First, then, we are still in need of an argument for why any property of manipulation that excludes moral responsibility should also be found in normal determined choices. How would one prove such a thing? Even if compatibilists were incapable of providing a counterexample, it wouldn't follow that none exists. But in fact, compatibilists can prove the premise false, by identifying that relevantly dis-analogous property. What they need in order to refute (23) is a property that: 1. is featured in cases of manipulation, 2. excludes moral responsibility, and 3. is not featured by compatibilist, determinist human free choices.

Let me then suggest that the relevant difference we are looking for is predicated upon a moral principle much like the following: "in order for a human choice to be morally responsible, it is necessary that the choice be made on the basis of that person's *God-given character and desires.*" In other words, for a choice to be free such that its maker is morally responsible, it need not be undetermined, but it does need to be determined (assuming determinism is true) by the agent's *own* desires, which flow from the agent's God-given character and inclinations. For example, when I chose to propose to my wife, the choice flowed out of my own character and desires, all of which I as a Calvinist still assert were providentially (and romantically!) predestined by my maker—in that sense, she truly *was* my destiny (and irresistible). On the other hand, when one engages in acts of manipulation (whether overriding or influencing at sufficient strength if there is such a thing), he "meddles" with another agent's God-given desires. He brings about a choice that is *not* made on the basis of this person's God-given character and desires, but instead desires that were humanly manufactured (either directly or indirectly), and for which the agent cannot be held morally responsible.

Several comments are in order.

First, this criterion is exactly the kind of property that incompatibilists were demanding, as it fulfills the three above conditions for a successful defeater: 1. the problematic meddling with God-given desires is obviously featured in cases of manipulation, 2. it excludes moral responsibility, and 3. it is absent on theological determinism in cases of normal, free choices made according to God-given desires. If this condition is properly understood, it is obvious that God-decreed compatibilist free choices satisfy it. In normal cases, the providential Calvinist God does not meddle with nor override our God-given desires; God simply providentially gives them: self-evidently, God is the giver of that which is God-given. God's divine work in our hearts is not a meddling interference in the way of our God-given characters and desires; it is their very legitimate creative source. So God's providential dealings in the normal cases cannot be said to feature this characteristic that excludes moral responsibility, whereas manipulation clearly does.

Secondly, I must note that its fulfillment of the three conditions is not even controversial, as it is not presupposing a compatibilist view of free will. It is quite compatible with indeterminism, because even incompatibilists are committed to the fact that if a person's character and desires are "meddled with" by a controlling agent who is not God, then it excludes moral responsibility. Of course, they would *also* believe that it does so when *God* controls the agent, which I don't, but that is irrelevant to my contention at hand. It remains that incompatibilists themselves are committed to the fact that my above condition is necessary for moral responsibility. And since this demand of free expression of one's God-given desires is not met by cases of manipulation and met by compatibilist free choices, it follows that it is a sufficient explanation for why determinism would not exclude moral responsibility even though manipulation does.

Thirdly, this criterion I'm suggesting isn't a complete novelty. In many respects, it is similar to statements made by both Brian Leftow and Susan Wolf when they each use the concept of a person's "real self," or John Martin Fischer when discussing "mechanism ownership." Susan Wolf speaks of a "real self" view,[7] according to which an agent is responsible if and only if choices are made or controlled by the "real self," captured by a set of values. The main difference between this and my view is that I claim that the real self of an individual is God-given, whereas she says: "But it does not matter where her real self comes from."[8] So naturally, she argues that one may manipulate the content of the real self, whereas it is impossible on my view: only God sets the real self. As to Brian Leftow, he writes:

> On the "expressivist" account, I am responsible for whatever appropriately expresses my rational judgments, values or character. It does not matter that I cannot do otherwise; I am responsible because the act is a genuine outflow (in the circumstances) of my real self.[9]

These remarks mesh well with the presently offered condition: moral responsibility ascribes praise or blame for the outflow of one's God-given character, or one's "real self." My model is also reminiscent of John Martin Fischer's notion of "mechanism ownership"[10]: whether we speak of "real self," or "ownership of the mechanism," it seems we are all trying to identify the same sort of condition of authenticity for a free, un-manipulated choice. My model simply suggests that the proper source of one's "real self" or "mechanism ownership" is God as creator.

Finally, and contrary to what will likely be the chief incompatibilist objection, my criterion is *not* arbitrary. What amounts to manipulation for any human being may very well not be so for their creator *in virtue of who God is*. As Paul Helm points out,

> It may be that whenever one creature governs another, the one governed suffers a diminution of his personal responsibility. Even if this is true, it does not follow that when God governs his creatures they are not responsible for what they do.[11]

7. Wolf, *Freedom Within Reason*, 23–45.
8. Ibid., 37.
9. Leftow, "Tempting God," 20.
10. See Fischer and Ravizza, *Responsibility and Control*.
11. Helm, *Providence of God*, 33.

Compatibilist or incompatibilist, on anyone's view that purports to be biblical, God almighty's position is radically different from that of his creatures. When it is forbidden for us to go and kill our neighbors, it is perfectly within God's prerogative, as the author of life, to give it and to take it away. God comfortably exercises this prerogative and quite openly declares this much in scripture: "I kill and make alive, I wound and I heal" (Deut 32:39); "The LORD kills and brings to life; he brings down to Sheol and raises up" (1 Sam 2:6). It is no more arbitrary that God can providentially determine human choices while for me to do so would be manipulation, than it is that God can take life as he pleases while for me to do so would be murder.

To drive the point home and put to rest the charge of arbitrariness, it is helpful to note that something like the criterion of God-given-ness as a necessary condition for authenticity holds true in other fields than ethics, such as aesthetics or athletics. A person's beauty, in a certain sense, is authentic only if it is God-given,[12] and not the product of man-made plastic surgery. Similarly, a person's athletic performance is recognized to be genuine only if it is the labor of God-given abilities and not doping with man-made, performance-enhancing drugs. That our moral responsibility would be dependent in this way on the God-given-ness of our characters and desires should not baffle us any more than it does in these less controversial fields: God is our rightful maker, and who or how we truly, genuinely, authentically are is to be found in how God—not a plastic surgeon, not a steroids syringe and not a mad scientist manipulator—makes us. As such, it is not special pleading to assert that God can and indeed does do things that we cannot and should not do. The way Calvinists see it, providentially determining human choices is one such thing.

Another objection might concern my appeal to God. At the onset of this work, I listed two different sorts of determinism: one wherein choices are determined by God: theological determinism, and another one wherein choices are determined by the laws of nature regardless of whether God exists. Since I am now appealing to God in my response to the manipulation argument, one may object that I am only defending the compatibility of moral responsibility with *theological* determinism, and fail to defend

12. The modest sense that is in view here does not intend to claim that plastic surgery is always wrong, or that some plastic surgery cannot be seen as "God-given" also in another sense. One could certainly say that God, in his general providence, has graciously "given" plastic surgery, let's say for folks who suffered face-altering injuries to recover a more pleasing silhouette. There is nothing wrong with that use of the phrase; it is just not the sense of God-given-ness that is in view here. Rather, the intended sense is simply the one according to which my wife's natural beauty is "God-given" in a way that it would not be if she had a forehead full of Botox, silicon in her lips and collagen in her cheeks. This much should be uncontroversial.

compatibilism with respect to merely physical, secular determinism, which would be a failure to defend compatibilism *simpliciter*. In response, I shall simply plead guilty. I agree that I find it very hard to think of a relevant difference between cases of manipulation and cases of normal, determined choices if God does not exist. That is a tacit admission that for all I know, manipulation arguments might very well be successful against non-theological determinism. It is therefore a good reason to adopt theological determinism, and in effect amounts to an argument for the existence of God for compatibilists! I doubt that many atheist philosophers will find it compelling, but that is not the point: it remains that if God exists, as I happily affirm, my above answer *is* available, and successfully preserves the compatibility of moral responsibility with theological determinism, the sort of determinism upheld by Calvinists.

One final objection might be a complaint that if our choices are determined by our fallen-ness, that fallen-ness might count as a case of manipulation, since it was human-caused by Adam—thus our fallen-ness would undermine moral responsibility. Alternatively, if we say that our fallen condition is actually God-given (to avoid the manipulation charge), that may seem theologically problematic. To this, I respond first that Adam's action, whatever else it was, does not seem to meet either definitions of what I have called influencing or overriding manipulation. My criterion for assessing the moral responsibility of a manipulated party may thus not even be relevant here: Adam is not sending us misinformation, or subliminal messages, or love potions, or manipulating our brains with electrodes, etc. But secondly, if one wants to press Adam's influence on us as a case of overriding manipulation, it seems to me that this influence is not *operated* by Adam. In the words of Romans 5, Adam is the person who brought *condemnation* on the human race, but the condemnation is very much God's. "The judgment following one trespass brought condemnation" (Rom 5:16): it is Adam's trespass, but God's judgment. Now of course, if one thinks that original sin is itself theologically problematic in that way, that is a separate objection, one that targets original sin and not my criterion of God-given-ness for assessing manipulation; but if one admits that the doctrine of original sin is unobjectionable, and that God's condemnation is just and righteous, then it is not "theologically problematic" to think God is the one who carries out this judgment and righteously applies the negative consequences of the fall to our natures as part of said condemnation. On this view, God would do so as our rightful maker, in a way that still counts as the proper source of our characters and identities, leaving intact our moral responsibility regardless of the fallen-ness of our natures. Our characters, while including desires affected by the fall, would remain God-given in the relevant sense.

At this point, technically, enough has been said to consider the manipulation argument refuted, but in order to appreciate how my above criterion of "God-given-ness" fares in responding to such incompatibilist accusations of special pleading, it is helpful to apply it to several more specific formulations of the manipulation argument: the famous "four case" argument by Derk Pereboom, the "zygote" argument by Alfred Mele, the "Walden Two" argument by Robert Kane, and finally the "Divine Controller" argument for incompatibilism suggested by Kane and developed by Katherin Rogers.

## Derk Pereboom's "four case" argument

The so-called "four case" argument by Derk Pereboom is precisely an instance of the manipulation argument as has just been discussed, pressing that manipulation and determinism are relevantly analogous, so that "causal determinism is in principle as much of a threat to moral responsibility as is covert manipulation."[13] Pereboom attempts to support this charge by offering "a series of cases culminating in a deterministic situation that is ordinary from the compatibilist point of view," and which aims to show that "an agent's non-responsibility under covert manipulation generalizes to the ordinary situation."[14] To that end, Pereboom tells four successive stories of a certain professor Plum who kills a certain Ms. White, and in each case, Pereboom only modifies a few small features about professor Plum, which he contends ought not make a difference to the question of Plum's moral responsibility. In this way, since his first telling of the story (as we will see) obviously excludes Plum's moral responsibility, Pereboom aims to show that each case, especially the fourth and last one, no less excludes moral responsibility. He thus explains his target:

> If I am right, it will turn out that no relevant difference can be found among these cases that would justify denying responsibility under covert manipulation while affirming it in ordinary deterministic circumstances, and this would force an incompatibilist conclusion.[15]

Finding this "relevant difference" is precisely what I claimed to have done with my above criterion of "God-given-ness," so let us see if it successfully adjudicates Pereboom's stories, thereby refuting his charge of special pleading and undercutting his unwarranted "incompatibilist conclusion."

13. Pereboom, *Living*, 89.
14. Ibid., 112.
15. Ibid.

It is worth noting that in each retelling of his story, Pereboom says a great deal about professor Plum's so-called "higher-order desires," or the "reasons-responsiveness" of his decision making process, the "resistibility" of his desire, its flowing out of his "constant character," and his possessing "powers of reflective self-control." All of these exotically named items come straight from the literature on free will, and constitute certain conditions that have been proposed by important compatibilist philosophers, as being sufficient for moral responsibility (and of course compatible with determinism).[16] Pereboom goes out of his way to show that Plum in each case satisfies all these conditions, so that if and when Plum is found not to be morally responsible, it will follow that these compatibilist conditions fail to be sufficient for moral responsibility. But since I neither endorse these complete analyses myself nor even aim at this point to offer a sufficient condition of my own,[17] I have no interest in defending these particular compatibilist accounts. What matters is that I be able to properly exclude moral responsibility when manipulation requires it, and yet coherently maintain moral responsibility in cases of normal determinist free choices. My retelling of Pereboom's stories will therefore gain much in simplicity as I omit all this specific and irrelevant material, and simply mention the parts that are relevant to the manipulation argument at hand, i.e., the parts that seek to establish that manipulation and determinism are relevantly analogous.

Case 1 is described as follows:

> Professor Plum was created by neuroscientists, who can manipulate him directly through the use of radio-like technology, but he is as much like an ordinary human being as is possible, given this history. Suppose these neuroscientists "locally" manipulate him to undertake the process of reasoning by which his desires are brought about and modified—directly producing his every state from moment to moment. The neuroscientists manipulate him by, among other things, pushing a series of buttons just before he begins to reason about his situation, thereby causing his reasoning process to be rationally egoistic.[18]

Pereboom calls for our agreement that Plum is not morally responsible under this kind of manipulation. I happily grant this conclusion: Plum here suffers from what I have called above "overriding manipulation"—which I

---

16. Each is briefly discussed by Pereboom right before he formulates this four case argument of his. He lists them as coming from the pens of David Hume, A. J. Ayer, Harry Frankfurt, John Martin Fischer and Mark Ravizza, and R. Jay Wallace.

17. See chapter 7 for a discussion of such sufficient conditions.

18. Pereboom, *Living*, 112–13.

affirmed in premise (21) excludes moral responsibility—and thus I need not reject any of the contentions of Case 1.

Pereboom goes on to tweak the story of Case 1 to offer Case 2, wherein Plum is no longer "locally" manipulated; but rather, though his decision to kill Ms White still results from the neuroscientists' programming, this programming is now supposed to have taken place once for all in the distant past, rather than at the moment of Plum's choice. Here again, Pereboom's ensuing contentions are most agreeable:

> it would seem unprincipled to claim that here, by contrast with Case 1, Plum is morally responsible because the length of time between the programming and the action is great enough. Whether the programming takes place two seconds or thirty years before the action seems irrelevant to the question of moral responsibility.[19]

All this is well. Plum in Case 2 is still manipulated (by means of over-riding manipulation) and is not morally responsible.

Pereboom continues his tweaking, to produce Case 3, wherein this time,

> Plum is an ordinary human being, except that he was deter-mined by the rigorous training practices of his home and com-munity so that he is often but not exclusively rationally egoistic (exactly as egoistic as in Cases 1 and 2). His training took place at too early an age for him to have had the ability to prevent or alter the practices that determined his character.[20]

And as expected, Pereboom's Case 3 supposes that this instilled ego-istic character leads Plum to murder Ms. White once again. So what is a compatibilist to do with Case 3? It depends. A first difficulty is that Case 3 introduces *two* important changes at once. The first change is that Pereboom has now removed the direct overriding manipulation by neuroscientists. This is where my criterion of God-given-ness helpfully comes in, to justify why Plum, who was not morally responsible in previous cases, could now possibly be: his choice is no longer the fruit of a bypass of his inner, God-given character and desires by means of overriding manipulation. On that basis, since Plum clearly satisfies my offered necessary condition in Case 3 and not in Case 2, it would accordingly be consistent for the compatibilist to maintain that Plum is morally responsible in Case 3 while not in Case

19. Ibid., 114.
20. Ibid.

2—keeping in mind the burden of proving this to be inconsistent is still on the shoulders of the incompatibilist anyway.

But is Plum in fact morally responsible in Case 3? It is hard to tell, because the second change Pereboom introduced simultaneously in Case 3 is now a possible instance of *influencing* manipulation. Plum is no longer the brainchild of neuroscientists; he is a bona fide human being whom compatibilist theists are free to see as being created by God with his own God-given character and desires, but we are now told that he suffered from "the rigorous training practices of his home and community." So what does that mean? There lies the second difficulty in adjudicating Case 3: we are not told enough about these influencing practices. If they amount to improper influencing manipulation tactics such as I described above, to a degree that meets or surpasses the threshold of what would excuse the killing of Ms. White (if there is such a threshold), then Plum cannot be held morally responsible in Case 3 indeed, but that would be because the influencing manipulation—*newly introduced* in Case 3—improperly meddled with his God-given character and desires; *not* because Case 3 was kept analogous to Case 2. If on the other hand these practices only amount to a proper parental and societal influence in the upbringing of any normally responsible child, then nothing compels compatibilists to think Plum should be excused in Case 3. His moral responsibility can be coherently maintained in light of my above-suggested relevant difference: in Case 3, Plum's choice to murder Ms. White springs out of his God-given character and desires in the absence of an improper manipulation (overriding or influencing) by human meddling. The charge of special pleading (between Cases 2 and 3) is thus successfully countered at this point of the argument.

Finally, Pereboom brings his argument to completion by offering Case 4 wherein Plum's choice is a fully normal, determinist choice, as free as any ever is on the compatibilist view. Pereboom here argues that there is no relevant difference between Case 4 and Case 3 that would exclude moral responsibility in Case 3 and rescue it in Case 4, so that without special pleading against cases of covert manipulation, compatibilists cannot maintain moral responsibility in the normal cases as long as they affirm determinism. But as has now become clear, Case 4 may already no longer *need* to be relevantly dissimilar to Case 3. It all depends on which of the two conclusions was adopted previously for Case 3. If Case 3 was judged not to feature influencing manipulation, then Case 4 does indeed not introduce any relevant difference, but in that case Plum will coherently be seen as morally responsible in both Case 4 and 3, justified by the fact that neither case involves a problematic manipulation, as Plum's choice to murder issues from his un-meddled-with God-given character and desires. On the other hand, if Case 3 was judged to feature influencing manipulation to a degree that excludes moral responsibility, then certainly, Case 4 can only rescue moral responsibility by pointing out a relevant difference with Case 3, but that difference is now made obvious. On that view of Case 3, Plum suffered from influencing manipulation whereas Case 4 explicitly removed this constraint, thereby making it explicitly dis-analogous. Whichever way one understands the influencing manipulation of Case 3, then, no special pleading is involved in maintaining moral responsibility on normal cases of determinist free choices as described in Pereboom's Case 4. In conclusion, the four case argument is successfully refuted by continuing to discriminate between determinism and covert manipulation on the basis that a covert manipulator—whether influencing or overriding—is "improperly meddling with an agent's God-given character and desires," a responsibility-undermining practice, which is obviously absent in normal cases of determinist, compatibilist free choices made by agents who freely act out of their God-given characters and desires. The four case argument thus fails to establish that determinism and manipulation are analogous.

## Alfred Mele's "zygote" argument

Alfred Mele's version of the same puzzle is rather similar to Pereboom's, but operates with only two cases, which, if they are analogous, show that determinism excludes moral responsibility. He describes the first case as follows:

> Diana creates a zygote Z in Mary. She combines Z's atoms as she does because she wants a certain event E to occur thirty years later. From her knowledge of the state of the universe just prior to her creating Z and the laws of nature of her deterministic universe, she deduces that a zygote with precisely Z's constitution located in Mary will develop into an ideally self-controlled agent who, in thirty years, will judge, on the basis of rational deliberation, that it is best to A and will A on the basis of that judgement, thereby bringing about E. . . . Thirty years later, Ernie is a mentally healthy, ideally self-controlled person who regularly exercised his powers of self-control and has no relevant compelled or coercively produced attitudes.[21]

In this story, it is expected that all concede that Ernie cannot be held morally responsible for his action. With that concession in place, Mele compares this story to a normal case of a human choice made on determinism:

21. Mele, "Manipulation," 278, quoted in Timpe, *Sourcehood*, 137.

> Compare Ernie with Bernie, who also satisfies [a set of] com-
> patibilist sufficient conditions for free action. The zygote that
> developed into Bernie came to be in the normal way. A major
> challenge for any compatibilist who claims that Ernie A-s un-
> freely whereas Bernie A-s freely is to explain how the differences
> in the causes of the two zygotes has this consequence. Why
> should that historical difference matter, given the properties the
> two agents share?[22]

That is indeed the challenge facing the compatibilist, but my above criterion of God-given-ness satisfies that demand: Bernie's choice is made on the basis of his God-given character and desires, which we are told were brought about "in the normal way," whereas Ernie's wasn't. Diana was improperly meddling with Ernie's God-given character, and so my criterion offers a coherent account of why Bernie is responsible in spite of Ernie's exemption.

## Robert Kane's "Walden Two" argument

Robert Kane also attempts to press the charge that determinism is analogous to manipulation, with the following strategy: he first considers B. F. Skinner's tale of the "Walden Two" utopia, wherein all persons are controlled through behavioral engineering, and he rightly points out that even though these people do what they want, we are all inclined to affirm that they are not really free; they are not really making their "own" choices, and presumably should not be morally responsible for them. Kane concludes that if such manipulation excludes moral responsibility, then determinism must equally do so.[23] He then identifies correctly the task at hand for compatibilists who like me want to decisively refute the charge of special pleading: "The problem is to locate the relevant difference between the two that makes one of them (CNC control [covert nonconstraining control]) objectionable and the other (mere determination) not."[24] My above criterion, if coherent, accomplishes exactly that. It explains why B. F. Skinner-type manipulation excludes moral responsibility—the behavioral engineering is tampering with the agents' God-given characters and desires, not permitting the free expression of who God made them to be—while God's decrees

---

22. Ibid.

23. Kane, *Significance*, 65–68. Peter van Inwagen offers virtually the same argument by analogy, using the story of "Deltas" and "Epsilons" from Aldous Huxley's novel *A Brave New World*. See van Inwagen, "Argument from Evil," 66.

24. Kane, *Significance*, 68.

on determinism do not. Hence my criterion successfully refutes the charge of special pleading.

But what is more, by "mere determination" what Kane has now in view is a determination by atheistic, merely natural causes, not the supernatural decree of a providential God. Though he gave brief consideration to the all-determining God of Jonathan Edwards, Kane disqualified his "predestinationism" as having lost its popularity among theists, for excluding human free will and making God responsible for evil (our two objections from Romans 9 once again!)[25] So Edwards's view ends up in the same bag as B. F. Skinner's case, excluding moral responsibility on the basis of manipulation.

From that point, Kane still presses the charge of special pleading for those who agree Skinner's case and Edwards's view exclude moral responsibility while mere naturalist determinism doesn't. This very argument is picked up by Katherin Rogers who names it "the divine controller argument for incompatibilism."[26]

## Katherin Rogers's "divine controller" argument

Rogers essentially defends the same contention that was suggested by Kane, but she helpfully provides the formal structure of the argument as follows:

1. If God causally necessitates your choice, then you are not morally responsible for it.

2. Causal necessitation of your choice due to natural causes in a deterministic universe is relevantly similar to divine causal necessitation.

   *Therefore*

3. If natural causes in a deterministic universe causally necessitate your choice, you are not morally responsible for it.[27]

This is clearly enough an attempt to show that people are engaging in special pleading when they affirm both that an all-determining God would exclude moral responsibility, and at the same time that we live in a deterministic universe with moral responsibility. So in straightforward logic, the audience that this argument now addresses is that consisting of

25. "Predestinationism of the kind defended by Hobbes and by some of his compatibilist successors, such as Jonathan Edwards, is no longer as popular as it once was among theists because it seems to take away a significant freedom from humans while passing ultimate responsibility for evil on to God." Ibid., 67.

26. Rogers, "Divine Controller Argument," 275–94.

27. Ibid., 277.

atheist compatibilist determinists who believe in moral responsibility and yet maintain that *if* an all-determining God existed, it *would* exclude moral responsibility. This restricted scope misses Calvinists by a long shot. Whether or not premise 2 is true, it is useless to establish incompatibilism against Christian theists who may reject premise 1, a premise which Rogers leaves unsupported and even explains why she does:

> The premise in the divine controller argument says that if God causes your choice you are not morally responsible. So, for example, it just isn't *fair* for God, or anyone, to punish you for a murder that God caused you to choose and commit. I take this to be an intuitive claim which is immediate (you see it as soon as you understand the terms), powerful, and widely accepted.[28]

That it is widely accepted is certainly true—there are lots of Arminians, after all—but that it is immediately obvious or even true at all is precisely what is disputed by Calvinists, so that the argument is irrelevant to our immediate controversy, as it offers no reason why given God's existence, determinism excludes moral responsibility.

Rogers and Kane's unsuccessful argument illustrates an interesting point nonetheless, in that it shows by its incorrect assumption where our relevantly dis-analogous feature actually lies: its presupposition in premise 2 was that whether they be manipulators, mindless universes, mad scientists, demons, or gods, all relevant controllers are created equal. But if God exists, that's a controller who's neither equal nor created, and who by his otherness refutes the charge of special pleading. God is relevantly *dis*-analogous to all human manipulators, covert or visible, influencing or overriding. It is thus shown false that determinism and manipulation are relevantly analogous, and hence the manipulation argument is no more successful than the coercion argument was in establishing incompatibilism.

---

28. Ibid., 286.

# The mental illness argument

A FINAL CONDITION (OR cluster of conditions) that allegedly excludes moral responsibility and may possibly be brought forward to support incompatibilism is mental illness.

## Does determinism entail mental illness?

As was the case with coercion and manipulation, mental illness can probably be the occasion of a handful of distinct arguments for (or minimally gestures in the direction of) incompatibilism, the first of which could once again be a direct claim of logical entailment as follows:

24. If determinism is true, then humans are mentally ill.

25. Mental illness excludes moral responsibility.

*Therefore*

6. Determinism is incompatible with moral responsibility.

Contrary to the coercion or manipulation arguments above, however, in the case of mental illness, I suspect that this direct form of the argument will hardly find any proponent, because premise (24) is so obviously false. It is quite clear that none of the pathologies that we call "mental illness" follows from mere determinism. These mental illnesses, or psychoses, have certain medical, psychiatric symptoms: cognitive handicaps, delusions, paranoia, etc. (more on these below), all of which are evidently absent from normal cases of free choices on the compatibilist determinist account. From this, it follows that determinism does not entail mental illness, and hence the best hope of a successful incompatibilist argument will once again have to be based on analogy. It will be the charge that determinism and mental illness are relevantly *analogous*; that whatever excludes moral responsibility for the mentally ill should equally do so for those whose choices are determined.

## Is determinism analogous to mental illness?

The first question to be raised in assessing this argument will be whether mental illness in fact excludes moral responsibility. Does it? To answer that question, one first needs to know what mental illness is. Without offering an unreasonably voluminous medical survey of psychiatry, at least some degree of specification is necessary, of exactly what sorts of conditions are in view. What is "mental illness"? As it turns out, it is hard to think of a more difficult question. If coercion was already hard to pin down, how much more is it the case with mental illness? For all the impressive advance of modern medicine, the notably difficult field of psychiatry is still greatly controversial, and finding a strong consensus on the relevant issues promises to be difficult.

A decent starting point nevertheless would be to list some of the diseases that can properly be described as "psychosis" or "mental illness." For this purpose, one would like to turn to a reference work, but not everyone uses the same classifications. In the United States, the American Psychiatric Association publishes its voluminous *Diagnostic and Statistical Manual of Mental Disorders* (or *DSM*, now in its fifth edition, DSM-5), which would seem like a reputable reference work to turn to, but its content is far from uncontroversial; it has been and continues to be criticized by important voices in the field.[1] In the U.K., the standard work employed instead is the World Health Organization's *International Classification of Diseases* (or *ICD*, now in its eleventh edition, ICD-11), the "Mental and behavioral disorders" section of which already differs from the DSM in non-trivial ways.[2] It is thus clear that any philosophical argument that aims to offer somewhat uncontroversial premises will need to go beyond the general level of "mental illness" as allegedly defined by any given reference work, and apply its claims to more specific designations of properly identified mental disorders. This restriction of the scope of diseases becomes all the more necessary anyway when we turn to the question of moral responsibility: does "mental illness" exclude moral responsibility? Surely not *all* mental disorders listed in either the DSM or the ICD remove a patient's moral responsibility for what they do. I even venture to say that some of the "disorders" listed by the DSM are just putting a strange label on normal albeit problematic behaviors, without much evidence that those behaviors are anything more than our normal,

1. See Allen Frances, chair of DSM-IV task force, strongly criticizing DSM-5 for the medicalization of normal life behaviors. Frances, *Saving Normal*.

2. Upon surveying the similarities and differences of DSM-IV-TR and ICD-10, Dr. Michael First reports his findings that "of the 176 criteria sets in both systems, only one, transient tic disorder, is identical. Twenty-one per cent had conceptually based differences and 78% had non-conceptually based differences." First, "Harmonization," 382.

freely chosen responses to various temptations, or normal life occurrences, rather than mental illnesses. For example, Allen Frances complains that the DSM-5 has turned tamper tantrums into "Disruptive Mood Dysregulation Disorder," gluttony into "Binge Eating Disorder," normal grief into "Major Depressive Disorder," the forgetting seen in old age into "Mild Neurocognitive Disorder," and that most of us will qualify for adult "Attention-Deficit Hyperactivity Disorder."[3] While the full critique of psychiatry's excesses should be left to competent psychiatrists, philosophers and theologians are probably safe in agreeing with Frances, and declaring these "conditions" to be neither mental illnesses, nor the occasion for an exclusion of moral responsibility. In any case, even without going this far, at the very least, incompatibilists will recognize that if their argument by analogy based on mental illness is to be at all convincing, it simply cannot rest on a blanket statement that all these conditions exclude moral responsibility. Instead, it will have to enter the inevitably messy business of declaring which psychoses exclude moral responsibility (at least relatively uncontroversially), and which ones do not.

For the time being, let us take as uncontroversial an example as we can find. Let us consider a most severe case of say autism, where the person is severely impaired in all social interactions, communication, does not control his own behavior, and whatever else any philosopher would demand for this person to be morally excused. Not everyone agrees on what those conditions are, but all should reasonably agree that there *are* such conditions for such mental illnesses. In this uncontroversial example, then, we would hold a case of a mentally ill person whose mental illness removes his moral responsibility. What then will the incompatibilist argument consist in? It will be the claim that this sort of mentally ill patient's actions are *analogous* to those of a person whose choices are determined; that whatever ingredient in this mental illness excludes moral responsibility is also present in any case of determined choice, thereby annulling moral responsibility on determinism.

The compatibilist responses to this argument will follow the same pattern as they did above in cases of coercion or manipulation, as the same several points can be made once again: first, if determinism in general does not entail mental illness, then the argument no longer is about mental illness *proper*, and the incompatibilist is invited to identify the alleged relevantly shared property of mental illness and determinism which excludes moral responsibility; otherwise the unsubstantiated claim that this property exists

3. Frances, *Saving Normal*, 177–205.

is just begging the question. And secondly, in order to refute the charge, we must once again formulate it in its rigorous syllogistic form as follows:

26. Choices made by mentally ill persons have a property that excludes moral responsibility.

27. If choices made by mentally ill persons have a property that excludes moral responsibility, then that property is also possessed by any choices made on determinism.

*Therefore*

19. Choices made on determinism have a property that excludes moral responsibility.

Notice that I am once more presupposing that the proponent of this argument by analogy is pressing the stronger claim that "there exists no relevant difference between determinism and mental illness," rather than the weaker claim that "there exists one relevant similarity between determinism and mental illness." See my discussion of this matter in the "pets and puppets" argument, as well as its use in the coercion argument and the manipulation argument above: I respond to the stronger claim, because the weaker claim is too obviously begging the question.

But once the argument pressing the stronger claim is put in this clearer form, our same two compatibilist complaints about premise (27) reappear: 1. it is still question-begging, because no reason is given to support the claim that whatever removes moral responsibility in the case of the mentally ill is necessarily present in the case of normal determinist choices; and 2. it is false, which can be shown by compatibilists identifying a relevant property such that: 1. it is present in the relevant cases of mental illness, 2. it excludes moral responsibility, and 3. it is not present in compatibilist, determinist human free choices.

Let me suggest the following as a relevant responsibility criterion: in order to be morally responsible, it is necessary that an individual either be appropriately aware of the relevant moral facts about what he is doing, or morally responsible for not being aware of them. He must either have moral consciousness in the process of decision-making, the awareness that what he is about to do (or not do) is evil (or good), or be morally responsible in the first place for not knowing it. This second disjunct is here to make room for the process of conscience cauterization, for example, when a wrongdoer becomes so hardened that he no longer even knows that what he is doing is wrong. It also allows to render a proper judgment in special cases like the one that follows: a person wants to rob a bank, but also wants to avoid moral blame, so he takes a newly invented drug ("Conscience-B-Gone"), which disables his moral awareness for two hours, during which he robs the bank. If we only considered his immediate moral ignorance, my criterion would excuse him; but with the caveat of the second disjunct in place, we can recognize that his ignorance is culpable, and hence he remains blameworthy for the robbery.[4] Leaving these special cases aside, the first disjunct of my criterion allows us, for example, to declare that I am not morally responsible if I pour sugar in my wife's coffee and it turns out that unbeknownst to me the sugar in the jar has been replaced with poison: I am not guilty for killing my wife, because I did not know that it was wrong to pour that thing in her coffee. That such epistemic conditions for moral responsibility are necessary should not be all that controversial.

Accordingly, this sort of necessary epistemic condition provides compatibilists with the following candidate for a dis-analogous feature between mental illness and determinism: "the individual's (non-culpable) ignorance that he is doing anything wrong." Does this property then satisfy conditions 1, 2, and 3 laid out above? First, it satisfies items 2 and 3: clearly enough, a person cannot be blamed if he is neither aware that he is doing anything wrong, nor culpable for that ignorance, and in normal cases of determinist compatibilist free choices, the self-conscious individual is normally aware of what he is doing when acting immorally. Item 1, however, might be a bit more controversial. Is it necessarily the case that mentally ill patients who are morally excusable lack the awareness that they are doing something wrong? This difficult, controversial, yet central question before us amounts to the following: "what does it take for a mentally ill person to be morally excused for their wrongful actions?" We presumably all agree that the mildest dysfunctions listed by the DSM do not qualify, so from there on up, as mental disorders increase in severity, at which level should we place a threshold to properly conclude that a patient is no longer morally responsible? My condition offered above suggests that the relevant threshold may be that of self-conscious awareness of the moral facts of the situation, or something like it. When the mentally ill patient is so impaired that he is no longer aware that his act is wrong, he can no longer properly be blamed. Without being too dogmatic on this point (as a sober theologian ought be on controversial matters of psychiatry), it strikes me as a good, non-arbitrary measure of moral responsibility for the mentally ill, and it will successfully refute the argument from analogy between mental illness and determinism.

William Rowe disagrees with this criterion. He presents the case of Andrea Yates, a mentally ill woman who drowned her five children in 2001

4. This special case was suggested to me by James N. Anderson.

in Texas. She had a long history of hallucinations, delusions, and heavy medical treatments, and the defense argued that she was insane at the time of the crimes and should hence be declared "not guilty" by reason of insanity. The prosecution disagreed, maintained that she was sane when she killed her children, and sought the death penalty. Interestingly enough, the criterion used by Texas law to determine whether a mentally ill patient should be declared "not guilty" was precisely that which I suggested above. As Rowe explains, "According to Texas law, the defense had the burden of proving not only that Andrea suffered from a severe mental disease but also that she didn't know the difference between right and wrong at the time of the drownings."[5] As it turns out, she failed to meet that criterion. Evidence was brought forward and found convincing that she *did* know what she was doing, that she called her husband to tell him what she had done, and that she seemed aware that it was morally wrong. Accordingly, she was found guilty and sentenced to life in prison.[6]

Rowe finds this judgment inappropriate, and argues that the condition for mental illness to exclude moral responsibility should be much more modest. He writes:

> Why does the defense have this burden? Couldn't someone be so insane as to be *incapable* of not committing a horrible crime while at the same time knowing that it is a crime? Does the mere fact that one knows that something is morally wrong suffice to show that one is not insane when one does that thing? Just to ask the question is to invite a negative answer![7]

Given how obvious Rowe thinks the answer is, we are not really offered an argument that we could refute,[8] but I think we can properly unpack the claim by pointing out a likely equivocation in Rowe's usage of the word "insane." The word can be used to describe one of two things: either 1. that

5. Rowe, *Can God Be Free?* 66.

6. Note that in 2005, a year after the publication of Rowe's book, the Texas Court of Appeals reversed the convictions, and in 2006, Andrea Yates was tried again, and this time was found not guilty by reason of insanity. The legal criterion had not changed, however, which means that the later jury concluded that she in fact did *not* know that what she was doing was wrong. The two juries are thus in direct contradiction on that one question, but this work is no place to discuss which of the two juries was mistaken. Whether or not Yates in fact met the criterion is of little relevance to our present discussion of whether or not the criterion is appropriate.

7. Rowe, *Can God Be Free?* 66.

8. Rowe's contention at hand does raise the question of being "incapable of not committing a horrible crime," but I shall delay my response to this issue until later in the present work when the preliminary issues have been properly established. For this discussion of moral responsibility in light of the "ability to do otherwise," see chapter 5.

a person suffers from a mental disorder without additional qualification, or
2. that a person suffers from a mental disorder *that qualifies him as lacking
moral responsibility*.[9] If this latter meaning is what Rowe has in mind, then it
is not at all obvious that being conscious of the moral facts doesn't exclude
one's being insane in that sense: deserving to be exempted for reason of
insanity. That is the very debated question before us, isn't it? On the other
hand, if by "insane" Rowe means the former, that is, just any sort of mental
disorder, then "just to ask the question" is, I agree, to invite a negative answer indeed: "does the mere fact that one knows that something is morally
wrong suffice to show that one is not insane in the sense of having some
sort of mental disorder?" Obviously not. It is certainly possible to suffer
from some sort of mental disorder and still know what one is doing. But
unfortunately, with this modest meaning of "insanity," Rowe's question no
longer has any bearing on the issue of moral responsibility. As was pointed
out above, to suffer from just any sort of mental disorder is no sufficient
reason to exclude moral responsibility. As a matter of fact, on the Christian
view, this would entail the absurd conclusion that no one is *ever* morally
responsible for anything wrong that they do, because at bottom, sin is just
that: a mental "disorder" of some sort; a dysfunction of one's decision-
making faculties. In the initial, pre-lapsarian, perfectly good creation of
God, the proper "function" of our decision-making faculties was to issue
rational choices; good, rational decisions toward what is right and good to
choose. To sin instead, is to act irrationally; that is, to act out of a mental
"dysfunction." Just as Alvin Plantinga suggested that cases of human *knowledge* are found when our true beliefs issue from cognitive faculties that are
"functioning properly,"[10] we can understand human moral *righteousness* to
be found when our good *choices* are issued by *decision-making faculties* that
are "functioning properly."[11] Immoral choices, then, entail a dysfunction
of those faculties: literally, a mental "disorder." To act immorally, rebelling
against the perfect creator God is irrational; it is "insane" in that sense, and
the more wicked the sin, the more "insane" we are inclined to describe the
person. It is quite uncontroversial, say, that Adolf Hitler was "insane" in
that sense (or "insanely evil," one may say), but does this exclude his moral
responsibility? Certainly not, and it seems to me that the relevant criterion
to maintain his guilt in the face of his insane evil remains the one offered

9. Not all may see legal responsibility and moral responsibility as always equivalent, but I am here supposing that they are interchangeable, for the sake of argument.

10. See Plantinga, *Warranted Christian Belief*.

11. I leave to another the task of assessing how much of Plantinga's original insights
in the field of epistemology carry over to the fields of ethics and metaphysics in the way
I suggest here, but it seems to me that the parallel holds rather well.

above: he was either aware that what he was doing was wrong, or, if we suppose that his conscience was hardened enough that he genuinely no longer
knew, then he was culpable for this ignorance of his.

In conclusion, then, not only mental illness and determinism have
not been shown to be analogous, but a relevantly *dis-analogous* feature has
even been identified: plausibly, the mentally ill who are not morally responsible lack awareness that what they are doing is wrong, whereas normal,
free, determinist acts on compatibilism do feature a consciousness of what
one is doing, and the knowledge of right and wrong. If this criterion is accepted, it demonstrates that mental illness and determinism are relevantly
dis-analogous. If it is rejected, then it remains that no relevantly analogous
feature has been shown between determinism and mental illness, so that
the incompatibilist contention if not proven false at least remains question-
begging. In each case, the mental illness argument is seen to fail, and hence
determinism does not exclude moral responsibility on the basis that it is
analogous to mental illness.

## Conceding the obvious: difficult questions remain

Now before this nicely vindicatory conclusion of mine is accused of being
over-simplistic and unrealistically tidy for a messy field like psychiatry, let
me add a few words to concede the obvious: despite the reasonable, partial
answers provided above, a host of difficult psychiatric and moral questions
certainly remain. These complexities unarguably abide, and we are left with
problem cases in which it is very difficult to assess properly whether or not
an individual is morally responsible. Psychopathic killers come to mind.
Well beyond the above case of Andrea Yates, some more complicated and
remarkable cases are mentioned in the literature on free will, usually for
the very purpose of underscoring from the onset just how difficult these
issues can be, before (and even after!) philosophers begin to think about
them and attempt to sort some of them out. John Martin Fischer opens his
collection of essays on free will with the troubling case of Michael Bruce
Ross, who brutally raped and murdered eight women aged between fourteen and twenty-five in the early 1980s.[12] Ross explained he was mentally ill
and suffered from constant, graphic, and powerful impulses to rape and kill
women; impulses that he himself deplored and sought to terminate by use
of drugs or chemical castration. While in prison, a certain drug was able to
successfully isolate these impulses and offer him a degree of peace, but the
violent impulses returned when the drug's use had to be discontinued. What

12. Fischer, "Framework for Moral Responsibility," 1–5.

is disturbing is that aside from all this, Ross is an otherwise surprisingly well-spoken Cornell graduate, whose letters exhibit impressive rationality, clarity, and moderation regarding his condition and its ramifications. The sexually violent impulses are described as foreign to him, unwanted and overwhelming, and Fischer's retelling of his story makes it plausible that the crimes would not have happened, had Ross been taking that special drug to kill the sadistic impulses all along. So what do we make of all this when pondering the question of his moral responsibility? I do not know.

Ishtiyaque Haji opens his book-length assessment of incompatibilism with the case of Robert Alton Harris who murdered two teenage boys in San Diego in 1978, with a complete apathy for the victims, viciously dwelling in sadistic laughter at their demise.[13] Haji then explains that Harris was brutalized literally from the womb: he was born two months early as a result of his father punching his pregnant mother in the abdomen out of jealous rage under the accusation that the child was not his. Both of his parents were alcoholics and Robert is believed to have suffered from fetal alcohol syndrome; his mother came to resent him for the difficulties she thought he caused in her marriage; he was especially targeted by his father for abuse because he was believed to be illegitimate, and he was abandoned at the age of fourteen. Unloved, unwanted, physically abused literally from the womb, and abandoned by his parents as a child; he was the perfect recipe for a disaster. In this light, what part of his adult rage and psychopathy are we prepared to say he was personally morally responsible for? I will not be quick to say. These cases are so complex that I would not presume to know whether and to what extent[14] these individuals were morally responsible, nor do I know what exact criteria would successfully adjudicate them.

Is this then a weak point in the compatibilist armor? It is unlikely. Admittedly, since these cases raise questions to which I do not have answers, it is always theoretically possible that the right answers would be found to be available to incompatibilists only, but consider what would have to be the

---

13. Haji, *Incompatibilism's Allure*, 11–13.

14. Indeed, moral responsibility may very well come in degrees. A person who is not free and hence not morally responsible for an action cannot be blamed, and one who is entirely free can be fully blamed, but it seems to me there is room in the middle to say that a person was free enough to receive some degree of blame, all the while maintaining that the presence of some mitigating factors alleviated some of his responsibility. In that case, we would say the person deserved some amount of blame that falls short of the full amount the same action *would* have called for if performed without those mitigating circumstances. The disturbing cases of psychopathic killers are likely to fall somewhere in that grey area, where they can be blameworthy to a certain extent, while their tragic upbringing alleviates some of their responsibility even if we should suppose that it doesn't annul it entirely.

case. One of two things would have to be true: either 1. these individuals are morally responsible and only incompatibilist criteria justify their blame, or 2. these individuals are not morally responsible and only incompatibilist criteria successfully exempt them. Neither scenario seems likely at this point. Scenario 1 is rendered implausible by the fact that incompatibilism is a thesis that *excludes* moral responsibility (namely when determinism is true), and doesn't seem equipped to yield judgments that *condemn* people whom any other compatibilist criteria would excuse. As to the second scenario and the need for criteria that properly exclude moral responsibility when needed, even if the compatibilist partial criteria I have offered above fail to solve these moral puzzles, what sort of criteria would the incompatibilist suggest in their place? Are incompatibilists prepared to argue that these individuals could only be exempted if it were found that they were not in possession of an indeterminist, libertarian free will? How would anyone justify that they weren't? And importantly, how would anyone (let alone a jury in the courtroom) *measure* that? We just don't have the mechanisms in place to observe whether a choice had determining antecedents or not. And if we cannot do so in normal cases, how much less can we assess the tortured lives of Michael Ross and Robert Harris? Whatever complexities are featured by these individuals, then, must be faced by incompatibilists and compatibilists alike, and if either camp ever comes to offer ground-breaking suggestions on how to understand these men's moral responsibility, it is unlikely that they will rest on a measure of determinism or indeterminism. So unless and until an incompatibilist comes up with a criterion that successfully and uncontroversially adjudicates all these cases and entails incompatibilism, we can safely set these cases aside in our debate as interesting, disturbing, puzzling cases with little present relevance to the question of compatibilism.

In conclusion, the mental illness argument has been found to be indefensible if taken as a claim that determinism entails mental illness, and unsupported or even refuted if based on a mere claim that determinism and mental illness are analogous. Complexities in the field were clearly seen to remain, but enough has been said to appreciate that the mental illness argument does not at this point support any incompatibilist conclusion.

# Biblical interlude: "not the will of man"

HAVING THUS FAR REFUTED the incompatibilist claims that determinism respectively nullifies "choices" or "free will," or amounts to "coercion," or "manipulation," or even "mental illness," a brief pause marked by irony is called for, to consider that some biblical evidence actually does at times lean in the direction of a denial of free will. While in a sense even Calvinists are not prepared to do so, some biblical passages seem to outright deny the reality of human choices in the decision to follow Christ. Romans 9 goes so far as to say in verse 16, "So then it depends not on human will or exertion, but on God, who has mercy." John 1:12–13 explains the way in which sinners become born again: John says of Jesus that, "to all who did receive him, who believed in his name, he gave the right to become children of God, who were born, not of blood nor of the will of the flesh *nor of the will of man*, but of God." In John 15:16, Jesus tells his disciples, "You did not choose me, but I chose you."

"*Not* on human will or exertion," "you did *not* choose me," "*not* the will of man," the Bible does not thereby deny the philosophical reality of morally responsible, human free choices, but it does put it under the providential grace of God. Calvinists offer both of these features with their compatibilist view of free will, and hence can rest confident that their view sits well (or minimally *aims* to sit well) with both strands of biblical teaching.

# 5

# The consequence argument and the principle of alternate possibilities

## Incompatibilism, burden of proof, and begging the question

THE HANDFUL OF OBJECTIONS surveyed above can properly be classified as "straw-men" arguments inasmuch as they object to various elements (denial of choice, denial of free will, affirmation of coercion, affirmation of manipulation, affirmation of mental illness, etc.), which are not believed by compatibilists (nor are they shown to follow from beliefs they do hold, for that matter). A second sort of incompatibilist claim must at present be rejected, not for failing to represent the compatibilist view accurately, but for now failing to establish incompatibilism in a non-circular fashion. For interesting reasons which themselves will be discussed later,[1] it is not uncommon for libertarian objectors to Calvinism to assume the truth of incompatibilism, to simply assert that "If all human actions are causally determined, then no one is ever morally responsible for any action,"[2] and to leave the assertion more or less unsupported as self-evident. Jerry Walls even asserts his incompatibilism as a basic belief that *cannot* be supported by any argument:

> We believe that libertarian free will is intrinsic to the very notion of moral responsibility. That is, a person cannot be held morally responsible for an act unless he or she was free to perform that act and free to refrain from it. This is a basic moral intuition, and we do not believe there are any relevant moral convictions more basic than this one that could serve as premises to prove it.[3]

Just like that, the perceived force of the claim itself leads incompatibilists to rest on the mere assertion, beg the question in favor of incompatibilism,

---

1. See chapter 5 and its analysis of why the incompatibilist principle of alternate possibilities invalidly borrows its plausibility from a similar but compatibilist principle.
2. Hasker, *Metaphysics*, 46.
3. Walls and Dongell, *Not a Calvinist*, 105.

and improperly shift the burden of proof back onto compatibilists. Consistently with this, Randall Basinger demands: "The Calvinist must . . . explain . . . how a God who decreed what each person will do can hold them accountable for what they in fact do."[4] But the Calvinist faces no such obligation quite yet. As a compatibilist, the Calvinist indeed maintains that God "decrees what each person will do," and "holds them accountable for what they in fact do." If a contradiction is featured or entailed by the above pair of beliefs, the onus is on incompatibilists to uncover it before they can expect any sort of compatibilist counter-argument.

Unfortunately, this strategy has enough intuitive pull that Calvinists at times take the bait and answer the charge prematurely and too timidly. They respond with embarrassment, start confessing their rational limitations, argue for mystery in the face of the unknown, and some get dangerously close to admitting irrationality. A brief sample will illustrate the point. Calvinist Edwin Palmer unduly shoots himself in the foot: "the Calvinist freely admits that his position is illogical, ridiculous, nonsensical, and foolish."[5] Likewise, and although he was very careful not to concede a "contradiction," J. I. Packer has spoken of an "antinomy" in his Calvinist view, thereby provoking much controversy.[6] Paul Helm appropriately reframes the sentiment: "how it happens that what someone is decreed to do he may nonetheless be responsible for doing, is somewhat mysterious."[7] This much we should rationally concede, with John MacArthur's qualification that "it is a mystery only to us. I don't know how God resolves it but I am content to leave it with Him."[8] Yet when Thomas Schreiner humbly confesses that "The final resolution of the problem of human responsibility and divine justice is beyond our rational capacity" and that there are "some mysteries that we cannot unravel" so that "ultimately the logical problems posed cannot be fully resolved,"[9] I think it is surrendering a bit too much. We can appreciate a refreshing Calvinist epistemic humility, but let us not confuse ourselves about the "logical problems posed." The burden of proof is *not* on the shoulders of the Calvinist, and since no contradiction has been shown between determinism and moral responsibility, Calvinists must take a deep breath, relax, and deal with the arguments. It is somewhat ironic that this sober

4. Basinger, "Exhaustive Divine Sovereignty," 191.

5. Palmer, *Five Points*, 104.

6. See Walls and Dongell, *Not a Calvinist*, 115–16 and Helm, *Providence of God*, 62–66.

7. Helm and Tiessen, "Room for Middle Knowledge?" 446.

8. MacArthur, *Body Dynamics*, 28, quoted in Walls and Dongell, *Not a Calvinist*, 155.

9. Schreiner, "Prevenient Grace," 245.

response would even be handed to them by an open theist, David Basinger: "If the truths in question have not clearly been shown to be contradictory, then no 'logical solution' or 'defiance of logic' is required. . . . If the truths are not clearly contradictory there is no logical problem as of yet to worry about."[10] And it is exactly the case! The burden of proof is still firmly on the shoulders of the incompatibilist, and we are still looking for an argument to support the incompatibilist thesis.

## The consequence argument

Not all incompatibilists are happy to leave the thesis unsupported, however, and some do try to offer the missing step, the missing argument to substantiate the claim that moral responsibility is incompatible with determinism. Peter van Inwagen pre-eminently attempted to do just that, by crafting just such an argument, the so-called "consequence argument" for incompatibilism.[11] He formulates the main thrust of his argument as follows:

> If determinism is true, then our acts are the consequences of the laws of nature and events in the remote past. But it is not up to us what went on before we were born; and neither is it up to us what the laws of nature are. Therefore the consequences of these things (including our own acts) are not up to us.[12]

From this general formulation, van Inwagen proceeds to offer three arguments, or three different specific articulations of what he sees as essentially the same broad argument for incompatibilism: the consequence argument. Each of these will be shown to be unsound.

## General formulation

An important shortcoming of van Inwagen's argument is that it understands "incompatibilism" differently than it has been defined so far. Traditionally, and in the present work, incompatibilism has been defined as the thesis that determinism is incompatible with *moral responsibility*. Instead, van Inwagen's argument aims to establish the thesis that determinism is incompatible

---

10. Basinger, "Biblical Paradox," 211.

11. Modern-times defenders of the consequence argument include Carl Ginet, David Wiggins, James Lamb, and Nelson Pike, all listed in Kane, "Introduction," 10. And Ishtiyaque Haji traces back the argument to Wiggins, and Ginet before him. Haji, *Incompatibilism's Allure*, 29n1.

12. Van Inwagen, *Essay*, 16.

with *"free will"*[13]—in his words, the thesis that "If determinism is true, there is no free will."[14] Now if "free will" in this sentence of his were understood in the same modest, compatibility-agnostic way I have understood it above, as a mere expression that is equivalent to "the freedom of will which is necessary and sufficient in the area of control for moral responsibility," then this argument would establish incompatibilism indeed. It would show that determinism is incompatible with that relevant kind of free will; an incompatibility that entails that determinism excludes moral responsibility. Unfortunately, this is not how van Inwagen understands the unqualified expression "free will." He makes clear both in his definition of the phrase[15] and in his usage of the concept in the consequence argument[16] that what he has in view is *libertarian* free will. And of course, the incompatibility of determinism and *libertarian* free will is rather uncontroversial and requires little argumentation; it is definitional! But from this, the usual (and the only interesting) understanding of incompatibilism, the thesis that determinism excludes *moral responsibility*, simply does not follow. I shall therefore examine these three formulations of his, each of which I assert establishes what I happily concede, namely that libertarian free will is incompatible with determinism, but falls short of refuting compatibilism.

At the onset, a quick word can be said about the general formulation of the consequence argument as quoted above. Already, it can be pointed out where the argument exhibits circularity. The compatibilist is free to agree with all of the claims of the argument, and grant its conclusion that on determinism our acts are not *ultimately* "up to us" in a certain sense. As long as compatibilists do not assent to the alleged equivalence between: 1. choices and actions being "up to us" *in a libertarian sense* and 2. their being "morally responsible," the consequence argument still falls short of establishing the thesis of incompatibilism under dispute. It fails to tell us what sense of "ultimacy" or "up-to-us-ness" is necessary for ascriptions of moral responsibility.

As I will now document, this failure is in turn not made good by any of the three specific articulations of the consequence argument.

---

13. "I shall argue that free will is incompatible with determinism." Van Inwagen, *Essay*, 13.

14. Van Inwagen, *Essay*, 106.

15. "To be morally responsible for some act or failure to act is at least to be able to have acted otherwise, whatever else it may involve; to be able to have acted otherwise is to have free will." Ibid., 162.

16. See my review of his three formulations of the consequence argument below.

## First formulation

The first formulation consists in the claim that if determinism is true, then humans do not have it in their power to "falsify propositions" about what they choose and do. It is formally laid out by van Inwagen as follows, with J being any given person (specifically a judge in his example), T an instant at which J chose not to raise his hand in a vote, $T_0$ any instant before J's birth, $P_0$ a proposition that expresses the state of the world at $T_0$, P a proposition that expresses the state of the world at T (hence including J's not raising his hand), and L the conjunction into a single proposition of all the laws of nature.

1. If determinism is true, then the conjunction of $P_0$ and L entails P

2. It is not possible that J have raised his hand at T and P be true

3. If (2) is true, then if J could have raised his hand at T, J could have rendered P false

4. If J could have rendered P false, and if the conjunction of $P_0$ and L entails P, then J could have rendered the conjunction of $P_0$ and L false

5. If J could have rendered the conjunction of $P_0$ and L false, then J could have rendered L false

6. J could not have rendered L false

7. If determinism is true, J could not have raised his hand at T[17]

All of these claims can without a fight be conceded by the coherent compatibilist. This formulation makes it very clear that the conclusion, (7), is not the thesis of incompatibilism. The argument has not once made mention of moral responsibility. Rather, what this argument establishes is that if determinism is true, all things being as they are, humans "cannot do otherwise than they in fact do." In a sense that is correct, and compatibilists must in turn demand a reason to think that this kind of ability is necessary for moral responsibility. Much more will be said below in the current chapter about this "ability," "alternate possibilities," and their connection to moral responsibility, but for now it suffices to see that the first formulation of the consequence argument stops one long step short of living up to its ambition: it does not establish incompatibilism, and subsequent formulations fare no better.

17. Van Inwagen, *Essay*, 70.

## Second formulation

The second articulation of the consequence argument is based on the notion of "access to possible worlds." Although van Inwagen formally defines a handful of logical operators in order to express his argument compactly, they need not detain us and be reproduced here, because once again they only serve ultimately to establish truths that should be happily conceded by the compatibilist insofar as they still fall short of supporting incompatibilism. Therefore we can issue all these considerations a hall pass, and directly jump to van Inwagen's perfectly acceptable conclusion, without worrying about how he arrived there. He ultimately wraps up his (valid) argumentation: "We may put the conclusion of the Second Argument thus: if determinism is true, then no one has access to any non-actual world. That is, no one has an ability that may correctly be described as an ability to realize some in fact unrealized possibility."[18]

That is quite correct. Determinism does not permit a free agent in the actual world to "access" truly alternate possible worlds. Only an indeterminist, libertarian free will allows one the access to alternate possible worlds that share a past that is identical to the actual world with respect to all hard facts until the moment of free choice at which point they begin to differ. But then of course compatibilists will want to hear why *that* is relevant to ascriptions of moral responsibility. Why is it that moral responsibility is excluded by the sort of free will that does not give access to alternate possible worlds, but included by the sort that does give access to such worlds? Why would our determinist world's barring of access to distinct possible worlds write it off as unsuitable for moral responsibility? In short, still, why is libertarian free will required for moral responsibility? The second argument does not say, and since it is the question at the heart of the compatibility debate, this silence disqualifies it from serving the incompatibilist cause.

## Third formulation

The third and last articulation of the consequence argument introduces an operator, N, and two rules, α and β as follows:

For any sentence $p$, N$p$ is the proposition that "$p$ is true, and no one has, or ever had, any choice about whether $p$ is true."

α   $\Box p \vdash Np$

β   $N(p \supset q), Np \vdash Nq$[19]

18. Van Inwagen, *Essay*, 93.
19. Ibid., 93–94.

Having asserted and supported these two principles, van Inwagen supposes that $P_0$ is a proposition that expresses the state of the world at some time in the remote past, L is the conjunction of the laws of nature, and P is any true proposition. He then offers the following formulation of his consequence argument to establish that if determinism is true, N$p$ is true of every true proposition $p$:

1. $\Box\,((P_0 \,\&\, L) \supset P)$   (statement of determinism)

2. $\Box\,(P_0 \supset (L \supset P))$   (follows from (1))

3. N $(P_0 \supset (L \supset P))$   (follows from (2) and (α))

4. N $P_0$   (new premise)

5. N $(L \supset P)$   (follows from (3), (4), and (β))

6. N L   (new premise)

7. N P   (follows from (5), (6), and (β))

Our attitude toward this formulation of the argument will once again depend on how we are to analyze the word "choice" in N's definition. This definition doesn't tell us whether "having a choice" is to be analyzed in libertarian terms or not. If it is, then all the starting premises α, β, (4), and (6) are true indeed, and the conclusion (7) follows, establishing that if determinism is true, then for every true proposition $p$, no one has, or ever had any *libertarian* free will choice about whether $p$ is true.[20] That is hardly disputable. But once again, we are left asking why *libertarian* free will is necessary for moral responsibility.

## Van Inwagen on the compatibilist response

At the end of his defense of these three strands of the consequence argument, van Inwagen finally comes to acknowledge this, anticipating that compatibilists will likely find his argument question-begging (as I do) and his unqualified usage of "free will" or "choice" problematic. He writes that compatibilists may say something like this: "Your argument simply demonstrates that when you use phrases like 'could have done otherwise' or 'has a choice about,' you are giving them some meaning other than the meaning they have in our actual debates about moral responsibility."[21] As a matter of fact, it is not so much that he gives them a *different* meaning than is usual,

20. Unless the meaning of "choice" shifts between the premises and the conclusion, but then the argument would obviously be invalid because of the equivocation.

21. Ibid., 104.

but rather a *libertarian* meaning, which begs the question of incompatibilism with respect to moral responsibility. In response, van Inwagen says that all it takes to avoid the charge for the third argument (and in his view, for the two others *mutatis mutandis*) is a reformulation of the N principle to read: N*p* is the proposition that *p* is true and, "in just the sense of *having a choice* that is relevant in debates about moral responsibility, no one has, or ever had, any choice about whether *p*."[22]

But this will not do. If the sense of "choice" and "free will" that is employed in all three of the consequence argument's formulations is no longer supposed to be libertarian, then none of their negative conclusions follows from the mere truth of determinism. In the first argument, only a *libertarian* free will features an ability to do otherwise holding the past and the laws of nature in place. In the second argument, only a *libertarian* free will permits access to alternate possible worlds. And in the third argument, only a *libertarian* free will secures the truth of α, β, (4), and (6). I will further develop these facts below in this chapter, revisiting the consequence argument while discussing the issues of "ability" and "alternate possibilities," but a decisive conclusion is already secured: van Inwagen's argument does not establish incompatibilism, but only that determinism is incompatible with libertarian free will.

## Additional incompatibilist voices on the consequence argument

Lest we think the fault lies only with van Inwagen, let me assure incompatibilists that the problem comes from the argument, not the man. The argument exhibits the very same shortcoming when defended by other capable advocates: Daniel Speak openly introduces the consequence argument as his attempt to demonstrate "the thesis that, necessarily, if determinism is true, then no one enjoys free will."[23] And the equivocation-prone phrase "free will" employed here is not even left ambiguously unqualified either. Speak is open about its being libertarian, which begs the question of incompatibilism: "The proponents of the consequence argument typically *assume* that freedom involves alternative possibilities."[24] Precisely. The consequence argument is circular; it assumes what it needs to prove. Incompatibilist Robert Kane's attempt at supporting the consequence argument

22. Ibid.
23. Speak, "Consequence Argument Revisited," 116.
24. Ibid., 118.

further illustrates the point. He endorses its obvious premises, and restates its conclusion as follows:

> Since this argument can be applied to any agents and actions at any times, we can infer from it that *if determinism is true, no one can ever do otherwise*; and if free will requires the power to do otherwise than we actually do (as in the image of forking paths), then no one would have free will.[25]

To which compatibilists must say: fine! *If* free will requires the power to do otherwise than we actually do, *then* no one would have free will. But we still have not been given a reason to believe the all-important *if*.

It is now important to properly identify a concept that has at this point evidently entered our debate, while remaining unannounced thus far: when van Inwagen, Speak, and Kane reflect on the concept of "doing otherwise," or a freedom involving "alternate possibilities," or an "ability to do otherwise," they make use of a related but slightly distinct incompatibilist contention, called the "principle of alternate possibilities." It is the claim that if a person does not have the "ability to do otherwise," then he cannot be morally responsible. The consequence argument vitally depends on this principle since all it showed was that determinism excludes the ability to do otherwise all things being as they are; it would thus require the additional premise that this ability is necessary for moral responsibility. A full assessment of this principle of alternate possibilities is the object of the next section in this chapter, but we needed to recognize the principle here, because Robert Kane makes an interesting final statement about the consequence argument's use of the principle of alternate possibilities. After correctly identifying this principle, Kane goes on to note that compatibilists tend to work with a different understanding of what "can" means in the condition "can do otherwise." This is true, and I myself will proceed to do so in the present chapter,[26] but Kane mistakenly thinks that consequently, the debate gets stuck on this point, with equal charges of circular reasoning on each side of the debate. He writes,

> At this point, arguments over the Consequence Argument tend to reach an impasse. Incompatibilist defenders of the argument claim that compatibilist critics are begging the question by interpreting "can" in the Consequence Argument in a way that is compatible with determinism.[27]

25. Kane, "Libertarianism," 10–11.
26. See the upcoming introduction of a principle I name PAP$_{If}$.
27. Kane, "Libertarianism," 11.

But this stalemate ruling will not do. It misunderstands the dialectic situation of the participants in this debate. Who is making a controversial claim here? Who is making an argument? Who has the burden of proof? It is the incompatibilist. The consequence argument for incompatibilism is an attempt *by the incompatibilist*, to demonstrate incompatibilism (the thesis that moral responsibility is incompatible with determinism). So it is the incompatibilist who must shoulder the burden of proof and present supporting arguments for that conclusion. The compatibilist has no question to "beg" with respect to the consequence argument. He could perfectly rationally sit back, minimally voice his skepticism, and simply point out which steps of the argument have not been shown true—though I myself will do more than that. By so doing, since its conclusion no longer follows, the consequence argument fails.

Leigh Vicens also picks up the consequence argument, but her contribution has no bearing on the present controversy, because what she argues is that free will is no more compatible with theological determinism than it is with the natural determinism that was targeted by van Inwagen's version of the consequence argument.[28] Her point is that if one accepts that the consequence argument successfully establishes that moral responsibility excludes *natural* determinism, then it (or a slightly modified version of it) can also be marshaled to reject the compatibility of moral responsibility with *theological* determinism as well. This conditional claim is thus irrelevant here, as she readily acknowledges,[29] since its premise has been rejected: the consequence argument has failed to show that moral responsibility is incompatible with determinism, be it natural or theological.

Finally, skepticism about the consequence argument comes even from the incompatibilist camp. Thomas Flint sees the shortcoming I pointed out, and admits that because of it the argument is unsuccessful to establish incompatibilism. He concludes more or less as I did above: "if one can plausibly charge that the sense of unavoidability employed in the Argument is not relevant to the question of human freedom, the Argument will have failed to refute compatibilism."[30]

Now, as mentioned above, both Kane and Speak in their question-begging (or so I claimed) defense of the consequence argument have appealed to the notion of "alternative possibilities," or "the ability to do otherwise." As I mentioned, this is a separate incompatibilist contention in its own right,

28. Vicens, "Consequence Argument," 145–55.

29. "Of course, those who think that natural divine determinism *is* compatible with human freedom will not be persuaded to reject non-natural divine determinism by the argument I present in this chapter." Vicens, "Critical Consideration," 92.

30. Flint, "Argument from Unavoidability," 428.

on whose truth the consequence argument has been seen to depend, and to which we now turn.

## The principle of alternate possibilities (PAP)

In his famous 1969 essay "Alternate Possibilities and Moral Responsibility," Harry Frankfurt endeavored to evaluate (and repudiate) a widely accepted principle of moral responsibility, which he called the "principle of alternate possibilities" (or PAP). Frankfurt described the PAP as follows: "a person is morally responsible for what he has done only if he could have done otherwise."[31] This principle, which at first glance may seem intuitive, has been channeled for centuries by incompatibilist philosophers and theologians against determinist views of human free will,[32] and may very well be the most serious candidate for an incompatibilist argument. Since determinism asserts that the totality of antecedents at the moment of a choice determines the one and only choice that the agent can and will make, it follows that, all things being as they are, the agent does not have the ability to do otherwise than he does. This, the PAP asserts, would jettison the agent's moral responsibility for his decision and action. PAP is thereby used as ammunition against compatibilism, the view that moral responsibility is compatible with determinism.

To appreciate its force, it may be helpful to read it directly from the pen of its modern day proponents.

Alvin Plantinga asks: "How can I be responsible for my actions, if it was never within my power to perform any actions I didn't in fact perform, and never within my power to refrain from performing any I did perform?"[33]

Thomas Flint: "Surely no free action is one that is unavoidable for me, one over which I have no control."[34]

Richard Rice: "For human beings to be genuinely free, it seems, they must not only be able to do what they choose, they must also be able to choose otherwise."[35]

David Widerker: "An agent is morally blameworthy for performing a given act A only if he could have avoided performing it."[36]

---

31. Frankfurt, "Alternate Possibilities," 1.

32. It was Pelagius's contention against Augustine, Erasmus's against Luther, Calvin's opponents' against him, and Finney's and Wesley's against Calvinism.

33. Plantinga, "Advice to Christian Philosophers," 265.

34. Flint, *Divine Providence*, 27.

35. Rice, "Divine Foreknowledge," 125.

36. Widerker, "Blameworthiness and Frankfurt's Argument," 54.

And Peter van Inwagen: "To be morally responsible for some act or failure to act is at least to be able to have acted otherwise, whatever else it may involve; to be able to have acted otherwise is to have free will."[37]

Although not always with so many words, theologians like philosophers voice the same sentiment: cf. Olson,[38] Picirilli,[39] Geisler,[40] Reichenbach.[41]

As was explained earlier,[42] not all indeterminists about free will are incompatibilists, and not all incompatibilists endorse the PAP, but this principle "unpacks well" the alleged strength of the libertarian position: the fact that a libertarian is able to claim about any person committing an immoral act, "the agent is responsible for his misdeed, because though he trespassed, he was able to choose *not* to do so, all things being just the way they were," whereas the Calvinist, with his compatibilist determinist view of free will must say: "given all the circumstances and the state of his heart and mind, the agent did not have the ability to refrain from trespassing at that moment." This, the incompatibilist alleged, should be enough to render a "not-guilty" verdict.[43] What then is a compatibilist to respond? There are a number of points to make.

First, the PAP's formulation must be challenged on the charge of equivocation, an equivocation that conceals a question-begging incompatibilism. Compatibilists must first uncover the equivocation and challenge the unqualified PAP's incompatibilist assumptions. And secondly, while pointing out that the assumption of incompatibilism would be sufficient to undercut the incompatibilist argument and establish the PAP's failure, compatibilists can actually go on the offensive and offer several rebutting defeaters, or

37. Van Inwagen, *Essay*, 162.

38. "If people's decisions and actions are determined by anything such that they could not do otherwise than they do, wherein lies their moral accountability or guilt?" Olson, "Responses to Bruce A. Ware," 134.

39. "If, in fact, those who crucified Jesus *had* to do so, if God's foreordination by its own efficacy made their actions unavoidable, then they were not free to do otherwise—*could* not do otherwise—and were therefore not responsible." Picirilli, *Grace, Faith, Free Will*, 80.

40. "Free choice implies we could have actually done otherwise." Geisler, "Geisler's response (to Reichenbach)," 131.

41. "If we cannot but sin, we cannot be held morally accountable for our actions." Reichenbach, "Freedom, Justice and Moral Responsibility," 280.

42. See definitions of "libertarianism" and "libertarian free will" in the introductory section on definitions.

43. Once again, the caveat that we are here only speaking about directly free actions is important, since incompatibilists may wish to say that a certain action can be free even if presently such that the agent couldn't do otherwise, as long as he could have done otherwise in the past. For more on this distinction between directly free and derivatively free, see my discussion of the principle I call PAP$_{Past}$ in chapter 6.

arguments showing that the PAP in its incompatibilist form is not merely unproven, but is in fact false. Let me develop all of these responses.

## Question-begging camouflaged by equivocation

### Explaining the problem

As Frankfurt himself recognized, the criterion specified by the PAP is far from being univocal, "Its exact meaning is a matter of controversy."[44] More precisely, the equivocation resides in one's understanding of the "ability" the possession of which is said to be necessary for moral responsibility. I propose to remove the equivocation by making explicit two importantly distinct understandings of this "ability," and to articulate the two different moral principles of alternate possibilities that result from them:

Let $PAP_{All}$ be the principle that "a person is morally responsible for what he has done only if, *all things inside and outside the person being just as they are at the moment of choice*, he could have done otherwise."[45] Let us name this sort of ability a *categorical ability*.

And now, let $PAP_{If}$ instead be the principle that "a person is morally responsible for what he has done only if he could have done otherwise, *had his inner desires inclined him to do so at the moment of choice*." This modified criterion no longer requires a *categorical ability* to do otherwise while holding all other things in place; rather, it is a *conditional ability* that is in view:[46] *if* the person had wanted to, that is, *if*—contrary to fact—his heart and mind had inclined him to do so, *could* the person have followed up on these alternate desires and acted otherwise than he in fact did? If not, this newly introduced $PAP_{If}$ would declare on that condition that he is not morally responsible. Note that this is not an attempt to *define* the words "can" or "ability," so it should not be worrisome that the word "could" found its way again into my explanation. It is not a circular definition of the word, it is merely an attempt to capture one particular sense of ability—the conditional ability—that one can be said to have, if, assuming his desires

44. Frankfurt, "Alternate Possibilities," 1.

45. More precisely, by "all things," I technically mean "all hard facts," because clearly enough *some* things must be different in the alternate scenario: if nothing else, at least the *choice* is different. All I mean to say is that in the envisioned alternate scenario, we are keeping in place everything about the person and his environment that would influence the choice in any way.

46. Identical labels of "categorical ability" and "conditional ability" are found in Ekstrom, *Free Will*, 81. Joseph Campbell also points out G. E. Moore had called out the equivocation between "hypothetical" and "categorical" abilities in Moore, *Ethics*, quoted in Campbell, *Free Will*, 88.

were different, he could have acted on those desires and done otherwise. If, contrary to fact, the person had wanted to, would there have been something else besides his desires preventing him from executing the alternative course of action? If yes, the $PAP_{If}$ declares that he is not morally responsible for his failure to do otherwise.

In other words, $PAP_{All}$ says that a categorical ability to do otherwise is necessary for moral responsibility, while $PAP_{If}$ says that a conditional ability to do otherwise is necessary for moral responsibility.[47]

Once the ability is disambiguated as above, it becomes clear that of the two principles, only $PAP_{All}$ is incompatible with determinism. If the alternate possibility must be accessible by the agent's will all things being categorically just as they are, then it calls for indeterminism indeed. $PAP_{If}$ on the other hand, is quite compatible with determinism, because its built-in condition "had his inner desires inclined him to do so" permits a hypothetical, counterfactual modification of the antecedents (namely, the state of heart and mind of the agent prior to the choice), and thus opens the door to an alternate possibility (an alternate choice) without necessitating indeterminism.

As a compatibilist, I assert that $PAP_{All}$ is false, and $PAP_{If}$ is true.[48] This is highly controversial, of course. But once the equivocation is removed, the question-begging nature of the PAP is made apparent: $PAP_{All}$ has (at least thus far) no purchase on the compatibilist, and incompatibilists cannot assume its truth in order to assert incompatibilism; they must establish it. Hence, it will not do for incompatibilists to rest their case on the mere truth of $PAP_{If}$. Since $PAP_{If}$ is perfectly compatible with compatibilism, any premature conclusion of incompatibilism on the basis that $PAP_{If}$ is true is logically invalid as it commits a *non sequitur*.

47. These two senses of ability are similarly distinguished by Ishtiyaque Haji who names them "the hypothetical sense of 'can'" and "the categorical sense of 'can.'" Haji, *Incompatibilism's Allure*, 34–36. In the theological world, we find the same distinction in Jonathan Edwards and A. W. Pink. Edwards writes "of the distinction of natural and moral necessity, and inability" in Edwards, *Freedom of the Will*, 23–31 (Part I, section IV). As to A. W. Pink, all references to this distinction in the 1945 edition of *The Sovereignty of God* were unacceptably removed by the editors of the 1961 edition. See explanation and valid criticism of this move by Paul Helm at http://paulhelmsdeep. blogspot.com/2013/03/pink-and-murray-and-jonathan-edwards.html (accessed in February 2015).

48. At this point, all sorts of familiar alleged shortcomings of the $PAP_{If}$ may already be rearing their ugly heads, but I shall refrain from offering a proper defense of $PAP_{If}$ against them until later in this chapter.

## Tracking the problem

So how does this subtle yet invalid strategy practically take shape? Quite simply, an incompatibilist advocate of the PAP could for example contend that "it would be unreasonable to command someone to do something impossible for them to do. It would be like commanding an armless man to embrace you."[49] We can easily recognize that an armless man is not reasonably to be held morally responsible for his failure to embrace someone (in this case "you"). But what is the exact nature of the inability that so obviously disqualifies him as a proper target of blame? It is one rooted in the fact that without arms, this man could not embrace you *even if he wanted to*. Even if this man's inner desires at the moment of choice were such that he wanted to obey the command and embrace you, he would find himself unable to do so; in other words, upon his failure, it is not the case that he could have done otherwise had his inner desires inclined him to do so. The $PAP_{If}$ thus successfully declares him to be exempt of guilt, and it follows that a compatibilist who affirms $PAP_{If}$ need not accept $PAP_{All}$ in order to avoid the absurd conclusion that an armless man could be held morally guilty for his failure to embrace someone. $PAP_{If}$ is sufficient (and $PAP_{All}$ unnecessary) to successfully adjudicate such cases.

The exposed equivocation in turn explains very well why the ambiguous PAP is often left poorly (if at all) supported by its incompatibilist advocates: the true $PAP_{If}$ is found shining in plain sight for all to see, its high plausibility being strongly felt by us all, and with a subtle equivocation close at hand, the unsupported $PAP_{All}$ lying in the nearby bushes illicitly benefits from the plausibility of its true and intuitive neighbor, $PAP_{If}$. Fortunately for compatibilists, however, once one is aware of and on the lookout for such an unjustified transfer of plausibility, the maneuver (intentional or not) is easily uncovered in incompatibilist writings. Consider the following instances:

David Widerker imagines that Holly had promised to attend Sarah's big birthday party, and failed to do so. Sarah blamed Holly only later to find out that Holly could not do so due to a failed airline departure. Widerker concludes on his illustrative support of PAP: "it seems rationally incumbent upon Sarah to withdraw her blame and excuse Holly. Holly had no viable alternative to her failure to attend Sarah's party and, hence, is not morally responsible for her absence."[50] Yes indeed, barring any responsibility that Holly may bear for possibly making herself dependent on an untrustworthy airline in the first place, we can agree with Widerker that

49. This preliminary, illustrative case is taken from a real-world example of a popular source: Vines, "Sermon on John 3:16," 26.

50. McKenna and Widerker, "Introduction," 3.

she is not blameworthy; but that verdict is not arrived at on the basis of an unqualified PAP alone. The much more modest $PAP_{If}$ does the job just as well, yielding the correct result: Holly is not morally responsible, because the airline failure made it so that she could not have fulfilled her promise *even if she had wanted to*. Given the absence of available transportation, Holly failed to keep her promise, and upon her failure, it is not the case that she could have done otherwise *had her inner desires inclined her to do so*. As a matter of fact, if she is a decent friend, we can further suppose that her inner desires *did* incline her strongly to do so, though she sorrowfully could not. Here again, $PAP_{If}$ is demonstrably sufficient (and $PAP_{All}$ unnecessary) to successfully adjudicate Holly and Sarah's dispute, so that Widerker's case does not support $PAP_{All}$.

David Copp offers another story wherein a boss requires an employee to do something that the employee lacks the ability to do. "A supervisor at the post office might demand that a mail carrier cook a soufflé for everyone in the post office in the next five minutes when the mail carrier does not even know what a soufflé is."[51] Of course that carrier cannot be blamed for the failure, because she could not cook it *even if she wanted to*. The conditional $PAP_{If}$ is used once more to support an unqualified PAP, and thus falls short of the impossible task.

A final example comes from the pen of Peter van Inwagen who envisions someone charging you of not speaking up while Jones was being bad-mouthed. This person, van Inwagen says, "must withdraw his charge if you can convince him that you were bound and gagged while Jones was being maligned."[52] And this example is again used to support the unqualified claim that "ought implies can" (see next section in this chapter for the relationship of this similar claim to the PAP). The invalidity of this pattern must be clearly seen by now: you are not responsible if bound and gagged, because you could not have spoken *even if you had wanted to*. Upon failing to speak, it is not the case that you could have done otherwise had your inner desires inclined you to do so. $PAP_{If}$ is sufficient and $PAP_{All}$ unnecessary. Hence these cases do not support $PAP_{All}$; they only reaffirm a $PAP_{If}$ that I suggest ought to be rather uncontroversial.

## The maxim—does "ought" imply "can"?

As seen in van Inwagen's contention just above, there is another way of putting the principle of alternate possibilities, by affirming instead the maxim

51. Copp, "'Ought' Implies 'Can,'" 271.
52. Van Inwagen, *Essay*, 161.

that "ought implies can" (hereafter "the maxim").[53] Since the wording of the maxim is not strictly identical to that of the PAP, some may want to infuse the maxim with a slightly different truth claim than that made by the PAP, but I find no significant difference between the two in this context, and find it simpler to understand them as largely equivalent. This is even more or less justified on the following modest assumptions:

Let us imagine a person P who performs a morally significant action A. A being *morally* significant, it could be either morally good or morally evil. Let us suppose that A is morally evil, but the present analysis is unaffected by this supposition, as it applies to both cases symmetrically.

Let us suppose that ought implies can, and that P is morally responsible for his doing A, a morally evil, sinful action. By definition, (at the very least on the Christian view) if A is a morally evil, sinful action, it means that P ought to refrain from A; P ought to do "not-A" instead. Now since we supposed that ought implies can, and P ought to do "not-A," it follows that P can do "not-A," which is to say that P has the ability to do otherwise than A. This shows that if ought implies can, then moral responsibility requires the ability to do otherwise. The maxim entails the PAP.

Conversely, let us now suppose that moral responsibility requires the ability to do otherwise, and that P ought to do "not-A." If P *ought* to do "not-A," then P has a moral duty to do "not-A." Such a moral duty presumably entails that P is morally responsible for his choice as to whether he will do A or "not-A," because if P were not morally responsible for it, it would be unreasonable to place a *moral* duty on P to do "not-A." From P's moral responsibility and the presupposed principle of alternate possibility, it follows that P could do otherwise than he did; he could do otherwise than "not-A," which is to say P can do A. This shows that if moral responsibility entails the ability to do otherwise, then ought implies can. The PAP entails the maxim.

Hence, the two directions of the entailment are established on this understanding, and we have thus equivalence between the principle of alternate possibilities and the maxim "ought implies can." This being said, if others insist that a difference still needs to be maintained at any point between the two, nothing serious follows for the present debate: only a language barrier, in that different things will be meant by "ought implies can" in their writings than are meant by the same phrase in the present work. This would then allow one to decouple the claims of the maxim from those of the PAP, and see the PAP as supporting incompatibilism while the maxim does

---

53. Among others, this maxim is famously attributed to Kant. See Frankfurt, "We Are Morally Responsible," 95.

not, or vice versa.[54] No separate incompatibilist argument can be based on this, however, and remain untreated by my present critique, since both the PAP and the maxim are here assumed to have the strongest incompatibilist aspirations, and *on these incompatibilist readings* find themselves refuted by the present critique. Therefore, a disagreement on the precise meaning of the maxim does not weaken my defense against incompatibilism, and I am free to continue seeing the two as largely equivalent.

Furthermore, not only are these two equivalent in the truth claims I see them make, but they also both lend themselves to the same equivocation clarified above with respect to "ability." The unqualified "can" in "ought implies can" can be interpreted either conditionally or categorically, just as it could in the phrase "can do otherwise" of the PAP. Accordingly, the maxim must follow my above conclusions regarding the PAP: the maxim must be seen as compatibilist and true if "can" is understood conditionally, and incompatibilist but false (or at least so far unproven) if "can" is understood categorically. The equivocation between conditional and categorical abilities is the same as that identified above.

## Revisiting the consequence argument beyond this equivocation

Having introduced the coherent difference between categorical ability and conditional ability, it is a good place to take a moment and revisit the consequence argument with these distinctions in mind. The consequence

---

54. Note, for example, Ishtiyaque Haji, who as a compatibilist denies the PAP, but affirms the maxim: "If morality *requires* that you do something, then you can do it." Haji, *Incompatibilism's Allure*, 92. But of course as a compatibilist, what he means by "can" in the maxim is not a categorical ability, but a conditional ability, which makes his understanding of the maxim an equivalent of the $PAP_{If}$. This is verified by the fact that the two ensuing examples that he provides to support this maxim are clear cases where a *conditional* ability is lacking from an agent, entailing his lack of moral responsibility: "If you can't, for example, save the drowning child because you have been tethered to your seat, or because you have been overcome by paralysis, the 'ought' implies 'can' principle indicates that you don't have a moral obligation to save the child; morality can't require you to do what is not in your power to do." Ibid. Clearly enough, being tethered or paralyzed make you such that you could not save the child *even if you wanted*. No categorical, incompatibilist ability claim is meant here, and so Haji sees the maxim as conditional and compatibilist. And of course on this understanding of can, I would join Haji in affirming the maxim (as I do the $PAP_{If}$).

See also Harry Frankfurt who maintains "that renouncing PAP does not require denying that 'ought' implies 'can' and that PAP is not entailed by the Kantian view." So that Frankfurt presumably upholds the maxim even though he clearly rejects PAP. Frankfurt, "We Are Morally Responsible," 96

argument had been rejected above for failing to support incompatibilism because of its question-begging understanding of choice and free will, but in order to fully defuse its initial plausibility, we can now analyze its claims with a compatibilist, conditional analysis of ability, to see that so understood, this kind of ability *is* indeed truly necessary, and is I think what made the invalid argument partially convincing in the first place.

When van Inwagen argued that we cannot be morally responsible for "consequences" of the past and the laws of nature, it was convincing insofar as we all sense that one cannot be morally responsible for such consequences over which we have no "control." But the only control that is shown to be necessary is a conditional sense of control, and this conditional sense is very much (entirely, I claim) responsible for the intuitive plausibility unduly conceded to the consequence argument, because this conditional sense of ability is so obviously necessary for moral responsibility. With a conditional sense of ability, we certainly want to maintain our human freedom to control our choices; we want our choices to be "up to us," in that we have at least the ability to choose one way or the other according to our own desires. We want the ability to choose A or B *if we want to*. And in the absence of this ability, we cannot be held morally responsible: whatever else moral responsibility requires, it demands nothing less than this conditional ability.

## First formulation

So let us take the first articulation of the consequence argument, which concluded that "If determinism is true, J could not have raised his hand at T." If the sense of "could" is understood conditionally, then we can see that it excludes moral responsibility. If J has been handcuffed with his hands behind his back, he lacks the conditional ability to raise his hand, in that he could not raise his hand even if he wanted to. The consequence argument failed to show why a categorical ability would be necessary for moral responsibility, but a conditional ability is without controversy necessary for such.[55]

---

55. This fact is what leads Christopher Hill to criticize this first formulation of the consequence argument, on the grounds that van Inwagen's definition of "can" either presupposes incompatibilism, or does not sustain one of the argument's premises, namely that J could not have rendered L false (L being the conjunction of the laws of nature). Hill, "Van Inwagen on the Consequence Argument," 49–55. Hill says that there are analyses of "can" under which it is false that J could not have rendered L false. The response offered by van Inwagen is instructive: he doesn't give an argument in favor of the premise as understood with a categorical sense of "can," instead he says that to him (and hopefully an audience of undecided readers), the conditional sense of "can" is no ability worth the name. So van Inwagen lets his premise stand on its own, supposing it will be found true by his audience. Van Inwagen, "Reply to Christopher Hill," 56–61.

## Second formulation

The second formulation of the consequence argument was phrased in terms of access to possible worlds. It was there established that only a libertarian free will provides an agent with access to alternate possible worlds that share a past identical in all things with the actual world. The argument failed to show why this kind of access was necessary for moral responsibility, but there is here again a close sense of ability, a conditional one, that is indeed necessary for moral responsibility. Phrased in terms of access to possible worlds, this conditional sense of ability would require that there exists a possible world in which the agent chooses otherwise than he does in the actual world, and that is identical to the actual world in all things up to the moment of choice, *except for the inner desires and inclination of the agent.* This difference between the pasts of the two possible worlds accounts for the compatibility of determinism with this conditional account. On this conditional analysis, the agent does not need to have a categorical ability to jump from one possible world to another that is strictly distinct; rather, he needs to be such that he could have brought about a different choice, *had he been in an alternate possible world that differs with the actual world only with respect to his inner inclinations.*[56] The consequence argument had failed to show why agents without a categorical ability to access alternate possible worlds could not be morally responsible, but the conditional ability to access such worlds as I just defined is certainly necessary for moral responsibility. If our judge J failed to raise his hand in the actual world, *and* could not have raised his hand even if he had found himself in an alternate possible world whose only difference with our world is that in it he genuinely wanted to do so, then it follows that he cannot be morally responsible for failing to raise

---

But once again, the issue is not that of defining the word "can"; it is about whether any sense of "can" is shown to be both necessary for moral responsibility and incompatible with determinism. So of course, to a compatibilist who thinks the argument is benefiting from the invalid transfer of plausibility between conditional and categorical senses of ability, all it shows is that a categorical ability is incompatible with determinism, but no reason is given to believe the question-begging assertion that a categorical ability to do otherwise is necessary for moral responsibility.

56. This conditional analysis of possible worlds is proposed in very similar terms by Keith Lehrer who suggests: "when we say that a person could have done something he did not do, we should not, and I believe do not, thereby affirm that every antecedent necessary condition of his performing the action is fulfilled. It is enough that there be some possible world minimally different from the actual world restricted in an appropriate way so that the person performs the action and those conditions are fulfilled. We may speak of worlds restricted in the appropriate way as possible worlds that are *accessible* to the agents from the actual world." Lehrer, "'Can' in Theory and Practice," 253–54, quoted in Fischer and Pendergraft, "Beg the Question?" 589.

his hand in the actual world. This is seen once more if we imagine him to be handcuffed in the actual world. There exists no possible world in which the handcuffed Judge has merely alternate inner desires, and is able to raise his hands, because the alternate desires in that alternate possible world are still blocked from being acted upon, by the handcuffs maintained in place in both worlds. This conditional sense of ability is seen to be necessary for moral responsibility, though compatible with determinism, while the categorical sense excluded determinism but was not shown to be necessary for moral responsibility.

## "Almost-possible worlds" (or "possible almost-worlds")

Now with respect to possible worlds, it might be objected that on certain compatibilist determinist accounts—for example, ones wherein there exists a best possible world, and God necessarily creates that one[57]—there really is no other possible world than the actual world. It would then seem to be impossible for anyone to be morally responsible on this account, if moral responsibility required the existence of *any* alternate possible world, even a modest one as I have defined, which does not have to match the actual world in *all* things prior to the moment of choice. Not even those exist, if there is only one possible world. Is this an insurmountable difficulty? I think not. A way around this would be to refine the description of this needed alternate "possible world," by removing from that world's book the propositions about why ultimately God providentially brought about any human choice rather than their contrary (and presumably all the true propositions that entail them). In other words, if say on this view God brought about in the actual world $W$ a human choice A rather than choice B, because God had a good purpose P behind the happening of A, then we could speak of the happening of B as belonging to an alternate possible world $W^*$ (both $W$ and $W^*$ being determinist here), if and only if we truncate and remove from $W^*$ the consideration of purpose P which on this view necessitated the actualization of A. We could name such a truncated possible world as $W^*$ a "possible almost-world." In considering its content for the sake of moral judgments in $W$, we would then be asking: "If God, supposing he did not

---

57. Hugh McCann discusses this question and argues in favor of such a view (that there is such a thing as a single best possible world), though to my knowledge he does not come out and conclude from this that there is only one possible world. This seems to be a good and necessary consequence of his view however, because if there is a best possible world, and God is the greatest conceivable being, God will necessarily pick this best possible world, and accordingly no other, lesser world remains truly possible, *given who God is.* See McCann, *Creation*, 155–75.

have purpose P for actualizing choice A, had actually, for some other reason, providentially inclined that person to choose B instead, then would
that person have been able to act on those desires and choose B, or not?" If
not, then the person is not morally responsible for his failure to act in the
actual world. I believe that this usage of hypothetical, truncated possible (al-
most-) worlds is coherent, useful, and quite intuitive. If libertarians are not
prepared to grant this much, however, all that follows is that the necessity of
a conditional ability to secure moral responsibility cannot here be *phrased*
*in terms of possible worlds*. It may be mildly disappointing for those of us
who think that possible worlds are useful tools (not to mention fun), but for
our immediate purposes, nothing hangs in the balance with respect to the
consequence argument's failure to establish that an access to fully specified,
alternate possible worlds is necessary for moral responsibility.

*Third formulation*

Finally, the third articulation of the consequence argument made use of the
operator N, and the rules α and β.

   N$p$ stood for "$p$ is true, and no one has, or ever had, any choice about
whether $p$ is true," and α and β were defined as:

α   $\Box p \vdash Np$

β   $N(p \supset q), Np \vdash Nq$

   Here, on a conditional analysis, it is "N$p$ excludes moral responsibility"
that is obviously true for every proposition $p$ about what a person chooses
and brings about. If a person does not have and never had any choice (understood conditionally) about what he does, then he cannot be held morally
responsible for his choosing it and acting on it.

   On the conditional analysis, however, α is false, because if we consider
a proposition $p$ describing the outcome of a person's free choice, even if
$p$ is necessarily true, it does not exclude the possibility that the choice be
made freely in the conditional sense, i.e. in the sense that the person could
have done otherwise, if only his fully specified inner state and desires, which
on determinism render $p$ necessary, had been different, and thus no longer
necessitated $p$.

   As to β, it is I concede evidently true, first, for any propositions $p$ and $q$
that do not describe human choices. If no one has or ever had a choice about
the truth of the law of gravity, and no one has or ever had a choice about
the fact that if the law of gravity is true apples will fall from trees, then no
one has or ever had a choice about the fact that apples fall from trees. And

secondly, we recognized earlier that β was indeed true as well of human choices, if the choice in N was understood in a libertarian sense.

Could it be however that β is false if we consider propositions $p$ and $q$ that have to do with human choices, and understand "choice" in N conditionally? On the conditional analysis, having a choice about $p$ means being able to bring about the truth or falsehood of $p$ if we suppose that the person's desires inclined him to. With this meaning of choice in view, let us consider whether a counterexample to β could be offered. On a Calvinist, determinist, compatibilist account of providence, the best candidate for such a counterexample to β would be to consider a human free choice understood conditionally and deterministically, and see whether a person could be said to make it freely in the conditional sense, while being such that the choice follows necessarily from antecedent conditions—namely God's decree—over which the agent has no choice (even conditionally), so as to prove β false. In other words, can we find propositions $p$ and $q$ such that $N(p \supset q)$ is true (where choice in N is understood conditionally), $Np$ is true (in the conditional sense of choice as well), and yet $Nq$ is false if choice is understood conditionally? This would yield the conclusion that β is false on the conditional understanding of choice, because its consequent would no longer follow necessarily from the truth of its antecedents. Let us then consider the relationship between a compatibilist free choice and its determining antecedent, God's prior decree, to see the parts over which the human agent can be said to have a choice understood conditionally. Let us consider an action A that a person P performs at a given instant t, and let $p$ be the proposition "God decreed that P would do A at instant t." Let $q$ be the proposition "P performs action A at t," and once again let $Np$ be the proposition that "$p$ is true and no one has or ever had a choice understood conditionally about whether $p$ is true." With those considerations in place, we can now evaluate if this best candidate constitutes a counterexample to rule β. For this to be the case, we would need to find that $N(p \supset q)$, and $Np$ are true, while $Nq$ is false.

First, $N(p \supset q)$ is indeed true. The agent P does not have a choice even conditionally over whether $p \supset q$. $p$ is God's decree that P would perform A, and $q$ is the fact that P performs A. Whatever A chooses, it is impossible for him to bring about that $p$ be true and $q$ be false, even if A wanted to. He does not have the conditional ability to bring about the falsehood of $p \supset q$, so we have $N(p \supset q)$ is true.

Secondly, $Nq$ (the consequent of β) is false indeed as long as the word "choice" in N is understood conditionally. If action A is a normal, determinist but compatibilist freely willed action, then it is the case that P could have refrained from performing it, *if he had wanted to*. If P's choice of performing

A satisfies the normal determinist compatibilist conditions for moral responsibility, P *does* have a choice, understood conditionally, about whether $q$ is true, insofar as he has the ability to follow his inner desires with respect to A, and *would* be able to choose *not* A, if he had so desired, that is, if God had purposed to incline P otherwise than God in fact did. In other words, God decrees the outcome, but P still has to make up his mind with respect to $q$ or *not q*. So P has a choice understood conditionally about whether to perform A, and thus N$q$ is false.

But is N$p$ true? For N$p$ to be true, it would have to be the case that P does not have a choice even understood conditionally about whether $p$ (God's decree that P would perform A). But that is likely not the case. It is true that if God decrees deterministically that P will perform A, then P cannot have a *categorical, libertarian* ability to refrain from doing A; but if P's choice is understood *conditionally*, then P *does* have a choice about whether or not $p$ was true. If P had wanted to refrain from A, that is, if—contrary to facts—P's desires had inclined him not to perform A, then it would have been the case that God's decree never included P's performing A. If P had wanted to, he could have refrained from A, and for this to happen, it would have had to be the case that $p$ was false. It remains that P has a choice understood conditionally about whether $p$ is true. Therefore N$p$ is false, and hence compatibilist free choices along with their determined antecedents do not constitute counterexamples to rule β where choice in N is understood conditionally. Since they are plausibly the best candidates for a counterexample to rule β, it is plausible that β is in fact true even on the conditional analysis.

So far, we have thus seen that on a conditional analysis of choice, while β is true, α is false. What does that mean for the conditional analysis of the third formulation of the consequence argument, though? Not much. Indeed, though α is false, it is only used in the argument to establish something that is nevertheless true. Let's recall the steps of the third formulation:

1. $\square\,((P_0\,\&\,L) \supset P)$   (statement of determinism)

2. $\square\,(P_0 \supset (L \supset P))$   (follows from (1))

3. $N\,(P_0 \supset (L \supset P))$   (follows from (2) and (α))

4. $N\,P_0$   (new premise)

5. $N\,(L \supset P)$   (follows from (3), (4), and (β))

6. $N\,L$   (new premise)

7. $N\,P$   (follows from (5), (6), and (β))

As is apparent above, α is only used to justify the inference from (2) to (3), but (3) is unobjectionable even on a conditional analysis: I think no one has or ever had a choice (even understood conditionally) over the fact that the past and the laws entail the present on determinism, or—to phrase the matter less in terms of natural determinism and more in terms of theological determinism—no one has or ever had a choice (even understood conditionally) over the fact that if God decreed something, that thing would come to past. No one could ever bring it about both that God decreed something, and yet that that thing not happen. So to use the language of premise (3), *even if, conditionally*, the person had wanted to, he could not have done anything that would falsify $P_0 \supset (L \supset P)$, on determinism. Therefore, premise (3) is fine even on a conditional analysis.

This is all and well, however, since on the conditional analysis, it is premise (4) that is false, for the very same reason that β was found true: namely, the conditional sense of choice is mild enough that a person can be said to have it even over things that happened in the past; it is a counterfactual sense of ability. While evidently no one has a *categorical* ability to falsify the past, the demands of a *conditional* ability accommodate this concept very well. To say that a person has a choice understood conditionally is precisely to say that the person could choose otherwise, *if only* something (like his inner desires) had been different, in the past. As I just showed in my discussion of rule β, on a conditional analysis of choice, not only is it coherent, but something like it is even *required* to affirm that a person has such a counterfactual, conditional choice over God's past decrees. He could choose otherwise than he does, *if only* his desires were different, that is, if only God's past decree of his inclination had been different. That clearly means premise (4) is false on a conditional analysis of choice.

I should add that although I thought it most plausible to focus in this fashion on premise (4) and its falsity on a conditional analysis, I suppose that one could instead (or also) offer a similar rejection of premise (6), contending as David Lewis does, that on a conditional analysis, a person *has* the ability, not to break the law, but to act in a way such that if he were so to act, something that is in fact a law would have been broken (and hence wouldn't have been a law).[58] And then again, if one makes this move, it also seems no less meaningful to reject (3) and (5) in this manner after all. If we follow Lewis and say a person has a conditional choice over whether a law really is a law, why not affirm this person has a conditional choice over whether $P_0 \supset (L \supset P)$? I think it more meaningful to understand a conditional choice to be a counterfactual power over the past statement of God's decree (and

58. See David Lewis, "Break the Laws?" 122–29.

hence reject (4)), but it's really a subjective matter as to which part of the past one thinks is more plausibly altered in the statement of the counterfactual condition required by the conditional analysis.[59]

Now let me reassert that the *truth*, or *sufficiency*, or *adequacies* of the conditional analysis are not the points debated here. I understand that libertarians find this conditional analysis most distasteful, and that is their right (more on that below in this chapter). My more modest point here is that premise (4) is not true on a conditional analysis, the only analysis of choice that has so far been shown (and admitted) to be necessary for moral responsibility.

In conclusion regarding this revisiting of the consequence argument, it has become clear in each of the three formulations, that the categorical ability is incompatible with determinism, but not shown to be necessary for moral responsibility; while the milder, conditional ability is necessary for moral responsibility, but compatible with determinism.

## The consequence argument and the necessity of the past

A bit of a different critique of the consequence argument has been offered by Joseph Campbell in an important paper that sparked an interesting conversation about another possible flaw in the argument. Since I don't personally exploit that possible weakness, I will not enter into much detail here about his concern, but it may be worth explaining it succinctly, to see how our respective responses to the consequence argument differ. Let's return to van Inwagen's premises in the third formulation of the consequence argument:

1. $\square ((P_0 \& L) \supset P)$   (statement of determinism)

2. $\square (P_0 \supset (L \supset P))$   (follows from (1))

3. $N (P_0 \supset (L \supset P))$   (follows from (2) and ($\alpha$))

4. $N P_0$   (new premise)

59. As a matter of fact, I think Lewis's suggestion can be plausibly reduced to mine after all. He is quite clear that he doesn't affirm the conditional analysis of choice as a power to bring about that something is both a law and broken; rather, it is the power to bring about that something which is in fact a law *would* have been broken, and hence wouldn't have been a law. That counterfactual alteration, it seems to me, amounts to changing the content of the past, i.e., changing $P_0$. If, say, *l* is in fact a law in the actual world, then the state of the world in the distant past, $P_0$, contains the state of affairs that *l* is a law. And hence the counterfactual Lewis envisions, that "if the person acted otherwise, *l* would not have been a law," is nothing less than a statement that if the person so acted, $P_0$ would have been different: it would have not contained the fact that *l* was a law.

5. N (L ⊃ P)      (follows from (3), (4), and (β))

6. N L          (new premise)

7. N P         (follows from (5), (6), and (β))

The conclusion N P expresses the (unacceptable) thesis that no one has or ever had a choice about any proposition P. We can now appreciate where Campbell and I each object. My response is, as explained above, that if "choice" is presupposed to be libertarian and to feature a categorical ability to do otherwise, then the entire argument is sound, but its conclusion is only that no one has or ever had a *libertarian* choice about P. That does follow uncontroversially from determinism, but doesn't establish incompatibilism until someone tells us why libertarian free will is necessary for moral responsibility. However, if we no longer suppose the choice to be libertarian, then I simply reject (4). If P now expresses the outcome of a free choice as I understand it, not presupposing it to be libertarian, then the more modest, conditional ability—the only one that is admitted to be necessary for moral responsibility—is quite possibly held by the person choosing P. Even if the choice is determined, we can suppose that the person *has* such a conditional ability to choose otherwise in a way that would make P false: he could, if he wanted. And in that case, it would indeed mean that $P_0$ had to be different, so in that sense, we would say that the person has a choice, conditionally speaking, over $P_0$, and reject (4). None of this is permitted indeed if we're talking about a categorical ability to do otherwise, but in a conditional, counterfactual sense, making $P_0$ false by supposing a slight modification of the past is exactly what we're doing in the expression of our subjunctive conditional: we are saying that if the person had had slightly different antecedent desires (in the past), he could have chosen otherwise without anything else standing in his way. So we see my point once again that the modest conditional ability to do otherwise is not excluded by determinism, and the categorical ability to do otherwise is not established to be necessary for moral responsibility.

This response of mine differs from Campbell's. He also rejects (4), but for a different reason. He doesn't protest the categorical ability to do otherwise that the argument assumes; rather he says—presumably even if the ability in view is categorical—that just because $P_0$ is in the past, it doesn't mean that no one has or ever had a choice about $P_0$. If the instant that $P_0$ describes is in the recent past when the person was alive, then although no one *now* has a choice about its content, someone may very well *have had* a choice about it. "The fact that no one *can* change the past is irrelevant to whether anyone ever *had* a choice about whether some true proposition about the past is true,"[60] he says. Instead, what would prevent anyone's ever having had a choice about $P_0$ would be the fact not merely that it was in the past, but that it was in the *remote* past: before anyone was born to make a choice about it. And in that case, what Campbell argues is that even if the argument is sound in our world, it presupposes the existence of a remote past, which he says is not a metaphysically necessary feature of the world, so that the argument fails to establish that determinism and free will are incompatible in every possible world. The consequence argument thereby fails to establish incompatibilism proper.

I think it is an interesting loophole in the consequence argument, and it has generated a good deal of stimulating conversation,[61] but I shall not make much of this point here, for the two following reasons. First, I believe that it is not very costly for incompatibilists to accept Campbell's objection, admit the shortcoming of the consequence argument, and regroup by simply adding the premise that there exists a remote past. They accordingly no longer establish the incompatibility of free will and determinism in every possible world (i.e., incompatibilism), but they still can claim to do so in every possible world that has a remote past, which ours does. After all, as Andrew Bailey has pointed out, "arguments for incompatibilism are of interest in part because of their connection to the question of whether *we* are free."[62]

And secondly, in any case, I believe my own response above has exposed a more fundamental problem for the argument, on which I am much more comfortable resting my case, and so I shall: the consequence argument successfully establishes that determinism is incompatible with libertarian free will, but fails to tell us why libertarian free will is necessary for moral responsibility, as it fails to disambiguate the sense of "choice" or "ability to do otherwise" that it employs in premise (4) and in its conclusion.

## Application to the deliberation argument—does one's rational deliberation presuppose one's belief in one's categorical ability to do otherwise?

As we endeavor to track and expose the equivocation between conditional and categorical abilities, and properly assess the role it plays in debates on free will, there is a final argument that calls for our attention. It is one that is

60. Campbell, "Necessity of the Past," 107.

61. For a good summary of the havoc that was caused by Campbell, see Bailey, "Incompatibilism and the Past," 351–75.

62. Ibid., 363.

no longer strictly about incompatibilism; it is one for indeterminism, but it remains helpful to evaluate here because it features the same call for alternate possibilities, and it plays off of the same equivocation that was just described between categorical and conditional abilities. I shall call it the deliberation argument. It is sometimes argued that the very act of decision-making by rational deliberation betrays a belief in one's ability to do otherwise. One does not deliberate about options that are known to be impossible, we are told; so deliberation itself is put forward as evidence of one's belief in one's categorical ability to choose this or that option. Peter van Inwagen argues:

> Anyone who rejected free will could not consistently deliberate about future courses of action. This is so, I shall argue, owing simply to the fact that one cannot deliberate without believing that the things about which one is deliberating are things it is possible for one to do.[63]

And just as before, by "free will," what is in view is "libertarian free will." Hugh McCann puts it this way: "Phenomena such as decision *smack of libertarianism*."[64]

The problem with this argument is that for rational deliberation no less than for moral judgments, what is known to be necessary is a *conditional* ability to choose, not a categorical one. What matters is that we believe that the options before us *would be* accessible *if* we were to choose them. Certainly, no one ever deliberates about options that would be impossible *even if one were to choose them*. John Martin Fischer illustrates this minimal notion of ability that we all see impacts rational deliberation:

> I can go to the movies later insofar as I would go to the movies, if I were to choose to go to the movies, and I can go to the lecture insofar as I would go to the lecture, if I were to choose to go to the lecture, and so forth. . . . I do not deliberate about whether to jump to the moon, because (in part at least) I would not successfully jump to the moon, even if I were to choose to jump to the moon.[65]

This is the compatibilist, conditional account of ability, and hence, all such conditional intuitions are insufficient to support the present libertarian contentions. Van Inwagen offers the following example in support of his above claim:

63. Van Inwagen, *Essay*, 19.
64. McCann, *Works of Agency*, 145.
65. Fischer, "Compatibilism," 49.

One cannot deliberate about whether to perform a certain act unless one believes it is possible for one to perform it. (Anyone who doubts that this is indeed the case may find it instructive to imagine that he is in a room with two doors and that he believes one of the doors to be unlocked and the other to be locked and impassable, though he has no idea which is which; let him then attempt to imagine himself deliberating about which door to leave by.)[66]

For a mere parenthetical comment, van Inwagen's story is in fact rather complex and somewhat under-explained. In fact, I contend that it is irrelevant to the libertarian conclusion it aims to support, whichever way one interprets it. The incompatibilist contention at hand is that deliberation entails a belief in one's categorical—not merely conditional—ability to perform the action that one is deliberating about. In order to support that, van Inwagen would need to put forward a story in which:

1. The agent lacks a belief in his categorical ability to perform an action,

2. The agent does not deliberate,

   *and,*

3. The *reason* why he does not deliberate is that he lacks a belief in his categorical ability to perform the action.

None of the available candidates for an action present in (or in the neighborhood of) van Inwagen's story satisfies these three conditions.

Let us consider first the exact deliberation mentioned by van Inwagen, a deliberation "about which door to leave by." This would mean deliberating about the actions "leaving through door A," or "leaving through door B." The agent knows that either door may be locked, so he lacks a belief in his categorical ability to *leave* through either of them. But then again, he *also* lacks a belief in his *conditional* ability to do so: knowing that either door may be locked, he does not believe that he *would* leave through either door, conditionally, *if only he chose to do so.* His choice would be insufficient; to succeed, the door would *also* have to happen to be unlocked. Why then couldn't his lack of *conditional* ability be the reason why he does not deliberate, given that compatibilists agree wholeheartedly that a belief in this sort of ability *is* necessary for rational deliberation? The story does not say, and hence it fails to discriminate between conditional and categorical abilities, which is to say, it fails to support indeterminism.

66. Van Inwagen, *Essay*, 154.

But what if the action under consideration now becomes "*attempting to leave through door A*," or "*attempting* to leave through door B"? In that case, the agent does possess the conditional ability to do either: regardless of their possibly being locked, the agent knows that he *would* attempt to open door A *if* he wanted to try, and he *would* attempt to open door B *if* he wanted to try. And yet again, we all agree that he will probably not deliberate about these two options either, contemplating their being locked or unlocked. But is it because he lacks a belief in his categorical ability to perform either action? Not at all.[67] The reason why it would be vain to deliberate about those is that he doesn't know which door is locked, and thus *as far as he knows*, whichever door he picks will have the exact same outcome. As far as he knows, choosing one or the other makes no difference. *That* is why no deliberation takes place. The point of deliberation is to weigh different outcomes based on our best knowledge of what would follow in each case, our knowledge of what difference the choice would make in the world. If we lack knowledge of any difference between two options before us, we will not deliberate about them indeed, but then nothing will follow about our belief in any categorical ability (or lack thereof) to choose one or the other. Nothing interesting will follow about the nature of our free will.

Now in order to identify and address all the intuitions at play in van Inwagen's example and its surroundings, let us consider a final revision of the story. Let us now suppose that the person is informed that "door A is locked and door B is open." In that case we all agree that he still would not deliberate about the impossible task of leaving through door A, nor even about *attempting* to open door A, but it wouldn't support indeterminist contentions any better, since clearly enough, it would be a case wherein the agent knows he lacks *conditional* ability. He would no longer deliberate about leaving through door A because he could not open it *even if he wanted*. Compatibilists wholeheartedly affirm the necessity of that sort of ability and possibility, but from it, the necessity of a categorical ability simply does not follow and hence intuitions about rational deliberation offer no support for the indeterminist view.

In conclusion, once the equivocation between abilities is uncovered, we see that a categorical ability is incompatible with determinism but not shown to be necessary for rational deliberation, while a conditional ability is necessary for rational deliberation but perfectly compatible with determinism.

---

67. As a matter of fact, if his free will is libertarian, then he *does* have the categorical ability to perform either action: he categorically *can* attempt to open door A or door B.

# The standard objection: the death of classical compatibilism and its distasteful conditional analysis

Having coherently distinguished between conditional and categorical analyses of ability, an all-important objection must now be addressed. Without fail, whenever the above concepts are mentioned, incompatibilists contend that in the absence of a categorical ability to do otherwise, one is left with a mere conditional analysis of abilities, which, we are told is not viable. The conditional analysis of ability is attributed to so-called "classical compatibilists," whose view has long been declared untenable.[68] More than this, it has been despised! Gary Watson reports that "This line of defence has seemed so plainly defective to its critics that they often entertain unfriendly suspicions about the philosophical integrity of those who pursue it."[69] William James and Immanuel Kant respectively called it a "quagmire of evasion" and a "wretched subterfuge."[70] So before we even consider my coming arguments to reject the $PAP_{All}$ with its categorical understanding of ability, we want to make sure that the conditional understanding of ability found in the remaining $PAP_{If}$ is not as distasteful as some philosophers say it is. Accordingly, let us ask the only relevant question: what exactly seems to be the problem with the conditional analysis of ability to do otherwise?

Three sorts of objections have been offered against it: some have found it to be question-begging, some have found it not to be *necessary*, and some have found it not to be *sufficient*. Let us review each problem in turn, to see that none of them should worry us much.

## *The charge of question begging*

First, then, is the charge that the conditional analysis is question-begging. Peter van Inwagen introduces the conditional analysis as one of the most important "argument[s] for the compatibility of free will and determinism,"[71] but remains largely unimpressed, and responds as follows:

> What does the [conditional] analysis do for us? How does it affect our understanding of the Compatibility Problem? It does very little for us, so far as I can see, unless we have some reason

68. Robert Kane attributes the invention of the label to Gary Watson, and lists the following philosophers as representatives: Thomas Hobbes, David Hume, John Stuart Mill, A.J. Ayer, Moritz Schlick, and Donald Davidson. See Kane, "Introduction," 11–16.

69. Watson, "Introduction," 4.

70. Both quoted in Dennett, *Elbow Room*, 131.

71. Van Inwagen, *Essay*, 114.

to think it is *correct*. Many compatibilists seem to think that they need only present a conditional analysis of ability, defend it against, or modify it in the face of, such counter-examples as may arise, and that they have thereby done what is necessary to defend compatibilism.

That is not how I see it. The particular analysis of ability that a compatibilist presents is, as I see it, simply one of his premisses; his central premiss, in fact. And premisses need to be defended.[72]

So van Inwagen essentially says that the conditional analysis of ability, taken as an argument for compatibilism, is question-begging. I think that is right, and compatibilists can join van Inwagen in his castigation: taken as an argument against incompatibilism, it "does very little for us" indeed. But all that means is that compatibilists should not use it like that. Instead, the only compatibilist claim worth making in this neighborhood is much more modest than that: it is simply one that says that a conditional analysis is compatible with determinism, and that it is the only analysis that has been shown to be necessary for moral responsibility and free will. This much I successfully defended above. So the conditional analysis is an utter failure indeed if taken as an attack upon incompatibilism, but it is just fine as a defense of compatibilism against the positive claim that moral responsibility and free will require an ability to do otherwise, a positive claim, which I explained above, begs the question of incompatibilism, a circular reasoning camouflaged by the equivocation on the word "ability."

## The necessity question

The second criticism of the conditional analysis is the claim that it is not *necessary*. To show that it's the case, i.e., that it's not necessary, van Inwagen again first points out in passing that "Napoleon could have won at Waterloo" can hardly mean "If Napoleon had chosen to win at Waterloo, Napoleon would have won at Waterloo."[73] He then points to the important work on the necessity question, by J. L. Austin. [74] Austin looked at the conditional meaning of "can" in statements of ability. He noted that when a person P is said to have the conditional ability to do action A, it must mean "P *would* do A *if A wanted to*." But Austin then found fault with this analysis of ability, because allegedly, "that P would do A if A wanted to" is not necessary for P

72. Ibid., 121.
73. Ibid., 115.
74. Ibid., 235n7.

to be said to have the ability to do A. Robert Kane explains Austin's classic counterexample, the golfer:

> For it is sometimes true that a person can (or could) do some-thing, but false that the person would do it (or would have done it), if he or she chose or tried. Austin's best-known example illustrating this point was one in which he imagined himself a golfer standing over a three-foot putt. It would be perfectly consistent, Austin argued, to say that he could (or had the power to) make the putt, though he might have missed it. For he has made many putts of this length in similar circumstances in the past—and also missed a few. His power to do it, therefore, does not imply that he *would* do it every time he wanted or tried.[75]

All of this is straightforward and convincing. Unfortunately, it fails to undermine any conditional claim worth making. What I contended for above in the present work was not at all that "any and all talk of ability must be interpreted conditionally as a counterfactual statement like the ones above." So it is perfectly fine to say that the golfer in a very real sense "has the ability" to make the shot even if his supposed desire does not ensure success. That kind of "guaranteed-success" conditional ability was never claimed to be necessary *for a proper usage of ability-language*. What the con-ditional analysis of the PAP (the PAP$_{If}$) was demanding a conditional ability to do otherwise for, was *moral responsibility*. It simply claimed that without a conditional ability to do A, P could not be morally responsible for failing to do A. The golfer example does not refute that. It does not even bear on matters of moral responsibility, as I would think obvious that barring very strange and unusual conditions, no one is ever shown righteous or evil for pushing (or failing to push) a golf ball into a hole on the green.

As a matter of fact, let us remove any and all suspicions regarding the compatibilist view in the face of the present objection, by considering Austin's own favored formulation of the conditional analysis—where "P could do A" is understood to mean "P would do A if P wanted to do A"—and his special feature of the golfer who may or may not pull off his shot, but this time introducing a moral situation into the example, to show that the PAP$_{If}$ does remain obviously true while being "merely conditional." The example would become something like this: imagine that Austin's golfer is preparing his shot on the green, when he sees an elderly woman being mugged on the golf course's parking lot, 50 yards from there. He cannot run there himself, nor alert anyone in time. Let's say that the way he sees it is correct: his only option to prevent the act would be to hit the mugger on

75. Kane, *Significance*, 54.

the head with the golf ball, a stunt whose precision he has matched many times in the past, but which he may still fail to pull off on any given off day. Let us now consider the following three possible ensuing scenarios: 1. He quickly aims, arms, and shoots, straight to the head of the mugger who falls unconscious. 2. He attempts the shot but fails, the ball is dodged, and the mugging still occurs. 3. He doesn't even attempt the shot, and watches by as the elderly woman gets mugged.

In each of these three scenarios, successfully making the shot is *not* something that the golfer "can" do in the above conditional sense that he "*would* do it if he wanted to," since we supposed that he might miss. Certainly, there is also another sense (contended for by Austin) in which we could meaningfully say he "can" do the shot, but that sense is neither here nor there; it is irrelevant to the rulings made by the $PAP_{If}$. On our former conditional understanding, it remains that the golfer cannot do the shot inasmuch as he cannot ensure success. Therefore, on scenario #2, per the $PAP_{If}$, he cannot be held morally responsible for failing to hit the man. He is not blameworthy for not stopping the mugging, because in that relevant conditional sense, he could not have hit him, even if he had wanted to. Now on scenario #3, it is not told whether he would or would not have succeeded if he had tried, and neither is it known by the golfer, so what we can say is that he is morally blameworthy for not *trying* to stop the mugging. We do know that he would have done *that*—the trying—if he had wanted. There was nothing else than his desires preventing him from *trying* to shoot the ball at the mugger, and hence no inability of his excluded moral responsibility. In each instance, the $PAP_{If}$ and its call for conditional ability are coherently upheld and convincingly applied: a conditional ability to do otherwise if one wants is and remains necessary for moral responsibility.

Now alternatively, if the claim of non-necessity at hand is no longer made regarding mere *ability language*, and actually says that a conditional ability is not necessary *for moral responsibility*, then the objection becomes wholly self-defeating, coming from incompatibilists who try with it to enforce the truth of the $PAP_{All}$. It is absurd to assert that the weaker, conditional ability is not necessary, while maintaining that the stronger, categorical ability is in fact necessary for moral responsibility. If one possesses a categorical ability, it follows that he also possesses a conditional ability;[76]

---

76. Someone might object that the conditional ability doesn't in fact follow from the categorical ability, since the former says the agent can do otherwise while holding all things in place, and the latter says the agent could do otherwise only if we suppose his desires are different. Phrased like that, it would indeed seem one ability doesn't say much about the other, but this is easily fixed by further specifying the conditional ability as follows: "the agent has the conditional ability to do otherwise if and only if he

and if one does not even possess a conditional ability, then it is hopeless to think he has a categorical ability. So if the lack of conditional ability to do otherwise does not exclude moral responsibility, then the lack of categorical ability does so even less. Hence, if $PAP_{If}$ is false, it follows that $PAP_{All}$ is false also, and by attacking the conditional analysis of ability as not necessary for moral responsibility, the libertarian provides the ammunition in premise (29) below to refute his own $PAP_{(All)}$ by *modus tollens*.

28.  $PAP_{All} \Rightarrow PAP_{If}$

29.  $\neg PAP_{If}$   (as per the objection)

   *Therefore*

30.  $\neg PAP_{All}$   (by *modus tollens*)

Therefore, the advocate of the PAP cannot possibly find fault with the conditional analysis of the ability to do otherwise on the basis that it is not *necessary*, without castigating his own non-conditional analysis.

In conclusion, the necessity objection is irrelevant if speaking about necessity *for proper descriptions of ability*, and it is self-defeating if speaking about necessity *for moral responsibility*. The *necessity* objection is thus a no-starter; let us then turn to the third of the alleged problems, the *sufficiency* question.

*The sufficiency question*

There are here again a couple of worries related to the conditional analysis of ability's not being sufficient. They are branded by incompatibilists as the alleged shortcomings of classical compatibilism and supposedly account for its deserved demise, but as was the case right above with the question of necessity, when assessing whether the conditional analysis is *sufficient*, not all incompatibilists actually complain about it being not sufficient *for the same thing*.

Some argue that the conditional analysis "person P would do action A if P wanted to" is not sufficient *to declare that P has the ability to do A*. To show that this is the case, a counterexample is offered wherein one has this kind of conditional ability to perform an action, but can still properly be said *not* to have the ability to perform it. Kane recounts Lehrer's classic example, red candy:

---

could do otherwise, while *allowing* for his desires to be different." This way, it is clear that one who has the stronger categorical ability also has the milder conditional ability, and nothing is altered in my discussion of $PAP_{If}$ and how it relates to determinism and compatibilism.

Suppose someone presents you with a tray of red candies. Nothing would prevent you from eating one of the candies, *if* you chose to. But you have a pathological fear of blood and of eating anything the color of blood, so you cannot *choose* to eat the candies; and so you cannot *eat* them.[77]

Kevin Timpe similarly argues that if Allison falls from the deck of a cruise ship, she "could do otherwise than drown if she were a mermaid," but in fact she "can do nothing else but drown."[78]

The compatibilist response to such examples is the same as was given above to the similar complaints about necessity. Just as conditional analyses are not meant to be *necessary* to encapsulate any and all statements of ability, they are not meant to be *sufficient* to encapsulate any and all such statements either. It is perfectly fine to say that in a real sense the haemophobic person "cannot" eat the red candy, and Allison "cannot" avoid drowning. It is just not the sense of ability that the $PAP_{If}$ is concerned about. The $PAP_{If}$ does not tell us what can sufficiently be the case in order to declare a person "able" in all senses. It merely tells us of one specific sort of inability that excludes moral responsibility. Therefore this first sufficiency objection is simply irrelevant to the truth of $PAP_{If}$ and its conditional analysis of ability.

The second and more serious worry of incompatibilists regarding the sufficiency of the conditional analysis of ability is that it fails to deliver the right conclusion in some important moral cases. They fear that in the absence of the $PAP_{All}$, the $PAP_{If}$ is inadequate to make proper judgments of moral responsibility as it allegedly fails to exculpate agents who are nevertheless obviously not responsible for their action. "One standard objection maintains that the mere fact that an agent acts on his preference or does 'as he pleases' is insufficient to sustain attributions of moral responsibility."[79] Hugh McCann thus objects:

> compulsives, addicts, people operating under duress—virtually everyone whose freedom to will differently we ordinarily view as compromised—would count by this criterion as free. Surely, if determinism is true, they would have willed differently had their strongest motives been different. Yet these are the people whose responsibility for decisions we would question, precisely *because* we think their strongest motive was too influential.[80]

77. Kane, *Significance*, 57.
78. Timpe, *Sourcehood*, 75–76.
79. Ciocchi, "Reconciling Divine Sovereignty," 409.
80. McCann, *Works of Agency*, 177.

These counter-examples brought forward by incompatibilists also include cases of pathological fear,[81] and cases of what I called "overriding manipulation" in chapter 3, where a skillful hypnotizer or a mad-scientist could use a laser to manipulate impulses in a patient's brain, and successfully control the patient's actions. If the mad scientist or hypnotizer uses his power to have the patient commit a moral wrong, the $PAP_{If}$ would be useless to exculpate the patient. Indeed, he "could have done otherwise *if his inner desires had inclined him to do so*," and of course for these desires to be such, it would have been necessary that the scientist not be present, but it remains that the patient has the conditional ability, and thus $PAP_{If}$ would fail to annul the patient's moral responsibility, whereas we all realize that he is neither free nor guilty because he is under the controlling scheme of the mad scientist or hypnotizer (we positively affirmed in chapter 3 that overriding manipulation excludes moral responsibility).

The problem with this objection, however, is that it is true but irrelevant. Why should one worry here about this kind of sufficiency? What claim or principle are incompatibilist writers contending against? The $PAP_{If}$ maintains that it is *necessary* to have the conditional ability to do otherwise if wanted, but it never said that this was *sufficient*. Daniel Speak objects that the "truth of the relevant conditional does not actually *suffice* for ability."[82] But this was never part of the claim. The $PAP_{If}$ tells us only that moral responsibility entails the conditional ability to do otherwise; it does not conversely tell us that the conditional ability to do otherwise *alone* entails moral responsibility. It tells us that if a person could not do otherwise even if his inner desires had inclined him to do so, then he lacks moral responsibility; but the $PAP_{If}$ says nothing about anything *else* that may jointly be required for securing moral responsibility. And here, the compatibilist is free to consider and accept any refined, convincing analysis he pleases, and list any number of possibly necessary items, which together do constitute a sufficient condition for moral responsibility.[83] Compatibilists are perfectly free to include many such items in that list;[84] they only maintain that "a categorical, libertarian ability to do otherwise" is not one of them.

81. Van Inwagen, *Essay*, 115.

82. Speak, "Consequence Argument Revisited," 123.

83. For example, with respect to manipulation cases, I introduced in chapter 3 the important condition of acting according to one's "God-given" character and desires. It successfully did then what $PAP_{If}$ is accused of failing to do now: it allowed one to coherently exclude moral responsibility in cases of manipulation (while maintaining it in normal cases of determinist free choice). $PAP_{If}$ is not the answer to such manipulation cases, but compatibilists have more than one string to their bows.

84. More will be said about this important "list" in chapter 7.

*Conclusion on conditional analyses: misplaced expectations*

These various misunderstandings of the real claim made by compatibilists with their modest $PAP_{If}$ have led incompatibilists to place unrealistic expectations on the so-called "conditional analysis" of ability. We saw above that they wanted it to deliver many things it was never intended to produce: an argument for compatibilism, a necessary condition for all descriptions of ability, a sufficient condition for all descriptions of ability, and a sufficient condition for attributions of moral responsibility; when all it really is is a necessary condition for attributions of moral responsibility. So of course these expectations are bound to be frustrated, but since I showed they do nothing to undermine compatibilism, that loss will not be grieved. The conditional analysis of ability in the modest $PAP_{If}$ really should not be this controversial, since $PAP_{If}$ is not only obviously true, but is also a firm commitment of incompatibilists themselves as soon as they put forward the $PAP_{All}$ anyway. What incompatibilists should say is not that this analysis is not "true," but rather that it is not "adequate," or "sufficient," for all sorts of *other* things they wished it did, but were never part of its claims.

So where does that leave us with respect to the much-proclaimed death of classical compatibilism? It depends on which truth claims we understand classical compatibilists to have made. If classical compatibilism is or ever was intended to claim any of the four misguided theses I rejected above regarding "the conditional analysis," then it belongs to the grave indeed. But did any compatibilist soberly ever make such sweeping claims?

If, however, one understands classical compatibilists to simply claim that a conditional ability to do otherwise is necessary for moral responsibility and a categorical ability is not, i.e., the truth of $PAP_{If}$ and the falsity of $PAP_{All}$, then I must count myself as one of them, and offer the present work as evidence that classical compatibilism so understood is alive and well.

Either way, whichever view one takes on what "classical compatibilism" ever meant, at this point the $PAP_{If}$ and its conditional analysis are safe, and our rejection of $PAP_{All}$ with its call for categorical ability does not commit us to any distasteful, untenable, or even dead position. With these considerations of ability in place, having properly defused the positive claims of the consequence argument and the deliberation argument and having defended the intellectual respectability of conditional analyses of ability, let us return to the PAP (on which we saw the consequence argument vitally depended) to finish the job, by moving beyond mere skepticism, and onto its positive refutation.

6

# Beyond mere skepticism

## Positive arguments against the principle of alternate possibilities and what its falsity means for incompatibilism

AT THIS POINT, THE principle of alternate possibilities has been shown to fall short of establishing incompatibilism, on the charge that it is equivocating and begging the question: on its conditional reading of ability ($PAP_{If}$) it is perfectly compatible with compatibilism, and on its incompatibilist, categorical reading of ability ($PAP_{All}$), it is begging the question in favor of incompatibilism. While this would be sufficient to declare the failure of PAP in establishing incompatibilism, the compatibilist defense has not spoken its final word yet. If it is fine to show an argument is invalid, it is even better to show its conclusion is false. In the present case, it so happens that compatibilists are in the comfortable position of being able to do so: beyond mere skepticism and accusations of begging the question as they offer undercutting considerations, Christian compatibilists have I believe good enough ground to go on the offensive, and offer rebutting defeaters, i.e., positive arguments of their own, why the PAP is not merely unproven, but is in fact *false*—and a fortiori cannot help the incompatibilist case.

In coming to do so, however, one must first ask: what exactly are compatibilists to refute? Frankfurt's essay famously attempted to refute "the principle of alternate possibilities," in its general form, unqualified as he stated it. But this should not be seen as an attempt on the part of compatibilists to refute any and all PAP—that is, both $PAP_{All}$ and $PAP_{If}$ indiscriminately. Indeed, in the absence of the above clarification, Frankfurt's ambiguous formulation of the PAP could be seen as a conjunction of both $PAP_{If}$ and $PAP_{All}$:

$$PAP = PAP_{If} \wedge PAP_{All}$$

In other words, PAP is true if and only if it is the case that both $PAP_{If}$ and $PAP_{All}$ are true. As such, if one endeavors to demonstrate the falsity of PAP as Frankfurt did, it need not entail the falsity of both $PAP_{If}$ and $PAP_{All}$. If PAP is proven false, all that follows is that *either* $PAP_{If}$ is false, *or* $PAP_{All}$ is false (or *possibly* both,[1] but *not* necessarily so):

$$\neg PAP = \neg (PAP_{If} \wedge PAP_{All}) = \neg PAP_{If} \vee \neg PAP_{All}$$

Another way to put the relationship between the various PAP would be to see that $PAP_{All}$ is more restrictive in its demand for alternate possibilities than $PAP_{If}$, so that PAP when unqualified stands merely for the all-encompassing $PAP_{All}$, and it entails $PAP_{If}$ with its more modest, conditional criterion:

$$PAP = PAP_{All}, \text{ and } PAP_{All} \Rightarrow PAP_{If}$$

Which again highlights that if $PAP_{If}$ were false, $PAP_{All}$ would be false as well, but if (as I will shortly argue) $PAP_{All}$ is false, nothing follows about the truth or falsity of $PAP_{If}$. And since compatibilists are open to the truth of $PAP_{If}$, they should not refute it; indeed they cannot, if as I believe and have affirmed above, $PAP_{If}$ is true. This explains why the rebutting defeaters that follow will only logically target the stricter, incompatibilist PAP: $PAP_{All}$.

As a starting point, I will now review the most famous argument against PAP called "the Frankfurt-style cases," which is a family of stories designed as counter-examples to the PAP. These famous cases have become the source of a voluminous literature debating their merits. Stifling all the suspense, let me announce right from the start that in spite of my predisposition as a compatibilist to root and cheer for anything that purports to refute the $PAP_{All}$, I will ultimately find Frankfurt-style cases inconclusive in refuting the unqualified PAP (that is, $PAP_{All}$). Nevertheless, I will subsequently offer two independent arguments, which I believe, on Christian principles, more decisively establish the falsity of the $PAP(_{All})$. Let me now deliver on these good promises.

## Frankfurt-style cases—a compatibilist's doubts

As mentioned above, Harry Frankfurt's classic article, "Alternate Possibilities and Moral Responsibility,"[2] made a unique contribution to debates on moral responsibility and free will, by offering what Frankfurt designed as counterexamples to the principle of alternate possibilities. While the PAP

1. Especially since I mentioned that $PAP_{All} \Rightarrow PAP_{If}$.
2. Frankfurt, "Alternate Possibilities," 1.

asserted that a person cannot be morally responsible for an action unless the person carrying it out "could have done otherwise," Frankfurt devised a certain type of story, the so-called "Frankfurt-style cases," wherein an individual is intuitively morally responsible for performing a certain action, and at the same time finds himself in a particular situation (albeit contrived) such that he could not in fact have done otherwise, regardless of the nature of his free will. Let me attempt a succinct retelling of Frankfurt's traditional story:

Black wants Jones to perform an action A and will do whatever it takes to bring about Jones's action, but he does not want to show his hand unnecessarily. To that effect, Black only observes Jones until the moment of choice, planning to force Jones to perform A only if it becomes apparent that Jones will not perform A on his own. But as it turns out, Jones does perform action A on his own, and Black need not interfere.[3] The conclusion drawn by Frankfurt from such stories, is that Jones is morally responsible for doing A—after all, he performed it freely and on his own—and at the same time Jones could not have refrained from doing A, because had he tried to, Black would have stepped in and forcefully brought about Jones's doing of A. This, Frankfurt argued, amounts to a counterexample of the PAP, since it is a case of a person being morally responsible for performing an action, without the ability to do otherwise.

While the literature on the topic is abundant, the main objections to the Frankfurt-style cases have been of two sorts. First, some have argued that the fail-safe mechanism cannot properly detect whether it needs to be activated without presupposing determinism;[4] and secondly, it has been argued that the "thing" for which Jones is responsible is not necessarily the same "thing" than which he cannot do otherwise, so that defenders of the PAP could coherently maintain that Jones either is in fact not morally

---

3. This example makes it evident that it is only one among many possible retellings of the story. In his own work, Frankfurt provides a helpful explanation of the key ingredients of such a story, for it to function as a Frankfurt-style case: "Constructing counterexamples to PAP is not difficult. It is necessary only to conceive circumstances which make it inevitable that a person will perform some action but which do not bring it about that he performs it. . . . The distinctively potent element in this sort of counterexample to PAP is a certain kind of overdetermination, which involves a sequential fail-safe arrangement such that one causally sufficient factor functions exclusively as backup for another. Thus the backup factor may contribute nothing whatever to bringing about the effect whose occurrence it guarantees." Frankfurt, "We Are Morally Responsible," 96.

4. See McCann, *Works of Agency*, 175–76 and Kane, *Significance*, 142–43.

responsible for doing *that* "thing," or in fact possesses the ability to do otherwise than that "thing."[5]

As a critic of Frankfurt-style cases (a friendly compatibilist one, but a critic nonetheless), I believe that both objections have some value, but let me focus on the second one, which seems to me the more serious. This difficulty with Frankfurt-style cases lies in the fact that regardless of the presence of Black (the counterfactual intervener), as long as the free will of Jones is not presupposed to be determinist, there will always remain *some sort* of alternate possibility categorically available to him. The counterfactual intervener may prevent Jones from "refraining to perform action A," but Jones can still use his libertarian free will to discriminate between two different scenarios: either "freely performing A on his own," or "freely beginning to choose *not* to perform A, and hence triggering the intervener and perform A forcibly as a result." This strictly provides a sound retort to the Frankfurt-style counterargument: there is no one "thing" for which Jones both is morally responsible, and than which he cannot do otherwise. The "thing" in question must be properly specified; this is a valid input of Peter van Inwagen, who differentiates between underspecified so-called "event universals" and fully specified "event particulars."[6] If we consider the underspecified operation "performing action A" (freely or not), then advocates of the PAP can readily concede that Jones cannot avoid it, and yet maintain that he is in fact *not* responsible for exactly that, "performing action A." Rather, they would say that Jones is responsible for "freely performing action A of his own inclination." This much he does have the categorical ability to refrain from, as long as he has libertarian free will. So the PAP would be coherently maintained in the face of Frankfurt-style cases.

The retort of Frankfurt-style defenders facing this objection has been to find fault with the content of the alternate scenario: that which happens if Jones were in fact to begin to exercise his libertarian free will to refrain from performing A. In that alternative scenario, Jones's prospects are less than great: because of Black's intervention, Jones does not in fact freely refrain from performing A; instead he is forcibly compelled to perform A regardless. This, defenders of Frankfurt-style cases have argued, is less than satisfying. Jones may have an alternate possibility, but it is a very crippled one. John Martin Fischer has dubbed the access to such poor alternatives

---

5. This line of defense is offered in van Inwagen, *Essay*, 166–80. See also Ginet, "Defense of the Principle," 75–90.

6. See further discussion of these two concepts in chapter 6 in the present work, and in van Inwagen, *Essay*, 171.

"flickers of freedom," and has contended that such flickers are not "robust" enough to sustain ascriptions of moral responsibility.[7]

On the one hand, one could wonder why compatibilist critics of the PAP would now demand "robust" alternate possibilities for moral responsibility, when their own view is that moral responsibility does not even demand *any* alternate possibility, much less robust ones. But I think the compatibilist contention is best read as follows: "if an agent can be morally responsible even when the only alternate possibility he faces is a crippled, mere flicker of freedom, then he might as well have no alternate possibility at all." Or in other words, "if Jones is not morally responsible when he has no alternate possibility, why think that adding a mere flicker of freedom all of a sudden rescues moral responsibility?"[8]

Unfortunately, I think incompatibilist advocates of the PAP can answer this challenging question very satisfyingly and quite ironically: why does adding a mere flicker of freedom rescue moral responsibility? Because PAP is true! While I believe PAP to be false myself, this strikes me as a fine answer. Contrary to appearances, it is not begging the question. At this point of the debate, the tables have already been turned, and PAP defenders are no longer in the position of *arguing* in favor of PAP; they are now merely defending it against the claims of Frankfurt-style cases aiming to refute it. Therefore it is not demanded of them that they provide an *argument* for why flickers of freedom are better than no alternate possibility at all, and they can simply hang this question on the sheer truth of the PAP as long as they believe PAP is true and obvious to them. The way they see it, PAP is true, and hence a morally responsible person must have the ability to do otherwise, even if that alternate possibility is a mere flicker of freedom. As Hugh McCann put it, in Frankfurt-style cases moral responsibility might very well hinge on a flicker of freedom, but if PAP is true, "a flicker shines like a beacon."[9] If PAP advocates are thus prepared to maintain the necessity of any alternate possibility albeit a flicker of freedom, there is not much else that proponents of Frankfurt-style cases can bring to bear on the question.[10] Therefore, the case

7. "Even if there is some sort of flicker of freedom here, it does not seem capable of playing the requisite role in grounding ascriptions of moral responsibility—it does not seem sufficiently robust." Fischer, "Responsibility and Alternative Possibilities," 47.

8. Fischer asks: "How can adding alternative pathways in which the fact that the contents are different from those of the actual pathway is entirely *accidental* and *flukish* render the agent morally responsible in the actual pathway?" Fischer, "Responsibility and Agent-Causation," 149–50.

9. McCann, *Works of Agency*, 175.

10. Even John Martin Fischer who champions Frankfurt-style cases admits this much in the midst of his arguments against "flicker theorists" as he points out "Despite the undeniable appeal of the flicker-of-freedom strategy, I believe that ultimately it is

against PAP must I think remain unsuccessful if restricted to considerations of Frankfurt-style counterfactual interveners.[11]

I suppose much more could be (and has been) said about the matter, so that defenders of Frankfurt-style cases might feel that my present brief refutation does not fully do justice to the voluminous literature, but for my immediate purposes, I see no reason to pursue much further arguments that I find implausible, albeit for a conclusion that I agree with. If I sense that Frankfurt-style cases are a weak ally in the war against incompatibilism, simply allow me now to flee this losing battle, quickly regroup, and launch a full-fledged assault on a front I find to be much more compelling for the Christian thinker. Accordingly, I will now offer two independently potent arguments, which I believe on Christian principles more decisively establish what Frankfurt-style cases failed to prove, namely that PAP is false.

## The praiseworthiness of impeccable righteousness

### The argument

A first argument which demonstrates on the Christian view that the principle of alternate possibilities (the claim that a categorical ability to do otherwise is necessary for moral responsibility) is false, is provided by the existence of God himself, as an essentially morally perfect agent who is also worthy of praise. The incompatibilist claim that moral responsibility (praiseworthiness or blameworthiness) requires the ability to do otherwise—or in the words of Norman Geisler: "praise and blame make no real sense unless those praised or blamed were free to do otherwise"[12]—is proven false by God himself in that God always, necessarily does what is morally righteous; God does not have the categorical ability to choose and act unrighteously, and yet God is praiseworthy for his righteous choices and actions, so that

---

not convincing. *I do not have a decisive argument against it,* but of course such arguments are few and far between in these realms." Fischer, "Responsibility and Alternative Possibilities," 45. And later on, "*I do not see any decisive way to rebut the current move by the flicker theorist,* but, again, I do not find it attractive," Ibid., 49; and again, "I believe that the arguments developed above against the flicker-of-freedom strategy are extremely plausible, *albeit not ineluctable,*" ibid., 50.

11. Ultimately, I believe that the most compatibilists can conclude from Frankfurt-style cases is the very modest statement by Derk Pereboom, that "Frankfurt-style arguments *substantially enliven the possibility* that facts about an action's actual causal history, rather than alternative possibilities, are pivotal in explaining an agent's moral responsibility." Pereboom, "Source Incompatibilism and Alternative Possibilities," 191.

12. Geisler, *Chosen But Free,* 43.

moral responsibility—in this case moral praiseworthiness—does not hang on the ability to do otherwise. The argument is a deductive one of the form:

31. God always chooses and acts righteously, and lacks the categorical ability to do otherwise than acting righteously.

32. God is morally praiseworthy, that is, he is morally responsible, for his righteous choices and actions.

*Therefore*

33. Moral responsibility does not require the ability to do otherwise.

Let us review each premise in turn.

## Divine impeccability

First, God always chooses and acts righteously, for he cannot sin. Given who he is, it is impossible for God to do anything but that which is righteous; it is impossible for God to do anything sinful, anything immoral, anything unrighteous. This attribute of God is called *impeccability*.

Biblically, the doctrine may be supported by a host of texts, which teach that God is holy (Ps 99; Rev 4:8), righteous (Ps 97; Rom 3:26), just (Ps 97:2; Gen 18:25), good (Ps 34:8; Mark 10:18) and all sorts of moral superlatives. These might in turn be said to teach that God *does* not sin, not that he *cannot* sin, but while this is strictly grammatically correct, two things must be pointed out in response. First, it would be very odd for these holy attributes to be touted so centrally in the biblical narrative about God if they happened to be merely accidental attributes of his, and not essential to the divine nature. When scripture affirms God is holy, holy, holy, it plausibly assumes that if God were *not* holy, he would not be God. In other words, holy is not just what God *happens* to be like, it is who God *is*, just as God doesn't just *happen to have* love, in a sense he *is* love, essentially (1 John 4:8). And secondly, a handful of scriptures do in fact bridge that gap for us, in affirming that God *cannot* lie (Heb 6:18; Titus 1:2) because he "*cannot* deny himself" (2 Tim 2:13); "God *cannot* be tempted with evil" (Jas 1:13). How could God possibly sin if he could not even be tempted? He does not, because he cannot. Divine impeccability seems at least biblically secured.

Philosophically, in any case, the matter is independently settled on the basis of perfect-being theology, and is almost universally conceded by compatibilists and incompatibilists alike without much of a dispute. This is not to suggest that there are absolutely no dissenting voices. For example, Wesley Morriston sees that divine impeccability threatens the incompatibilist understanding of "significant" free will, and hence to hold on to his incom-patibilism, he ultimately denies divine impeccability, affirming that God *could* act unrighteously: "if a person is significantly free, there must be worlds in which he goes wrong with respect to some action, and in those worlds he is not morally perfect."[13] In essence, there are possible worlds in which God actually goes wrong!

But to affirm this is I think a failure to appreciate an essential property of God. God is the greatest conceivable being. In the words of Daniel Hill, God, by definition as a divine being, exhibits "maximal greatness," one com-ponent of which is the property of being metaphysically necessarily sinless.[14] Sinlessness is a great-making property, and so any divine, maximally great being must exemplify it to its maximal degree, *ceteris paribus*. Of course Morriston might pick up on the *ceteris paribus* and object that all things are *not* equal. Since on his view impeccability conflicts with moral freedom, he might affirm that since God can only exhibit one of the two, it is better to be free than to be impeccable. That move might bring us to a conflict of intuitions, and if so, I am not sure how I would disprove the opposite view point, but it seems clear to me that it is far worse for God to be "unlimited" in his freedom but immoral, than to be "limited" in freedom and remain at least righteous. So I maintain that God's absolute goodness is part of his maximal greatness and as such is essential to the concept of God: to deny his impeccability is to deny his divinity. At the very least, it is to deny any orthodoxly conceived (and biblical) understanding of God.

Morriston's skepticism notwithstanding, we can thus pursue the pres-ent argument on the assumption that the orthodox view is right, since the vast majority of even incompatibilists (who are the targeted recipients of the present argument), for the above reasons, happily affirm impeccabil-ity. Open theist William Hasker has no trouble asserting: "if, as I believe, God's moral perfection is an essential part of his nature, then an action as being unfaithful to his promises is absolutely impossible for God; it is not one of the things he could possibly do."[15] And Arminius himself recog-nized that God "*cannot* will to do with His own what He cannot rightfully do, for His will is circumscribed within the bounds of justice."[16] They are right. God cannot sin. Phrased in terms of possible worlds, it means there exists no possible world in which God sins; God's sinlessness is broadly

13. Morriston, "Is God 'Significantly' Free?" 257–64. See also Guleserian, "Divine Freedom," 348–66.

14. See chapter 6 of Hill, *Maximal Greatness*, 192–227.

15. Hasker, "Philosophical Perspective," 135–36.

16. Arminius, "Friendly Conference," quoted in Sell, *The Great Debate*, 13, quoted in Olson, *Arminian Theology*, 119–20.

logically necessary. God is sinless in every possible world in which he exists—which supposing God's necessary existence, means God is sinless in every possible world.

Moreover, it can be pointed out that these contentions are unaffected by whichever view one adopts on the meta-ethical question of "voluntarism." This controversial question has to do with the grounding of moral values, and their relation to the will and commands of God. It asks the following about the moral good: is it good merely because God says so, or is it essentially good in such a way that God could not declare it nor have declared it to be otherwise?[17] One view on this question, called voluntarism, traditionally attributed to William Of Ockham,[18] sees fit to affirm that moral values are purely the determinations of God's will and commands, so that if God had declared that jealousy, hatred, murder, rape, and lies be morally good and desirable, and he had commanded us to engage in them for goodness' sake,[19] then they would indeed have been good and desirable ends for us to pursue in virtue of God's will and commands, making them our duty in obedience to him. On this view, then, the reason why God cannot sin is that whatever he happens to decide to do, becomes morally righteous in

17. This question is somewhat related to the so-called Euthyphro dilemma, a popular objection to divine command theories of ethics. The Euthyphro is an attempt to show that moral values and duties cannot be rooted in God's will, by asking of the good "is it good because God wills it, or does God will it because it is good?" The alleged dilemma pressed on divine command theorists is that moral values are either arbitrarily chosen by God, or recognized by God independently of himself, neither of which is presumably acceptable by the divine command theorist. In effect, the Euthyphro presses a dilemma between voluntarism and Platonism. I see two ways of fending off this objection: either point out that the Euthyphro is a false dilemma and offer a third alternative to voluntarism and Platonism, one which features moral values anchored in God's necessarily good nature, or else simply adopting voluntarism if one finds no problem with it. I am inclined to do the former, following William Lane Craig: "The arbitrariness horn of the [Euthyphro] dilemma . . . is avoided by rejecting voluntarism in favor of God's commands' being necessary expressions of his nature." Craig, "Most Gruesome of Guests," 172–73. Nevertheless, rescuing divine command theory from the grips of the Euthyphro is not my present burden, I just noted here that God's impeccability is coherently secured whether one adopts voluntarism or sees moral values as necessary, for being anchored in God's necessarily good nature.

18. "Ockham seems to have taught that God could in a certain sense make wrong into right, and could command men to hate himself." Kenny, *God of the Philosophers*, 9.

19. What I mean by the qualification "for goodness' sake" is that on voluntarism, these actions would be seen as truly good, and not local evils compensated by balancing goods, like we might say in the actual world that at times God may command us, say, to lie to a Nazi general, in order to preserve lives. In such cases, the lie is commanded for the sake of compensating goods, not as a good end in itself. Conversely, when God tells us to love one another, it is not a justifiable evil for bringing about some compensating good other end; love is good for "goodness' sake," as I understand here.

sheer virtue of having been willed and decided by God. On this view, there are no actions or moral proclamations that God just could not do because of who God is, but if God were to choose and perform them, they would accordingly become righteous.

On the other hand, on the non-Ockhamist, non-voluntarist view, it is in fact metaphysically impossible for God to make such pronouncements, because the good is not defined by a contingent and arbitrary divine decision, but rather by God's good commands, which flow necessarily from his nature, a divine nature that is necessarily good (in the sense of goodness that we know to be true in this world, i.e., that which is loving, just, caring, self-less, truthful, etc.) and could not be other than it is. And here again, obviously it is impossible that God sin, because his will is necessarily set on the good that flows from his nature.

Whichever view one adopts on the question of voluntarism, then, divine impeccability is equally safe: in one case (the Ockhamist view) it is guaranteed by the fact that God's decisions would redefine any actions that are evil in this world as good actions in alternate worlds in which God chooses them, and in the other case it is guaranteed by God's outright inability to choose any evil courses of action because God's perfect nature prevents him to. In either case, God cannot act unrighteously in any possible world; God is impeccable.

## Divine praiseworthiness

When we turn to premise (32), it is hardly disputed that God is morally responsible for this goodness of his. God is unqualifiedly and absolutely praiseworthy. Biblically, the psalmist does tell us to praise the Lord, for he is good and his love endures forever (Pss 106:1; 107:1; 135:3). "Great is the LORD, and greatly to be praised" (Pss 48:1; 145:3); "praise him for his mighty deeds; praise him according to his excellent greatness!" (Ps 150:2). Here again, it is hard to imagine Christian incompatibilists would disagree with this most biblical claim that God is worthy of praise for who he is and what he does. Arminians praise God! But then if that is true, all that remains to do is to put the two premises together, and see the absurd conclusion that it forces onto incompatibilist advocates of the PAP. Let us give Jonathan Edwards the honor of doing so, more eloquently than I possibly could. He noted that: 1. Arminians claim that without a categorical ability to do otherwise "there is no virtue or vice, reward or punishment, nothing to be commended or blamed," and 2. Arminians "acknowledge that God is necessarily holy, and his will necessarily determined to that which is good." And so Edwards concludes,

> So that putting these things together, the infinitely holy God who always used to be esteemed by God's people not only virtuous, but a Being in whom is all possible virtue, and every virtue in the most absolute purity and perfection, and in infinitely greater brightness and amiableness than in any creature: the most perfect pattern of virtue, and the fountain from whom all others' virtue is but as beams from the sun; and who has been supposed to be, on the account of his virtue and holiness, infinitely more worthy to be esteemed, loved, honoured, admired, commended, extolled, and praised, than any creature; and he who is thus every where represented in Scripture; I say, this Being, according to this notion of Dr Whitby, and other Arminians, has no virtue at all: virtue, when ascribed to him, is but an empty name; and he is deserving of no commendation or praise, because he is under necessity, he cannot avoid being holy and good as he is; therefore no thanks to him for it.[20]

Now, evidently and thankfully, incompatibilist Arminians do worship God as morally perfect and worthy of praise, but, to be consistent, they would have to concede that just as God cannot act unrighteously by a necessity of his own holy nature, and yet he remains morally praiseworthy, human beings who on Calvinism cannot but do what they are decreed to do, remain morally responsible for at least much of it, the good and the bad.

It's interesting to find traces of the argument long before Edwards in the work of John Calvin, who even threw in the devil into his version of the charge:

> Therefore, if the free will of God in doing good is not impeded, because he necessarily must do good; if the devil, who can do nothing but evil, nevertheless sins voluntarily; can it be said that man sins less voluntarily because he is under a necessity of sinning?[21]

It must be noted that "voluntary" (translated from the Latin *voluntate*) is a bit of an unfortunate word choice here. Even Arminians do not say that on Calvinism humans act involuntarily, only that they are not morally responsible. Involuntariness entails lack of moral responsibility, but lack of moral responsibility doesn't entail involuntariness. Nevertheless the spirit

20. Edwards, *Freedom of the Will*, 152–53.
21. Calvin, *Institutes*, Book Second, Chapter 3, Section 5, 181.

of the argument is there, albeit formulated with a less than philosophically rigorous term.

## Too good to be Calvinist

What then do Arminians have to say with respect to these compatibilist contentions? One of the things they do affirm is not without irony: Arminian controversialists frequently and passionately affirm the truth of my premise (31) (that God *cannot* act un-righteously), by contending that God could not possibly do at least one thing: act as a Calvinist God! God, they say, is too good to be Calvinist (or in some cases at least what they mistakenly perceive to be the God of Calvinism). They write as follows.

Jerry Wall and Joseph Dongell: "If it is a matter of sheer power, it is plausible that God could create a world in which many would be lost. But the God of holy love *not only would not but could not.*"[22]

William MacDonald: "God *cannot*—and to say the same thing—will not regenerate a heart that will not admit him."[23]

Norman Geisler: "An all-loving God, by nature, cannot *not* love all His creatures"[24] and "He is love, and He *cannot* be loving only to some people."[25]

Jack Cottrell: "Should sin occur, God's love was *bound* to express itself in grace, involving a plan of redemption centered around his incarnation and the offer of forgiveness for all who would accept it. In the face of sin his love *could not do otherwise*; his nature would *require* it."[26]

There it is: God, they say, does not have the ability to be an evil Calvinist God. But then on this view, if it is *impossible* for God to be Calvinist, is he not praiseworthy for his presumably superior Arminian benevolence? If God is praiseworthy in spite of the alleged impossibility, it follows that the PAP is false.

## Recognizing different levels of granularity for actions

One important front on which incompatibilists may now attempt to fault my argument is the question of whether it applies the PAP correctly, to the right sort of choices and actions. We must here consider whether my above

22. Walls and Dongell, *Not a Calvinist*, 218.
23. MacDonald, "Spirit of Grace," 86.
24. Geisler, *Chosen But Free*, 91.
25. Ibid., 150.
26. Cottrell, "Nature of the Divine Sovereignty," 109.

argument applies the PAP to single actions, or to classes of actions. More precisely, if my argument intends to apply the PAP to specific divine actions, an incompatibilist objector could find fault with premise (31), when it asserts that God "lacks the ability to do otherwise than acting righteously." This premise, they may say, presupposes a determinist view of God's choices, and thus begs the question of determinism at least for the divine will. God may lack the ability to "act unrighteously," the objection would go, but if God has libertarian free will (which of course libertarians would naturally affirm he does), then he does have the ability to "do otherwise" than the one option he in fact chooses nonetheless, and that may be the only sense of ability pressed by the PAP for moral responsibility. If that is true, an incompatibilist could maintain that God is impeccable, lacks the ability *to act unrighteously*, but has in all things which he freely chooses, the ability to *do otherwise than he does*, thereby satisfying the requirement of the PAP to permit his praise. Does this response succeed in answering the present argument?

It does not. Premise (31) does not in fact presuppose that God's choices are determinist, because it is not applied to any one specific action of God, but rather to a class of actions. It does not demand that God not have the ability to do *any* other thing than what he actually does, rather, it merely demands that God not have the ability to do otherwise *than acting righteously*. As this latter qualifier might throw off skeptical incompatibilist advocates of the PAP, let us unfold its exact meaning, and see that it is a coherent and legitimate application of the PAP. What this qualification calls for is a clarification of just what sort of things one is said to be morally responsible for, and just what sort of things that person could "avoid," or "do otherwise" than. In its standard form advocated by incompatibilists above, the PAP applied its contention to any "thing" that a person "does," as it claimed: "a person is morally responsible for *what* he has *done* only if he could have *done* otherwise" (And here again, this all-encompassing descriptor of "doing" includes one's "choosing, which is loosely something that one "does" too.) So what the PAP demands for a person to be morally responsible *for doing one thing* is that this person have the ability to do otherwise *than that very thing*. But in practice, how is one to describe a "thing" that we do? There are several levels of granularity, that is, levels of specificity one could use in describing a choice or action for which one can be morally responsible. Take by way of illustration the biblical story of Acts 5:1–11. It could be truthfully said of it that "Ananias and Sapphira falsely told the Holy Spirit that they had shared all the proceeds of their sale" (an act for which they received punishment, which presupposes that they performed it freely), and accordingly, Ananias and Sapphira were morally responsible (blameworthy) for that very same thing: "falsely telling the Holy Spirit that they had shared all the proceeds of their sale." But another way of analyzing their mischief is what scripture more generally declares that they did: they "lied to the Holy Spirit" (v. 3). This is the level of description at which scripture indicts these two, and so naturally, they were morally responsible for "lying to the Holy Spirit," just as much as they were morally responsible for "falsely telling the Holy Spirit that they had shared all the proceeds of their sale." Both are true, even though there were theoretically a multitude of possible different ways that these two could have "lied to the Holy Spirit" on that instant. At an even higher level, it could further be said that "Ananias and Sapphira lied," and "Ananias and Sapphira were morally responsible for lying." Or finally even higher, "Ananias and Sapphira sinned," and "Ananias and Sapphira were morally responsible for sinning," etc.

It seems rather uncontroversial, then, that the description of an action can legitimately be done at several levels of granularity, and it would be natural that the PAP, if true, apply at constant levels of granularity, since it links moral responsibility for a "thing" to the ability to do otherwise *than that same "thing."* This simply means that the action for which one is morally responsible must be described at the same level of granularity when asserting of it that the person "could have done otherwise." He could have done otherwise than *that very action, thus described, at that level of granularity.* The PAP asserts that if Ananias and Sapphira are morally responsible for "telling the Holy Spirit that they had shared all the proceeds of their sale," then Ananias and Sapphira had the ability to do otherwise than "telling the Holy Spirit that they had shared all the proceeds of their sale." It further asserts that if Ananias and Sapphira are morally responsible for "lying to the Holy Spirit," Ananias and Sapphira had the ability to do otherwise than "lying to the Holy Spirit." And again, it further asserts that if Ananias and Sapphira are morally responsible for "lying," then they had the ability to do otherwise than "lying."

We can put these contentions in more general and more symbolic logical terms. Let us imagine a fully specified situation for person P at time t, where a choice must and will be made by P. Presupposing a libertarian account of P's free will so as not to beg any question, it would follow that P has a collection of possible free will choices that is finite, but featuring more than one option. Some of them will be morally righteous, and some will be sinful; let us name them respectively $R_1$, $R_2$, . . . , $R_n$, and $S_1$, $S_2$, . . . , $S_m$. (Nothing hangs on there possibly existing morally neutral options as well.)

Let's suppose that P chooses and performs the sinful option $S_1$. If P is morally responsible for doing $S_1$, the PAP asserts that P was able to do otherwise than $S_1$. P could have done $\neg S_1$, which given the list of all options available to him, means that P could have done $(S_2 \vee S_3 \vee \ldots \vee S_m \vee R_1 \vee R_2 \vee \ldots \vee R_n)$.

In defining the S's and the R's, it was understood that they covered absolutely all the different, unique options that P could possibly choose, each being fully specified so that any minute difference between two possible courses of action—albeit similar ones—resulted in two different symbols ($R_x$ and $R_y$ with x≠y). This means that the S's and the R's each describe P's individual possible choices *at the most fully specified, lowest level of granularity.*

If we now wanted to describe what P chose and did at a higher level of granularity, considering not a single action but a class of actions, then we would simply regroup the S's and the R's according to common features that they share amongst each other. For example, if $S_1$ through $S_4$ consisted of all the "adulterous" decisions that P could have made at t, all the possible courses of action in which P's decision involves his committing adultery in one way or another, then "P decided to commit adultery" could be phrased "P decided to do $(S_1 \vee S_2 \vee S_3 \vee S_4)$." And accordingly, if we assert that "P is morally responsible for *committing adultery*," the PAP will entail that P was able to do otherwise than committing adultery, which means P was able to do $\neg(S_1 \vee S_2 \vee S_3 \vee S_4)$, hence he was able to do $(\neg S_1 \wedge \neg S_2 \wedge \neg S_3 \wedge \neg S_4)$, which here is the ability to do $(S_5 \vee S_6 \vee S_7 \vee \ldots \vee S_m \vee R_1 \vee R_2 \vee \ldots \vee R_n)$.

All of this seems to be a coherent, natural, and most plausible method of application of the PAP to the various levels of granularity of free choices and actions, and it is with this understanding of "thing" that my argument applied the PAP to an assessment of God's impeccability and praiseworthiness. If the usage rules of the PAP laid out above are correct, my above argument was a valid application of the PAP, since it contemplated God's moral praiseworthiness for doing a thing—"acting righteously"—*at the same level of granularity* as the thing other than which he is unable to do: "acting righteously." God is not able to do otherwise than "acting righteously" (described at just this level of granularity for action), and yet God is morally responsible—morally praiseworthy—for "acting righteously" (described at just this level of granularity for action).

When we apply to God the above naming of righteous options as R's and sinful options as S's facing an agent at a time t, we see that while libertarians may maintain that God has the categorical ability to choose between say $R_1$ and $R_2$ (because of God's allegedly libertarian free will), in virtue of his impeccability, he does not have the ability to choose among the S's. So God does not have the ability to do otherwise than $(R_1 \vee R_2 \vee \ldots \vee R_n)$, a conjunction which groups only and all righteous options, and was thus described in my argument as "acting righteously." At that level of granularity, then, PAP advocates would need to say that since God is not able to do otherwise than $(R_1 \vee R_2 \vee \ldots \vee R_n)$, he is not praiseworthy for doing $(R_1 \vee R_2 \vee \ldots \vee R_n)$; God is not praiseworthy for acting righteously. That is what my argument claims is absurd, and allows one to conclude that the PAP is false.

Once the issue of the scope of applicability of the PAP with respect to levels of granularity is thus clarified, it becomes easier to assess the possible escape routes that PAP advocates could suggest in order to avoid the conclusion of my argument.

On the one hand, if my argument applied the PAP at the lowest level of granularity for divine action, then we saw that they could object that premise (31) is question-begging by presupposing a determinist view of the divine will, wherein God does not have a categorical, libertarian ability to do otherwise than he does. This, I already replied, is not the case, because my argument did not in fact apply the PAP to any one specific divine action, but rather to a class of actions, at a higher level of granularity: that of all the righteous options.

But since that is so, there are now two final possible escape routes left for PAP advocates to take (and for me to block); two responses to my argument, to rescue God's praiseworthiness and impeccability in the face of the PAP: they can either: 1. prevent my application of the PAP to these higher levels of granularity, by revising the formulation of the PAP to add qualifications on the "thing" for which it says one is morally responsible, thereby making it so that it is no longer applicable to higher levels of granularity for action, or 2. accept that the PAP is in fact applicable to higher levels of granularity for action, and hence concede that God is not praiseworthy *for his choice being among the righteous options*, but maintain that God is still somehow praiseworthy, *for his choice being the specific one that it is*. Let us review these options in turn and show that neither is successful.

## Does the PAP not apply to all levels of granularity for action?

The first escape route, then, is for PAP advocates to try revising the PAP to apply only at the lowest level of granularity for action, and not at higher levels. Since it is at the lowest level of granularity (that of the fully specified, unique actions) that the PAP excludes compatibilism, and it is only at a higher level that my present argument applies the PAP to God, if the PAP turned out to be applicable at the lowest level of granularity and not above, then an incompatibilist could maintain that the PAP is true at the lowest level, refutes compatibilism, and yet does nothing to undermine God's impeccability and praiseworthiness for "acting righteously." That would be a coherent response. Unfortunately, two objections stand against this move.

First, it is an ad-hoc, arbitrary qualification. Why would the PAP, if true, be thus restricted in the levels of granularity at which it applies? Why would it be true of the lowest level, and false of any (every) other? The alleged intuitive warrant of the PAP that is claimed by incompatibilists would seem to equally support each level of granularity indiscriminately. If an inability to avoid "telling a specific lie L" in response to a question excludes moral responsibility for "telling specific lie L," why then would an inability to avoid "lying" not exclude moral responsibility for "lying"? The warrant for either assertion seems to be the same. And of course let it remain clear that my present claim is only a conditional one since I do not believe that PAP is true or warranted at *any* level; but if it *were* true at one, why would it not be true at (all) others?

I dare even say that this undifferentiated warrant (or lack thereof) is most likely why the PAP was found formulated unqualified by its advocates in the first place, in appropriately vague terms of "things" we do, because the level of granularity of these "things" does not matter in how convincing they think the principle appears. But seeing now that the lowest level of granularity is the only one that excludes compatibilism, without an explanation of why just this one is thought true and (all) others false, the PAP advocate is wide open to the charge of special pleading against compatibilism.

And secondly, I can simply point out that PAP advocates themselves, in their own writings, concede its applicability to various levels of granularity for action, including ones above the lowest level. The chief incompatibilist Peter van Inwagen distinguishes between what he calls events or states of affair "particulars," and events or states of affair "universals." The "particulars" would correspond to what I have called the lowest level of granularity, while the "universals" are any other levels above it. He very helpfully clarifies the distinction as follows:

> Just as there are many different ways the concrete particulars that make up our surroundings could be arranged that would be sufficient for the *truth* of a given proposition, so there are many different ways they could be arranged that would be sufficient for the *obtaining* of a given state of affairs. Consider, for example, the state of affairs that consists in Caesar's being murdered. This state of affairs obtains because certain conspirators stabbed Caesar in Rome in 44 BC, but, since it is a universal, *it*,

that very same state of affairs, might have obtained because, say, Cleopatra had poisoned him in Alexandria in 48 BC.[27]

With this distinction in mind between particulars and universals, van Inwagen explicitly applies his re-formulation of the PAP to fit each of these in turn: "PPP1 A person is morally responsible for a certain event particular only if he could have prevented it"[28] and later on, "let us now turn to a principle about universals: PPP2 A person is morally responsible for a certain state of affairs only if (that state of affairs obtains and) he could have prevented it from obtaining."[29]

This is as explicit as it could possibly be: the PAP is applied to particulars and universals, to low and high levels of granularity. Not all PAP advocates are this explicit, but they implicitly affirm the same thing whenever they voice the need for alternate possibility for an action, without carefully specifying it in all details down to the lowest level of granularity. Doing so would be cumbersome for them I admit, but anything short of that tacitly admits that the principle, if true, applies to universals as much as particulars and hence permits my *reductio* when applying it to God. Put in more formal terms, the matter of granularity levels can be expressed as the following *modus tollens*:

34. If PAP is true at the lowest level of granularity, then it is true at the higher levels.

35. Divine praiseworthiness and impeccability showed that PAP is false at the higher levels.

*Therefore*

36. PAP is false at the lowest level as well.

The PAP is thus shown false whichever level is in view, and hence distinguishing between a true and a false PAP at different levels of granularity for action is not a successful route to escape the present argument.

Accordingly, let us turn to the last possible escape that remained: affirming PAP at all levels, granting that God is not praiseworthy *for his choice being righteous*, but maintaining that God is praiseworthy *for his choice being the specific one that it is.*

27. Van Inwagen, *Essay*, 171.
28. Ibid., 167.
29. Ibid., 171.

## Just what is God praiseworthy for?

This second and last strategy that PAP advocates could theoretically adopt to avoid my present argument is to concede that the PAP does apply to the higher levels of granularity for actions, and hence permit that the PAP entails that God is not morally praiseworthy for "acting righteously" in the sense that God is not morally praiseworthy for the fact that his specific choice is found among the set of righteous, morally good options (since righteousness is all God can do); but maintain God's praiseworthiness inasmuch as God is morally praiseworthy for the specific righteous option he does pick, since he does have the ability to do otherwise than choose *that one*. God would not be praiseworthy for his pick of $(R_1 \lor R_2 \lor \ldots \lor R_n)$, but would be praiseworthy for his pick of say $R_2$ over the other R's: $R_1$, $R_3$, $\ldots$, and $R_n$. On this view, God is only morally responsible for his specific pick *among* the morally righteous options, but he is not responsible (that is, not praiseworthy) for the fact that his pick is righteous to begin with.

This option also must be rejected for two reasons. First, it is intuitive (not to mention biblical) that God is praiseworthy for his righteousness in general, just as much as in the particulars. God is worthy of praise *because* he is good, *as opposed to* being evil. Remember the psalmist praising the Lord *"for* he is good." "Praise him *according to* his excellent greatness!" (Ps. 150:2) God is worthy of praise for his discriminatingly doing that which is righteous, over that which is unrighteous. God knowingly, consciously, intently chooses to do what is righteous, *rather than* what is unrighteous, and by any Christian account, that choice is worthy of praise. As Daniel Hill correctly points out,

> [The theist] wants to say that every divine being is praisewor-
> thy not only for those things [deeds of supererogation similar
> to what I have described as picking $R_2$ over other R's], but
> also for refraining from evil, keeping promises, not lying etc.,
> even though no divine being could have a choice about these
> matters.[30]

And secondly, if one rejects God's praiseworthiness for his pick being righteous *rather than unrighteous*, then there remains no other ground of praiseworthiness left to uphold. What sort of praiseworthiness remains for God for his mere discrimination among the righteous options only? Answering that question inevitably first raises another more fundamental one: what exactly *are* those alleged options open to God in light of his divine freedom and perfection in the first place? And answering that latter

---

30. Hill, *Maximal Greatness*, 214.

question potentially takes us into the deep waters of a highly controversial and very prolific debate in the philosophical literature. Philosophers have a great deal to say about the possibilities available to God in his divine freedom and given his moral perfection. As they assess the matter and argue their case, though, God's freedom is typically discussed at the level of *possible worlds*, raising instead the question of which possible worlds God could actualize in creation. The question at hand is quite similar to this one in terms of the philosophical issues that they raise, because God's decision to actualize a particular possible world is really a conjunction of an immense number of his individual free decisions. It is the aggregate gathering of all of God's decisions regarding every single contingent[31] state of affairs whose obtaining depends on his creative decision and action. Therefore, the same sorts of considerations of goodness, righteousness, praiseworthiness, possibilities, and divine freedom are raised in discussing the actualization of possible worlds and whether God can pick possible world $W_1$ over possible world $W_2$, as would be raised in discussing individual divine actions and whether God can pick action A over action B. The present question could then lead us into lengthy discussions of the various ways in which possible worlds might be thought to be arranged: is there a single best possible world? Are there multiple best possible worlds? Is there no best world and instead an infinite set of continually increasing better worlds? Are possible worlds even commensurable?[32] These fascinating questions, however, need not detain us, as they can (and should) be short-circuited for our present purposes. There are, I maintain, in each of these scenarios, good reasons to think that God's praiseworthiness cannot be rescued *for merely picking one righteous option among the righteous ones* (picking $R_2$ over the other R's: $R_1$, $R_3$, . . . , and $R_n$), but proving such a claim is not necessary at this point, because the matter can be drastically simplified as follows. We can restrict our discussion to the case of a single divine action, where a single righteous alternative is available for God, and it will still establish the thesis at hand. The claim made by the PAP is a universally quantified one: it is said that moral responsibility entails the ability to do otherwise. All I need is a single counter-example wherein God cannot do otherwise and yet remains praise-

---

31. Here and on subsequent occasions, I intend the word "contingent" to refer simply to this uncontroversial fact: that the states of affairs in view "depend on God's creative decision and action." I thereby make no pronouncements as to whether these divine decisions and actions are themselves determined by other states of affairs about God's nature, or are instead categorically contingent in a way that they could have been otherwise all other things being just as they are.

32. For excellent discussions of these matters, see Rowe, *Can God Be Free?* and McCann, *Creation*, 155–75.

worthy. Whichever scenario is true with respect to how possible worlds are organized, I can always find such a situation (or even postulate a fictional one!) where God is facing a choice that features only one righteous option and God cannot fail to pick it in virtue of his impeccable righteousness. In that case, the escape route of the PAP advocate presently considered, that of maintaining praiseworthiness for the choice of a righteous act over other righteous ones is unavailable, because there *are* no other righteous ones. God's praiseworthiness cannot hang on his picking $R_2$ over the other R's if there are no other R's. In this fashion, consider the promises God made to Abraham. Once they are made, God is only facing two options on this matter: keep the promises or break the promises.[33] Could God fail to keep his promises to Abraham? No. Was God praiseworthy for keeping them? Certainly.[34] Could Jesus, being God, have failed to accomplish his Father's will and obediently give his life as a ransom for many? No. Was he praiseworthy for his sacrifice? Most certainly. So this escape route will not do, and it remains that if God's choices and actions are not praiseworthy for being righteous rather than unrighteous, neither are they praiseworthy for their mere discrimination among the righteous options alone. But then if God's choices and actions are praiseworthy at all, it follows that moral responsibility (in this case praiseworthiness) does not require the ability to do otherwise. The principle of alternate possibilities is thereby shown false for him who believes God is praiseworthy while impeccable.

## Atheists included

As announced above, this argument is mainly designed to appeal to Christians or at least theists, as long as they are committed to the existence of a maximally great, impeccable, and praiseworthy being. Beyond this primary audience, however, I want to point out that its scope may not in fact have to be so restricted. This argument has a decent potential to appeal to atheists

33. Against this, one might protest that even in this case, there are several possible ways in which God could have kept his promises to Abraham. I am once more skeptical that one can rescue divine praiseworthiness in this way, but let us, here again, bypass the debate by responding that even if God did not, God *could* have made the promise fully specified in such a way as to exclude a multiplicity of ways in which to fulfill it. The point remains that fulfilling it would be a praiseworthy thing for God to do.

34. See Mary and Zechariah praising God for keeping his promises to Abraham, respectively in Luke 1:55 and 1:73. The praiseworthiness of divine promise-keeping is explicitly presupposed in scripture by Solomon as well when he praises God for keeping the promises that God had made to his father David: "Blessed be the LORD, the God of Israel, who with his hand has fulfilled what he promised with his mouth to David my father" (2 Chr 6:4).

(and agnostics) as well, because it establishes that if the PAP is true, a praise-worthy impeccable being *cannot* exist, not merely that it *doesn't*. This means that if the PAP is true, the very idea of a praiseworthy person who is too good to sin (or to "act immorally," in non-religious moral language) is incoherent. This is a problematic feature for *any* moral system, whether or not one believes that such a being in fact exists, and whether or not this morally perfect being also happens to be an omnipotent creator of the universe who raised Jesus Christ from the dead. Whatever one's view of what grounds moral values and whether God has any business anchoring them, defining them, or revealing them, we need to maintain that in theory a person who would be so good as to make it incoherent that he act immorally, should possibly be praiseworthy for that impeccable goodness of his. Mark Twain, hardly a committed Christian, discerned this when he remarked tongue in cheek: "I am morally superior to George Washington. He couldn't tell a lie. I can and I don't."[35] What Mark Twain's sarcasm indirectly mocks should be rejected even by atheists, to recognize that one should not hang moral responsibility on the possibility to do otherwise irrespective of one's state of heart. And once again, *a fortiori*, what is absurd for Twain and Washington is absurd for Jesus and me. I am not better than Jesus for the fact that while neither of us has (so far) committed murder, I could and he couldn't. On the contrary, what grounds his inability to murder and my ability to do so are our moral characters and natures: his perfect and mine depraved, the very things that make me blameworthy and him gloriously worthy of praise.

## Turning the table around—a positive argument for compatibilism from the falsity of the PAP

Having offered a first argument for the falsity of the principle of alternate possibilities, and before we consider an additional, independent argument for that thesis, let us bring this line of reasoning to completion, develop-ing it all the way into a positive argument in favor of compatibilism. The principle of alternate possibilities was introduced as an argument in favor of incompatibilism: if the PAP were true, it would follow that determinism is incompatible with moral responsibility, which means that PAP entails in-compatibilism. When the PAP was refuted just above, it was therefore seen as a *premise* in an argument for incompatibilism. But to prove that a premise in an argument is false does not prove that the conclusion is also false. There-fore, if left at that, the above critique and refutation of the PAP *undercuts* the position of the incompatibilist, but it does not *rebut* it. If PAP is true,

35. Quoted in van Inwagen, *Essay*, 63–64.

incompatibilism follows, but the falsity of the PAP does not as of yet entail the falsity of incompatibilism (i.e., the truth of compatibilism).

Upon further examination, however, there *are* additional considerations that provide the necessary support for a full-front assault on incompatibilism on the basis that the PAP is false. I now contend that a refutation of the PAP does refute incompatibilism (and hence establishes compatibilism) based upon the fact that incompatibilism *does* entail the truth of the PAP, so that ultimately we do not just have PAP ⇒ Incompatibilism, but also Incompatibilism ⇒ PAP, which ties the demise of the PAP to that of incompatibilism.

## The argument

I propose the following argument:

37. Incompatibilism is the thesis that moral responsibility is incompatible with determinism.

    *(by definition)*

    *Therefore*

38. If incompatibilism is true, then moral responsibility entails indeterminism.

    *(follows from (37))*

39. If moral responsibility entails indeterminism, then moral responsibility entails libertarianism.

    *(uncontroversial premise)*

40. If incompatibilism is true, then moral responsibility entails libertarianism.

    *(follows from (38) and (39))*

41. The exercise of a libertarian free will entails the ability to do otherwise than one does.

    *(possibly controversial premise, to be supported below)*

    *Therefore*

42. If moral responsibility entails libertarianism, then moral responsibility entails the ability to do otherwise than one does.

    *(follows from (41))*

    *Therefore*

43. If moral responsibility entails libertarianism, then PAP is true.

    *(follows from (42) by definition of the PAP)*

    *Therefore*

44. Incompatibilism entails that PAP is true.

    *(follows from (40) and (43))*

    *But*

45. PAP is false.

    *(as argued above)*

    *Therefore*

46. Incompatibilism is false.

    *(follows from (44) and (45))*

    *Therefore*

47. Compatibilism is true.

For the sake of clarity, it can be restated more compactly if we define the following symbols:

COMP is the thesis of compatibilism,

INC stands for incompatibilism,

IND for indeterminism,

MR for moral responsibility (or the thesis that at least one person is, was, or will be morally responsible),

LFW stands for the thesis of libertarianism (or the thesis that at least one person has, had, or will have libertarian free will),

AP stands for alternate possibilities (or the thesis that at least one person has, had, or will have the ability to do otherwise than he does, did, or will do (respectively)),

and

PAP is the principle of alternate possibilities.

With those in place, the argument is stated as follows:

37. $INC =_{df} \neg \Diamond (MR \wedge \neg IND)$   (definition)

38. $INC \Rightarrow (MR \Rightarrow IND)$        (from (37))

39. $(MR \Rightarrow IND) \Rightarrow (MR \Rightarrow LFW)$ (premise)

40. INC $\Rightarrow$ (MR $\Rightarrow$ LFW)     (from (38), (39), *Hypothetical Syllogism*)

41. LFW $\Rightarrow$ AP     (premise)

42. (MR $\Rightarrow$ LFW) $\Rightarrow$ (MR $\Rightarrow$ AP)  (from (41), *Hypothetical Syllogism*)

43. (MR $\Rightarrow$ LFW) $\Rightarrow$ PAP     (from (42), definition of PAP)

44. INC $\Rightarrow$ PAP     (from (40), (43), *Hypothetical Syllogism*)

45. $\neg$ PAP     (from independent arguments)

46. $\neg$ INC     (from (44), (45), *Modus Tollens*)

47. COMP     (from (46))

Let us review each premise in turn.

(37) is merely the definition of incompatibilism: it is the thesis that moral responsibility is incompatible with determinism.

(38) follows directly from it, because if moral responsibility is incompatible with determinism, and moral responsibility is true, then determinism is false, which means that indeterminism is true.

(39) is the uncontroversial claim, upheld by incompatibilists themselves, that if moral responsibility requires indeterminism, it will not be just any kind of indeterminism.[36] If a fully determinist world excludes moral responsibility, then say the mere thesis that the radioactive decay of certain particles is not determined will do nothing to rescue moral responsibility. Rather, the sort of indeterminism that incompatibilist indeterminists contend must be true is one that is located in the activity of the will of moral agents, that is, in the exercise of their libertarian free will.[37] Our premise

---

36. "[F]or the libertarian, a necessary condition of free will is a view of the person as a substance that acts as an agent, that is, as a first cause or an unmoved mover. Thus determinism is sufficient for a denial of libertarian free will, since it says that all events are caused by prior events and there are no substantial agents that act as unmoved movers. But even if determinism is false, this alone does not establish libertarian free will, because completely uncaused events that randomly occur without reason, as in the quantum world, do not give the type of agency needed for libertarian free will, namely, the freedom by which the agent as a substance is in control of his actions. The main debate between compatibilists and libertarians is one about the nature of agency and not determinism per se, although the truth of determinism is sufficient for the denial of libertarianism, as was already mentioned." Moreland and Craig, *Philosophical Foundations*, 279.

37. Alfred Mele puts it this way: "to be sure, quantum mechanics, according to leading interpretations, is indeterministic. But indeterminism at that level does not ensure that any human brains themselves sometimes operate indeterministically, much less that they sometimes operate indeterministically in ways appropriate for free action and moral responsibility." Mele, *Free Will and Luck*, 10.

(39), therefore, follows straightforwardly: if moral responsibility entails indeterminism, then moral responsibility entails libertarianism.

(40) follows from (38) and (39) by *hypothetical syllogism*, the transitivity of the relation of logical entailment:

$$A \Rightarrow B$$

$$B \Rightarrow C$$

$$\overline{\phantom{A \Rightarrow C}}$$

$$A \Rightarrow C$$

If A entails B and B entails C, then A entails C. That premise (40) follows from (38) and (39) is an exemplification of this rule with A = "Incompatibilism is true," B = "Moral responsibility entails indeterminism," and C = "Moral responsibility entails libertarianism." This correctly yields the conclusion that if incompatibilism is true, then moral responsibility entails libertarianism.

We now come to premise (41), which might be appraised differently by different incompatibilists. Some will see it as straightforwardly true, and some will see it as the most controversial premise of this argument (aside from the rejection of PAP in (45), of course, but its defense was the purpose of earlier sections in this chapter). So what can be said in favor of premise (41), the claim that the exercise of a libertarian free will entails the ability to do otherwise than one does?

First, some—maybe most—incompatibilists will find no problem with that. Paul Franks indeed reports that "most philosophers identify libertarian freedom concerning some act with being able to refrain from performing that act."[38] Rescuing the ability to do otherwise than one does was the very purpose of libertarian free will. On libertarianism, an agent can freely choose A or B, all things being just as they are up to the moment of free choice. This is the categorical ability we have been discussing in this work, and as van Inwagen sees it, it's the very meaning of free will.[39]

But other incompatibilists have become convinced by some of the arguments opposing the PAP, and accordingly, they are inclined to reject it while still maintaining that determinism excludes moral responsibility, just not *in virtue* of excluding alternate possibilities. William Hasker mentions Linda Zagzebski and David Hunt as holding this view, and calls them "Frankfurt libertarians,"[40] since Frankfurt-style cases are one reason they

---

38. Franks, "Original Sin," 361.

39. "To be able to have acted otherwise is to have free will." Van Inwagen, *Essay*, 162.

40. Hasker, "Divine Knowledge," 48–49.

reject the PAP while remaining libertarian incompatibilists. William Lane Craig also rejects the PAP on the basis of Frankfurt-style cases,[41] and on the basis of the above argument that God is both praiseworthy and impeccable.[42] Yet as an incompatibilist, Craig too, maintains that while moral responsibility does not demand alternate possibilities, it does demand indeterminist, libertarian free will.[43] The same view is held by Eleonore Stump[44] and presumably Derk Pereboom[45] as well.[46] But is this position coherent? Can one maintain that morally responsible agents on the one hand have a libertarian free will and at the same time lack the categorical ability to do otherwise when performing a directly free act? One cannot in fact. By anyone's account of libertarianism, I contend that the two inevitably hang or fall together. A way to see this is to come back to definitions, and ask: what is libertarian free will, if not an ability to freely choose otherwise than one does? Incompatibilists will be hard-pressed to provide a definition of libertarian free will that does not in fact feature or logically entail the categorical ability to do otherwise in the way the $PAP_{All}$ demanded. If they do not with van Inwagen *define* libertarian free will as the ability to do otherwise, at the very least they are committed to describing it as "indeterminist." If they did not, then determinism would obtain, and on their incompatibilist view, it would exclude moral responsibility. So "indeterminist" free will is the most

41. William Lane Craig presents a Frankfurt-style case featuring a scientist supporter of Barack Obama, having implanted a chip in the brain of a voter, intending to secure that his vote will be made for Obama, and yet who does not need to press the button to activate the device because the voter picks Obama on his own. Craig, "Response to Gregory A. Boyd," 225.

42. He writes "This understanding of libertarian freedom has the advantage that it enables us to ascribe libertarian freedom to God himself and to Christ in resisting temptation." Ibid.

43. "What is essential to libertarian freedom is not the possibility of choosing otherwise but rather the absence of causal constraints outside oneself that determine how one chooses." Ibid.

44. "What is required for libertarian freedom and for moral responsibility, as I have argued elsewhere, is not that the agent could have done otherwise, but that the ultimate cause of the agent's act lie in the agent's own intellect and will, so that the agent himself is the ultimate source of what he does." Stump, "Responsibility Without Alternative Possibilities," 152.

45. "The incompatibilist condition for determinism that I favor makes no reference to alternative possibilities for action, but instead claims that for an agent to be morally responsible (accountable), her action cannot result from a deterministic causal process that traces back to factors beyond her control." Pereboom, *Living*, 124.

46. Pereboom's position might however be less exposed to the incoherence I am here denouncing, since he does not himself attempt to craft a coherent libertarian account that would satisfy the demands of his incompatibilism, but rather rejects compatibilist and libertarian accounts of free will altogether to deny moral responsibility.

modest descriptor that can be used to refer to libertarian free will without mention of alternate possibilities. But in turn, we must probe: what does indeterminism mean in the area of free will and what does it entail? On the one hand, it is not uncommon here again to see incompatibilists even *define* indeterminism in terms of alternate possibilities. Van Inwagen defines determinism as "the thesis that there is at any instant exactly one physically possible future."[47] This explicitly enough entails that indeterminism calls for *more* than one possible future, that is, it calls for alternate possible futures, brought about by the free choices of moral agents. It calls for alternate possibilities indeed. If on the other hand, one attempts to define indeterminism itself without reference to alternate possibilities, then once again the most modest affirmation that can be made is that on indeterminism, the free choices of moral agents are *undetermined*. That is what indeterminism is. So can this move avoid alternate possibilities? We must probe further and ask: what does it mean for choices to be *undetermined* in that way? It means that they are not *determined*, or *necessitated* by prior conditions, inside or outside the agent; that is, the totality of prior facts about the world does not suffice to determine the agent's choice. And there we must of necessity see alternate possibilities reappear: indeed, if the totality of prior facts about the world does not determine an agent's choice to be what it is, then it must mean that given all of these facts, the free choice could have been other than it is. If the choice could not have been other than it is while holding these other facts in place, then it is the case that these other facts did determine the one and only possible choice. This means that if the choice was undetermined, it entailed that the agent could have done otherwise. No matter how modestly one defines libertarianism and its underlying indeterminism, then, they necessarily entail the existence of alternate possibilities,[48] from which premise (41) follows: the possession of a libertarian free will entails the categorical ability to do otherwise than one does.

Two potential objections must now be addressed. First, in response to this claim, those so-called "Frankfurt-libertarians" could insist that Frankfurt-style cases are in fact examples wherein agents could have libertarian free will while lacking the ability to do otherwise, because of the

---

47. Van Inwagen, *Essay*, 3.

48. This much is affirmed by William Hasker, quoted by Kevin Timpe, and saying that alternate possibilities are "crucial" for the incompatibilist and libertarian positions. See Timpe, *Sourcehood*, 146. Timpe himself joins us on this point when he writes "the Source Incompatibilist should admit that her commitment to the sourcehood condition also carries with it a commitment to some alternate-possibilities condition, even if it is a very weak one which insists on no more leeway that the sourcehood condition's requirement of the falsity of causal determinism already secures." Ibid., 158.

counterfactual intervener. In response, I must simply reference my above rejection of Frankfurt-style cases as a successful argument for compatibilism. The reason why Frankfurt-style cases cannot establish the compatibility of libertarian free will with an inability to do otherwise is the same reason why they earlier failed to establish the compatibility of moral responsibility with an inability to do otherwise: they do not in fact feature a categorical inability to do otherwise, unless they additionally presuppose determinism. If instead we suppose that the agent *has* libertarian free will, then although he cannot do otherwise than perform the action (because of the counterfactual intervener), he does have the ability to do otherwise than "freely performing the action without the intervention of the counterfactual intervener," and the access to this alternate (though crippled) possibility hangs on the exercise of his libertarian free will. He has the ability to bring about this alternate possibility. This shortcoming of Frankfurt-style cases was the reason why Peter van Inwagen and I rejected them as a successful proof of compatibilism, but then it follows that they equally fail at dissociating libertarianism from the categorical ability to do otherwise, and hence fail to undermine the present argument for compatibilism.

A second objection is offered by Linda Zagzebski in a paper asking the question "Does Libertarian Freedom Require Alternate Possibilities?"[49] She answers that it does not, because she explains we must distinguish between two different senses of contingency: temporal contingency and causal contingency, defined as follows. A free action is *temporally contingent* if and only if an alternate action could have been performed while absolutely all things temporally prior to the action were kept in place, but a free action is *causally contingent*, if and only if an alternate action could have been performed while all *causally relevant* antecedents were kept in place. Clearly enough, not all things in the universe that temporally precede an action are causally relevant to that action, so temporal contingency entails causal contingency, but a causally contingent action need not be temporally contingent as well. Zagzebski takes the concept of divine foreknowledge as an example, contending that if God foreknew yesterday the outcome of a free choice that will be made tomorrow, then the choice is no longer temporally contingent—the agent cannot do otherwise than what God foreknew yesterday—but it is causally contingent, as the agent can do otherwise while all *causally relevant* antecedents remain the same: God's foreknowledge is temporally prior, but it is not causally relevant: it does not figure among the list of things that cause or influence the action.

49. Zagzebski, "Require Alternate Possibilities?" 231–48.

With these reasonable distinctions in place, Zagzebski argues that incompatibilism rests on the following principle she calls "LTR" for the "libertarian thesis on responsibility," stating that "An agent is morally responsible for her act only if the act is causally contingent."[50] Zagzebski contrasts it with the unqualified PAP, which she takes to demand temporal contingency when it contends that "An agent is morally responsible for her act only if she could have done otherwise."[51] Accordingly, she argues that "LTR may be true even if PAP is false."[52] This may seem to dispute my argument's premise (41), blocking the inference to (42) and (43), and rejecting (44), thereby maintaining incompatibilism in light of the LTR, but rejecting PAP to avoid the compatibilist conclusion that I claimed—in premise (46)—follows from PAP's falsity.

But nothing in my argument hangs or falls with what Zagzebski calls the temporal contingency for a libertarian free choice. The argument never presupposed that libertarianism required such a strong sense of contingency in an action as to be able to bring about the falsity of God's prior beliefs. Her qualifier of libertarian free will in terms of an ability to do otherwise all *causally relevant* things being equal is perfectly fine for all my present argument has to say, and hence I concede that what she calls LTR *is* the libertarian thesis on responsibility; but it is what in my argument is called PAP! It is with that more modest understanding of the categorical ability to do otherwise that my arguments are offered against the PAP. So as long as she affirms LTR as she does—which she must, as an incompatibilist—it concedes the truth of my premise (41). The separate question of whether libertarianism entails the stronger temporal contingency (and hence excludes things like infallible divine foreknowledge) is interesting, but irrelevant to the present work. These two objections of Frankfurt-libertarians notwithstanding, then, the exercise of a libertarian free will does involve the categorical ability to do otherwise, and that is premise (41).

Premise (42) then follows from (41) by *hypothetical syllogism* once again. If moral responsibility entails libertarianism and libertarianism entails the ability to do otherwise, then moral responsibility entails the ability to do otherwise. Thus, if moral responsibility entails libertarianism, then moral responsibility entails the ability to do otherwise.

(43) is merely a restatement of (42) whose consequent is identified as the PAP: if moral responsibility entails libertarianism, then PAP is true.

50. Ibid., 233.
51. Ibid.
52. Ibid., 234.

(44) is yet another application of *hypothetical syllogism* (A ⇒ B and B ⇒ C entail A ⇒ C), to premises (40) and (43), with A = "Incompatibilism is true," B = "Moral responsibility entails libertarianism" and C = "PAP is true." We have A entails B and B entails C, so A entails C, and that is premise (44): "Incompatibilism entails the PAP."

(45) is the rejection of PAP, for which a first argument was offered above, and a second one will come below.

(46) follows from (44) and (45) by *modus tollens*. If incompatibilism entails the PAP and the PAP is false, then incompatibilism is false.

This establishes that incompatibilism is false, and since compatibilism is its logical complement, it means (47): compatibilism is true.

We hold a sound argument that establishes the truth of compatibilism. *Et voilà.*

## The source incompatibilist response

To resist this conclusion, there is one possible route that has been employed by some incompatibilists. It consists in qualifying the principle of alternate possibilities to make a more modest demand in terms of ability, one that still asks *of humans* that they have the ability to do otherwise, but can tolerate *God's* inability to act unrighteously without excluding his praiseworthiness. These incompatibilists have pointed out what they take to be a relevant difference between humans and God: on determinism, humans are determined by *external* factors, which can be traced back to sources *outside* of themselves, whereas God's inability to act unrighteously stems from his own necessary and perfect nature; it is not determined by something or someone else. Michael Bergman and J. A. Cover phrase this condition in terms of the "causal buck" stopping with the agent: "As we shall be thinking of it, to be responsible for A involves being the front end of the causal chain issuing in A: S is responsible for her act A so long as the causal buck for A stops with S."[53] Daniel Hill explicitly draws the same sort of distinction in his definition of freedom: "My view is that an agent, S, freely performs an action, A, if and only if S is not ultimately caused to perform A by anything 'outside' S."[54] Determined humans would indeed fail to qualify as free on that account, and Paul Franks explains how God is thought not to be analogous to humans in that respect:

---

53. Bergmann and Cover, "Responsibility Without Divine Freedom," 392.
54. Hill, *Maximal Greatness*, 71.

However, when one asks why God always acts in accordance with the moral law, the whole story can be told without relying on anything external to God. Perfect intentional conformance to the moral law simply follows from his perfection. Unlike finite creatures, a perfect being's actions trace back to that being alone.[55]

That distinction between God and humans certainly holds true, so one could maintain that moral responsibility is not excluded in the case of God whose impeccability comes from within, while it is excluded for determined humans inasmuch as their determination would come from without, namely from the providential activity of their creator. I honestly must admit that this is a rather effective defensive move, and a *prima facie* coherent position to take, but let me offer three responses to try and convince even such incompatibilists.

First, one could press on and object that this distinction is in fact not the relevant criterion for ascriptions of moral responsibility in this case. While a God who is impeccable by nature and humans whose natures guarantee the outcome of their choices are different with respect to the source of their natures, they remain identical with respect to what seems to be the most important and striking fact: *they did not choose to have the natures that they have.* The rightness (or wrongness) of their choices is secured by their natures, and not by "them." In the face of this contention, an interesting attempt to meet the challenge is made by Alexander Pruss who uses a formulation of the doctrine of divine simplicity according to which God is identical with his nature. If that is the case, then the goodness of God's choices being secured by his nature *does* mean that they are secured by him, since his nature *is* him.[56] But it is doubtful that this will work: first, the doctrine of divine simplicity understood in those terms is itself rejected by many if not most incompatibilists;[57] but most importantly, even then, one can rephrase the relevant fact without banking on God not being identical to his nature. All one needs to point out is that the goodness of God's choices, just like that of causally determined humans, is *determined by states of affairs that they did not themselves choose.* This seems to be the relevant fact, it is true whether or not God is identical to his nature, and it is unaffected by whether one's nature is created or uncreated, contingent or necessary. Now of course, there can still be those incompatibilists who will say they disagree on that being the

55. Franks, "Divine Freedom," 117.

56. Pruss, "Essential Divine-Perfection Objection," 443.

57. See a full discussion by Plantinga who calls the doctrine "a dark saying indeed" in Plantinga, *Does God Have a Nature?* 27.

relevant fact. They may insist the internal or external *origin* of one's nature is what matters, regardless of the fact that neither God nor determined humans got to *choose* their natures. They may say *source* is relevant, and *fixity* is not. What can be said in response? Without claiming that this is a rebutting defeater—as it would be shifting the burden of proof, quite clearly—I can at least modestly point out that my argument has shaved off any motivation to adopt this view, since the issue of fixity, that of being determined by factors beyond one's choosing, was rather central in the incompatibilist complaint about determinism, even if its being the relevant factor is no longer conceded to my case. It certainly was the allegedly relevant fact on which the *consequence argument* banked everything, and yet, we now could run a consequence-argument-style syllogism that backfires against God's praiseworthiness in light of what I (and the consequence argument) claimed to be the relevant fact of fixity in premise (48) below:

48. God never chose to have the nature that he has.

49. God never chose the fact that if God has such a nature then he cannot act unrighteously.

*Therefore*

50. God never chose to never act unrighteously (and hence isn't praiseworthy for that feat).

So the incompatibilist who maintains that the source and not the fixity of one's nature is what is relevant here, must at the very least give up the consequence argument or reject divine praiseworthiness. But can anything else be said to convince them that fixity is more relevant than source? Wes Morriston[58] and Joshua Rasmussen[59] both suggest interesting thought experiments (involving, for example, uncreated impeccable human beings, who presumably shouldn't be relevantly different from created ones) to try and stir the intuition that fixity—and not origin—is what matters. This case is rather convincing, but at the end of the day, since the burden of proof is still on the shoulders of the compatibilist, I don't think it's strictly possible to block this incompatibilist escape route altogether, because at one point or another, the argument must move from something that is true of God, to something that it claims is true of men. When that move is made, I suppose incompatibilists always have the option of claiming there remained a relevant difference in something that is true of God and false of men. Fair enough; that may be the final defensive position out of which I am unable to

58. Morriston, "What is So Good," 350–52.
59. Rasmussen, "Freedom to Do Evil," 420.

dislodge them, though I hope to have shown that this move, if not incoherent, is at least unattractive.

Secondly, even if this response from the incompatibilist turned out to be appealing to some, one can now point out just how much it still concedes. The source incompatibilist who makes this move in response to my present argument *is* in fact admitting that compatibilism is true! Indeed, it is now admitted that what excludes moral responsibility in the case of humans is *not* that they are entirely determined. It is that they are determined *by the wrong kind of factors*. Kevin Timpe, arguing for this appropriately named "source incompatibilism," puts it in those terms: "insofar as I'm an incompatibilist, I don't think a choice can be free if it is causally determined by factors external to the agent, that is, if there exists an externally sufficient causal chain which brings about that action."[60] Exactly: the determinations that are said to exclude moral responsibility are those "external to the agent," but insofar as some determinations can arise internally (and in fact do so in the case of God), moral responsibility is compatible with determinism. So we now all agree on this: being determined isn't the problem; it's *how* one is determined that counts. The debate on compatibilism itself has been surrendered.

Now, I should of course point out that "source incompatibilists" who make the above move still find fault with Calvinist determinism, because human choices that are determined by God do not pass even the revised, more modest source incompatibilist criterion for moral responsibility: they *are* determined by factors outside themselves. But it is now clear that the debate has significantly shifted: compatibilism, the thesis that *determinism is incompatible with moral responsibility*, is no longer at stake; rather, we are back to raising the more specific question of whether being determined *by something or someone outside oneself* removes moral responsibility. In many respects, it is the problem of being "manipulated" from the outside, which was fully treated in chapter 3, and there it was argued that there is no successful manipulation argument against compatibilism.

Finally, I will simply note that the very next argument against the PAP (and for compatibilism by *modus tollens*) will exclude this escape route altogether. The next argument won't allow any such loophole based upon a determination being internal or external, since it will focus exclusively on human beings. I shall argue that fallen humans who lack the ability to live a sinless life remain morally responsible for their failure to do so. Given the nature of the case, no internal/external distinction will be available to rescue moral responsibility in the face of even a revised PAP.

---

60. Timpe, *Philosophical Theology*, 109.

To this argument we now turn.

## The blameworthiness of original sin—a "Pelagian or universalist" unorthodox dilemma

Even more so than the previous one, this next argument features premises that are designed to appeal to traditional Christians. It does not weigh much in interactions with advocates of incompatibilism who also reject traditional Christian orthodoxy, but for those committed to fairly essential Christian doctrines, it should make the acceptance of PAP$_{All}$ very costly.[61]

## The argument

"If the Diatribe's inference stands good, the Pelagians have clearly won the day"[62]—Martin Luther

The impetus for the present argument is found in Luther's *Bondage of the Will*, his lively refutation of Erasmus's *Diatribe on Free Will*. In it, Luther trumpeted the following claims *ad nauseam*: "If there were enough good in 'free-will' for it to apply itself to good, it would have no need of grace!"[63] and "What need is there of the Spirit, or Christ, or God, if 'free-will' can overcome the motions of the mind to evil?"[64]

According to Luther, if the PAP as defended by Erasmus proves anything, it proves "that 'free-will' has, not just some small degree of endeavor or desire, but full force and completely free power to do all things, without the grace of God and without the Holy Spirit."[65] Luther seems to claim that if the PAP is true, it can and hence must be applied to the full series of one's life choices, and yield the conclusion that any human being albeit fallen can live, or could have lived, a perfect sinless life—which is supposed to be absurd per Christian belief. In other words, if free will can do one thing, it can do everything. Unfortunately, since the PAP may or may not be so aggregated, modern philosophers may be tempted to dismiss Luther's quick and rough formulation above on the alleged grounds that it is an unsupported slip-

---

61. This reduced scope of relevance may not be too costly a sacrifice however, because it seems to me atheist philosophers of free will tend to be compatibilists, and therefore need no refutation of the PAP$_{All}$.

62. Luther, *Bondage of the Will*, 155.

63. Ibid., 145.

64. Ibid., 157.

65. Ibid., 174.

pery slope or an outright *fallacy of composition*. To prevent this move, the argument should be formulated rigorously, and I propose to set it forth as a *reductio* as follows.

Let us assume the truth of $PAP_{All}$, and let us consider a person P in the present world, who in the course of his finite earthly lifetime, is confronted with a finite number n of instants where an opportunity presents itself for making a free will choice between a sinful action and a righteous deed. Let those instants be chronologically ordered and named $t_1, t_2, \ldots, t_n$.

At any such instant $t_i$, P will either freely commit sin $S_i$, or freely choose the righteous option $R_i$,[66] so that we can organize P's life decisions chronologically as they occurred (or will occur) in the present world, say: $R_1, R_2, S_3, R_4, S_5, S_6, \ldots, S_n$.

Let us focus on the first sin in the sequence, which in P's case is $S_3$. $S_3$ was defined as an actual free will sin, which we suppose fulfilled all the individually necessary and jointly sufficient conditions for P to be morally responsible for doing $S_3$ at $t_3$.

According to the $PAP_{All}$, since P is morally responsible for doing $S_3$, it follows that P had the ability to avoid $S_3$, all things being just as they were up until instant $t_3$. Using the semantic of possible worlds, it means that there is a possible world, say $W^3$, whose history is identical to that of the present world (let us name it $W^0$) in all respects up until $t_3$, and wherein P refrains from doing $S_3$, to presumably perform righteous deed $R_3$ instead. If an advocate of the PAP is inclined at this point to object that the alternate possibility need not be righteous, but could just be another sinful one, then I will redirect him to my above discussion of the so-called "levels of granularity" for the PAP: we saw in earlier sections of this chapter, that the PAP, if true, must apply not only to specific actions, but more generally to classes of actions. With that in mind, we are here supposing that P is morally responsible, not just for specifically "doing $S_3$ at $t_3$," but more generally for "sinning at $t_3$," which means that P must have the ability not just to avoid doing $S_3$ at $t_3$, but to avoid sinning altogether at $t_3$. Of course, the alternative to $S_3$ need not be positively righteous, it could be morally neutral if there is such a thing, but the point is that it is no longer sinful, and hence this step of the argument goes through, as $S_3$ has been rectified into a non-sinful action at $t_3$ in $W^3$. I will thus continue referring to that alternate, non-sinful action, as $R_3$.

In $W^3$, the composition of P's lifetime choices may thus be $R_1, R_2, R_3, R_4, S_5, S_6, \ldots, S_n$ where only $R_3$ has taken the place of $S_3$. But in fact, no one is committed to thinking that after $t_3$ in $W^3$, the rest of P's choices should be

---

66. I realize that libertarians would affirm that more than two options are open in any such instance, but the foregoing reasoning will not be negatively affected in any relevant aspect by this admitted simplification.

identical to those in $W^0$. Indeed, this would actually be extremely unlikely, because P's better choice at $t_3$ in $W^3$ most likely sends a ripple effect into P's future, as he is now avoiding the negative consequences that followed from $S_3$ in $W^0$, and is therefore likely not only to fare better at $t_5$, $t_6$, and the rest of the series in $W^3$ than he did in $W^0$, but also to encounter wholly different free will choice opportunities because of the life scenario difference introduced at $t_3$. This is fine, and is taken into account merely by adjusting the R's and the S's after $t_3$ in P's combination of choices in $W^3$. What is important is that all choices are identical *up until t3* between $W^0$ and $W^3$ as dictated by the $PAP_{All}$.

Let us now consider the content of $W^3$, and in it, jump to the next instance of sin by P, say $S_5$. The present argument must now assume that $PAP_{All}$ is also true in $W^3$. Is that assumption justified? It is quite true that for all we know, a proponent of $PAP_{All}$ in our world $W^0$ need not believe that $PAP_{All}$ is a broadly logically necessary truth, that is, true in every possible world. But all the present argument needs to assume is that $PAP_{All}$ is true in every possible world that differs from $W^0$ only with respect to the free choices that P makes. *Those* possible worlds certainly include the truth of $PAP_{All}$, since it would be absurd to think that P in $W^0$ has it in his power of free choice to do something such that, were he to do it, this metaphysical principle of moral responsibility would be false. Thus $PAP_{All}$ holds in $W^3$, and can be applied again to the next instance of sin $S_5$ that P commits in $W^3$. The application of $PAP_{All}$ to $S_5$ then tells us that since P is responsible for $S_5$ in $W^3$, he must have the ability to choose otherwise than $S_5$ at $t_5$, all things being equal prior to $t_5$. This means that there is a possible world $W^5$ identical to $W^3$ in every respect up until $t_5$, wherein P does not commit $S_5$, and chooses $R_5$ instead, and so on.

The above reasoning can be pursued by recurrence as many times as needed, jumping from possible world to possible world, "rectifying" the list of P's sinful choices, by identifying nearby possible worlds in which those sins are replaced by righteous deeds. The length of the list of free will choices will certainly vary from one possible world to another, but as long as the list remains finite in any given possible world, our reasoning by recurrence will succeed to reach completion, and will in the end give us the existence of a possible world, accessible by P provided that he just exercise his free will, in which P does not commit a single sin, and lives a perfect moral life.[67]

---

67. I suppose that one could argue against the successful completion of the recurrence if the list of such choices were to become infinite in case P enjoyed an eternal earthly life, but incidentally, since in the Christian view death is the wages of *sin* (Rom 6:23), the cause of such an eternal earthly life would be precisely that which the argument aims to establish: the absence of sin in a possible world's earthly life of P.

But then the existence of that finally identified possible world means that though he failed in $W^0$, it was within P's actual power of will, all things being just as they were, to live a perfect, sinless life, thereby working himself to heaven. As Christians recognize, this doctrinal conclusion is part of the unorthodox outlook on humanity named Pelagianism, involving a denial of the doctrine of original sin.

In order to avoid this most inconvenient conclusion, a Christian must identify which premise in the above argument he rejects. His alternatives come down to:

#1. Rejecting the $PAP_{All}$

#2. Rejecting the assumption that P is morally responsible for his sins $S_i$, so that the $PAP_{All}$ no longer applies to them in the above recurrence. Unfortunately, that entails that P cannot be judged for his failure to live a sinless life, and since no special assumption was made about P, the reasoning can and must be applied to all humans, and that entails the doctrine of universalism. All sinners make it to heaven, because no one morally deserves judgment for failing to live a sinless life. Traditional Christians also recognize that option as unorthodox for denying the reality of the eschatological wrath of God (John 3:36) flowing from his righteousness, and which Jesus says will justly cause weeping and gnashing of teeth (Matt 8:12; 25:30).[68]

Or finally,

#3. Accepting the conclusion that it is within a fallen man's power of will to live an absolutely sinless life and hence work his way to heaven. That thesis is minimally a part of the unorthodox view of Pelagianism, and does not belong in a Christian anthropology, wherein we fallen descendants of Adam are children of wrath *by nature*, and not by accident (Eph 2:1-3). I should note that the precise definition of "Pelagianism" is not entirely uncontroversial, as Pelagius probably taught a constellation of related but different theses, not all of which need to be affirmed for one to qualify as "Pelagian." For example, Kevin Timpe focuses instead on the equally

---

68. I should add that my present case doesn't even presuppose the view that eschatological condemnation is eternal (though I take it to be biblical. Cf. Matt 25:46; 2 Thess 1:7–10; Heb 6:1–2; Rev 14:9–12). My argument goes through even if one is an annihilationist, because if humans are not morally responsible, then they don't deserve *any* condemnation—eternal or temporal—and hence nothing short of universalism will do for him who affirms the principle of alternate possibilities while denying that fallen humans are able to live a sinless life. And finally, even some versions of *universalism* are insufficient to evade the present argument, because a universalist who says all sinners are ultimately forgiven and covered by the atonement of Christ still affirms at least that the sinners were morally responsible in the first place, before being all forgiven. The present argument pushes one to the more radical view that no sinner ever was guilty in the first place: they were not morally responsible.

Pelagian thesis that humans can freely choose the good without any grace from God. Timpe takes it that his model successfully dodges the charge of Pelagianism if it satisfies the "anti-Pelagian constraint" which he carefully states as "No fallen human individual is able to cause or will any good, including the will of her coming to saving faith, apart from a unique grace."[69] I agree that this constraint is necessary to avoid charges of Pelagianism (and concede that Timpe's model satisfies it), but I dispute that it is sufficient for such, since one is still left with fallen sinners who out of their free will can full well live a perfect sinless life and gain heaven by their good works. That is still Pelagian.

Finally, coming back to universalism, it's important to note as well that not just any kind of universalism will do. The sort of universalism taught for example by Thomas Talbott[70] or Robin Parry[71] is insufficient here; it's still too orthodox. It maintains that all humans will eventually be *reconciled* to God for their sins, all of which they are nevertheless *culpable* for. Robin Parry maintains that "without divine redemptive grace, human beings (and creation as a whole) are doomed to futility. Do we deserve divine punishment? Yes."[72] But the $PAP_{All}$ leaves no room for even this: instead, it demands the sort of universalism taught by Derk Pereboom,[73] wherein all humans go to heaven *because none of them is responsible in the first place*; because failing to live a sinless life isn't something they're blameworthy for. Even those who teach eventual, universal reconciliation should recognize that this consequence of the $PAP_{All}$ is beyond the bounds of orthodoxy.

In conclusion, the true dilemma for Christian advocates of the $PAP_{All}$ (#1), is therefore universalism (#2), or Pelagianism (#3). In the event that both #2 and #3 are seen individually as too high a price to pay for traditional orthodox Christians, they must recognize that $PAP_{All}$ is false, so that no acceptable PAP can be marshaled against compatibilism.

## Incompatibilist responses and compatibilist rejoinders

What might an orthodox Christian incompatibilist do to salvage the $PAP_{All}$ and its attendant incompatibilism?

---

69. Timpe, *Philosophical Theology*, 13.
70. Talbott, "Universal Reconciliation."
71. Parry, "Universalist View."
72. Ibid., 105–6.
73. Pereboom, "Free Will, Evil, and Divine Providence," 320–21.

## Blaming today's sin on yesterday's

A first strategy adopted by incompatibilists in the literature consists in softening the PAP into a version that is more modest, more plausible, and less obviously Pelagian.

Kenneth Keathley proposes the following: "The fellow who robs a convenience store had the ability to refrain from doing so or in a previous will-setting moment had the ability to refrain. For that reason, he is morally responsible for his crime."[74] Alfred Mele acknowledges similar distinctions,[75] and Robert Kane includes this criterion as part of what he calls "Ultimate Responsibility":

> This condition of Ultimate Responsibility . . . does not require that we could have done otherwise . . . for *every* act done of our own free wills. But it does require that we could have done otherwise with respect to *some* acts in our past life histories by which we formed our present characters.[76]

He adds,

> Often we act from a will already formed, but it is "our own free will" by virtue of the fact that *we* formed it by other choices or actions in the past . . . for which we *could* have done otherwise.[77]

Let $PAP_{Past}$ be this principle that "a person is morally responsible for what he has done only if he could have done otherwise all things being just the way they were either in that instance, or at some relevant point in his past."[78] If this new and more modest $PAP_{Past}$ is true, it still follows that compatibilism is false because determinism permits neither of the two items in the disjunction sported by the $PAP_{Past}$: on determinism, the agent could (categorically) do otherwise neither on that instance nor on any other before it. The $PAP_{Past}$

---

74. Keathley, *Salvation and Sovereignty*, 88.

75. "For example, they [libertarians] can claim that an agent freely A-ed at *t* only if, at *t*, he could have done otherwise than A then or claim instead that an agent who could not have done otherwise at *t* than A then may nevertheless freely A at *t*, provided that he earlier performed some relevant free action or actions at a time or times at which he could have done otherwise than perform those actions." Mele, *Free Will and Luck*, 6.

76. Kane, "Libertarianism," 14.

77. Ibid., 15.

78. Van Inwagen acknowledges this qualification of the principle in van Inwagen, *Essay*, 161–62, and Ishtiyaque Haji introduces the same concept by distinguishing between what he calls a "directly free" action, and an "indirectly free" action. Haji, *Incompatibilism's Allure*, 43. Laura Ekstrom also offers a replacement to the PAP along those lines in Ekstrom, *Free Will*, 211.

would hence exclude moral responsibility on determinism, which is to say it entails that compatibilism is false. Since its conclusion has the same force, then, readjusting the $PAP_{All}$ into a $PAP_{Past}$ is a step in the right direction for incompatibilists, because even the most convinced libertarians recognize that at times, say an alcoholic can reach a point in his addiction where he literally no longer has the ability to refrain from drinking, or even more obviously, that if he's driving home drunk enough, he might very well have put himself in a situation where he literally no longer has the ability to avoid crashing into another driver's vehicle. At that point, even a proponent of a PAP of sorts will want to say that the sinner is still responsible, because he had the choice to refrain from drinking in the past, before alcohol got the best of him. While the $PAP_{All}$ is too blunt for this (and thus stands refuted by such easy counter-examples), the $PAP_{Past}$ yields the correct conclusion.

Unfortunately, the $PAP_{Past}$ will not solve the problem at hand for in-compatibilists attempting to shake off Pelagianism. Indeed, the above rea-soning by recurrence is just as effective with the $PAP_{Past}$ as it was with the $PAP_{All}$, because in each of the possible worlds $W^i$ under consideration, a PAP was applied exclusively to the supposed very first free-will sin in P's life. On those instances, even $PAP_{Past}$ either excludes moral responsibility or pro-duces the existence of the next possible world in the recurrence chain. Put another way, we cannot go back in time indefinitely, continuing to blame earlier free choices. Is the sinner morally responsible for his very first free-will sin? If he lacked the ability to refrain from the first sin, he is not morally guilty on this view, and we are back to universalism. If on the other hand he continually has the ability to refrain from committing a first sin, then he can live a sinless life, and we are back to Pelagianism.[79] Hence, despite its initial allure, the $PAP_{Past}$ offers its advocates no way out of the above dilemma.

It is worth noting here that in the literature, the $PAP_{Past}$ is also em-ployed to respond to a similar problem for the PAP that I chose not to press in the present work: the freedom of the glorified saints in heaven and the unrepentant in hell. Understanding that the former no longer have the abil-ity to sin, that the latter no longer have the ability to repent, and yet that all remain morally responsible, one can press them as rebutting defeaters of the unqualified PAP: at least some people are morally responsible while

79. So which of these two heresies does Keathley reject in the end? Pelagianism. He writes: "Soft libertarianism contends that though depravity makes sin inevitable, it does not make any particular sin necessary." *Salvation and Sovereignty*, 88. Essentially, he rejects Pelagianism, grants original sin, and says that we cannot avoid sinning. All that we can choose is which sin to indulge in. In other words, you *must* commit a sin, but you have a libertarian free will to pick which one you want. This is not a very liberating way of rejecting the compatibilism of Calvinists, but at any rate, by Keathley's own criterion, it would jettison moral responsibility and entail universalism.

lacking the ability to do otherwise.[80] The standard incompatibilist response is to posit something very much like the $PAP_{Past}$, affirming that the saints in heaven and the sinners in hell remain responsible based upon the fact that at some point in the past, they had the categorical ability to make different choices that would have avoided their present, unalterable condition. Thus Kevin Timpe and Timothy Pawl argue:

> On our view, while an agent must have alternative possibilities open to her at some time in order to be free, the agent need not always have alternative possibilities open to her. She may freely form her character such that she *can't* choose *not* to perform some particular action at a later time, and nevertheless do the latter action freely.[81]

The distinction is offered in similar terms by Joshua Rasmussen[82] and Paul Franks,[83] and I concede here that it is a coherent one to make. It is still not entirely without difficulties, because one may then ask what exactly happens at death, that the damned instantly lose the categorical ability to repent and the redeemed instantly lose their categorical ability to sin, but this in turn gets us into rather controversial discussions, which are entirely bypassed by my present argument as it simply focuses on the earthly lifespan of the fallen: they are blameworthy for their failure to live a perfect life, while lacking a categorical ability to do so, present *or past*.

### Implausible possibilities

One could offer another critique of my argument that would be as follows: all that the present argument shows is that $PAP_{All}$ makes sinless perfection "possible," as a matter of "mere" logical possibility, one could say, but that may not be a very *probable* possibility. It may even be an extremely *improbable* possibility, in light of environmental factors, and other influencing considerations one might offer. So someone committed to the $PAP_{All}$ might allow for the mere logical possibility of sinless perfection, and yet maintain that its extremely low probability renders it irrelevant; its high improbability makes it virtually impossible.

The problem with this response is that nothing in the present argument presupposes or requires that this possibility be in fact even remotely

---

80. See for example Cowan, "Sinlessness of the Redeemed," 416–31.

81. Pawl and Timpe, "Free Will in Heaven," 400.

82. "At least some of the goods in heaven depend for their existence on there being persons who *had* moral freedom." Rasmussen, "Freedom to Do Evil," 422.

83. See chapter 3, "Heaven," in Franks, "Rational Problem of Evil."

probable. Pelagianism does not call for probable and numerous sinless humans, but only for their sheer possibility. It asserts that sin is not *necessary*, which is to say that sinlessness is *possible* regardless of Adam's fall. Even one who asserts that there is *in fact* no such sinless descendant of Adam, but still maintains that there *could* be some who thus work their way to heaven without sin, is still Pelagian. The orthodox denial of Pelagianism is only achieved by one who affirms the biblical teaching that working one's way to heaven is *impossible*, not merely difficult, improbable or accidentally unattained. Accidental, contingent sinfulness still falls short of original sin. In light of original sin, there is no possible world (not even a few) in which a fallen descendant of Adam works his way to heaven. Biblically, fallen humans are *by nature* "children of wrath" (Eph 2:3); not by accident, however probable an accident it may be.

In any case, the problem will not go away by berating the "mere possibility" to do otherwise, since this possibility is the very thing that the PAP values so much and demands for moral responsibility. Like a bump in the carpet that is pushed down at one point only to reappear at another, the affirmation of "mere possibility" will inevitably come back and haunt him who tries to salvage the PAP while avoiding Pelagianism: if environmental considerations make sinless perfection virtually impossible, are then humans virtually irresponsible? This link instated by the PAP between moral responsibility and the possibility to do otherwise will not be severed half way through the argument, to affirm one and reject the other. The problematic connection must be thrown away altogether, and one who rejects Pelagianism must reject the PAP. Biblical anthropology must both maintain true—not merely virtual—*inability*, and true—not merely virtual—*responsibility*. Upholding these two means rejecting the PAP.

*Sinners who don't sin—readjusting original sin*

Another position that incompatibilist advocates of the PAP could take is one that attempts to maintain "original sin," but simply to "readjust" the doctrine, to accommodate its compatibility with the PAP. Let us clarify exactly what the stakes are.

Traditionally, the doctrine of "original sin" has been understood to encapsulate two distinct truth claims: 1. original guilt, and 2. original inclination. *Original guilt* is the claim that in virtue of Adam's sin, all of his descendants (except Jesus) stand morally guilty. According to this doctrine, regardless of their own personal sins, all humans stand legally condemned on the basis of Adam's sin; his sin is "imputed" to them; it brought moral guilt and legal condemnation on himself and on all his descendants (except Jesus). I should note that I personally have some reservations about the name "original guilt," since strictly speaking, I see "guilt" as referring to the quality of being morally responsible for an action that one actually committed, and as such, it cannot be transferred; rather, what I think is transferred on this view is the legal *debt* and moral *condemnation*, so that the affected party stands condemned *as if* he were himself personally guilty. But let's leave these minor linguistic issues aside, as the big idea of original guilt remains rather clear: Adam sins, and all stand legally condemned as a result.

*Original inclination*, on the other hand, is the related though distinct claim that in virtue of Adam's sin, all his descendants are born with a sinful *nature*; one that results in them all inevitably committing personal sins. This "original inclination" is a sort of handicap that prevents Adam's fallen descendants from living a perfect, sinless life.

With enthusiastically Reformed convictions, I take it that both doctrines—original guilt and original inclination—are true, important, and biblically taught at least in Romans 5 if nowhere else. They together form my understanding of what a solid view of original sin demands. This being said, not everyone may agree and understand original sin in this fashion. After all, there is no philosophically rigorous, agreed-upon definition in any inspired dictionary of theology, of exactly what "original sin" (itself an extrabiblical expression for a biblical teaching) should or should not include; so it is proper to see what can be said if theologians do make the jump and reject either of the above doctrines, whether or not they are prepared to reject all use of the phrase "original sin."

## Rejecting Original Guilt

The first of these to be rejected is usually original guilt. Arminians particularly have traditionally found it hard to accept that human beings may be morally condemned—in the sense of contracting legal guilt—for a sin that they did not personally commit. Wayne Grudem reports that "not all evangelical theologians, however, agree that we are counted guilty because of Adam's sin. Some, especially Arminian theologians, think this to be unfair of God and do not believe that it is taught in Romans 5."[84] The thought is confirmed by libertarian Paul Franks, who finds it "not likely that a broad free-will defense will succeed if one ascribes to original guilt,"[85] which is

---

another way of saying that original guilt is found to be incongruent with libertarian free will.

I should note that I myself don't believe the two are contradictory, nor jointly entail any contradiction. It seems to me perfectly consistent to affirm the imputation of Adam's guilt to all his descendants and maintain at the same time that their free will is libertarian. As a compatibilist Calvinist, I do reject libertarianism for a number of reasons, but my embrace of original guilt is not one of them. So why do libertarians tend to reject original guilt? I am not sure. Perhaps they feel like imputing guilt to unborn persons comes too close to a Calvinist doctrine of predestination or unconditional election? Maybe their libertarianism is premised on a sort of egalitarianism, according to which in order to possess free will we should not only start our lives with a level playing field, but with a blank sheet as well? I can only guess.[86] At any rate, it remains that for whatever reason, Arminianism is thought to be unfriendly toward original guilt. It has thus been judged attractive by libertarians to reject original guilt, deny that Adam's sin and guilt are imputed to his descendants, and instead hang the doctrine of original sin on original inclination alone. This is the route taken for example by Paul Copan,[87] Alvin Plantinga,[88] or Keith Wyma,[89] who all appear to affirm original sin understood as original inclination, but reject original guilt.[90]

In response to this view, it would certainly be edifying to offer an imperforate defense of original guilt, but this work is not the place for it, for two reasons. First, I don't know that I am able to do such a thing myself,[91]

---

86. As a matter of fact, one plausible guess is that original guilt is perceived to contradict the incompatibilist principle of alternate possibilities as well. Adam's sin is not something we could have prevented, so it is thought we cannot be guilty for it in the sense required by moral responsibility. But in fact, it is a different sense of guilt that is in view here. As I pointed out, the admittedly poorly named doctrine of original guilt doesn't claim that we truly *are* morally responsible for Adam's sin, only that the legal guilt for it is *imputed* or *transferred* to us, in the same sense that Jesus isn't really *guilty* of the sins of the elect, their guilt is only imputed to him. So I maintain that libertarianism and incompatibilism are both consistent with original guilt, and thus continue to find its rejection by Arminians unnecessary.

87. Copan, "Original Sin," 519–31 quoted in Franks, "Original Sin," 356.

88. Plantinga, *Warranted Christian Belief*, 207–9 quoted in Franks, "Original Sin," 356.

89. Wyma, "Innocent Sinfulness, Guilty Sin," 271–72.

90. While none of them seems to utilize both terms "original guilt" and "original inclination," Franks's exegesis of their writings leaves no doubt that their position is a clear affirmation of the latter and rejection of the former.

91. As mentioned above, I do maintain that original guilt is taught in Romans 5, in the sense that original guilt is the *best* interpretation of the passage; it enjoys the *most* support from the text. But it may not be the *only* possible interpretation; alternate

and second, for now, it suffices to see that this doctrine is not directly relevant to the present argument. All that was assumed in the above reasoning is that it is impossible for fallen human beings to live a perfect sinless life. That was thus an affirmation of original *inclination*, and would yield the exact same conclusion that PAP is false, whether or not fallen humans *additionally* contracted moral guilt in virtue of Adam's sin. Original *inclination*—not guilt—was shown above to exclude the PAP, and hence the position of Plantinga, Copan, and Wyma fails to avoid the conclusion that PAP is false since it stands refuted even by the modest truth of original inclination, a doctrine that they wish to maintain.

It is nevertheless interesting to note that these writers do aim to rescue the PAP, as they maintain that even though it is necessary that at least one sin be committed, no single particular instance of sin is necessitated. As Copan puts it, "we do not sin necessarily (that is, it is not assured that we must commit this or that particular sin), we sin inevitably (that is, in addition to our propensity to sin, given the vast array of opportunities to sin, we eventually do sin at some point)."[92] While no individual sin is necessitated, it is necessary that one sin or another be committed at one point or another. Making that exact point, Jerry Walls and David Baggett helpfully distinguish between (Q) "we can avoid all sin" (which they say is false), and (Q$_I$) "For any x, if x is a sin, then we can avoid x" (which they maintain is true). Their response to Calvinists who argue against PAP on the basis that fallen humans cannot avoid all sin is then to accuse them of equivocation on the word "all," allegedly confusing between (Q) and (Q$_I$).[93] This critique fails to apply to my above argument. I have not equivocated between (Q) and (Q$_I$), I have *demonstrated* by recurrence that (Q) follows from (Q$_I$), thereby establishing that their attempt to affirm (Q$_I$) and reject (Q) is incoherent. To illustrate the obvious point that not all properties of a part aggregate to a property of the whole (that is, after all, the straightforward fallacy of composition), they offer the following example, which I suppose they take to be analogous to our present case:

> In a restaurant, a friend, concerned about food allergies, might ask if we can eat everything on the menu; after glancing at it, we may affirm truthfully we can, without implying we're either

---

interpretations while less plausible are not entirely impossible, and hence while I believe Romans 5 is best interpreted to entail original guilt when teaching that "one trespass led to condemnation for all men" (v. 18), I don't necessarily know how to logically enforce this understanding with someone who is otherwise committed to its being impossible that Adam's guilt be imputed to us all.

92. Copan, "Original Sin," 519–31, quoted in Franks, "Original Sin," 356.

93. Baggett and Walls, *Good God*, 70.

able or willing to break the standing Guinness record for food consumption.[94]

Several responses must be made. First, the example itself is confusing, because *it* now equivocates on the words "can eat," meaning at one point "being able to eat without having an allergic reaction," and at another point "being able to eat without having an indigestion." They do need that shift in meaning, because the ability to eat any one item without having an allergic reaction *does* entail that one is able to eat the full menu without an allergic reaction,[95] just not without indigestion. Avoiding the equivocation, however, their simple point would have been made if they had only considered the indigestion and not the allergy. Indeed, being able to eat any single item on the menu without indigestion doesn't mean one can eat the whole menu without indigestion. So the question now becomes: is the indigestion case relevantly analogous to the case of living a sinless life? It demonstrably isn't. What eventually causes the indigestion is that every time the eater consumes one more item, it reduces his ability to eat another one after it, thereby entailing that he cannot consume the whole series. But no such diminution of ability exists in the case of the fallen man: every time a man avoids a sin, it obviously doesn't reduce his ability to avoid future sin; on the very contrary, the less one sins, the less prone to sin he will be! So this case is not relevantly analogous, and does nothing to undermine my above demonstration.

That this position of Plantinga, Copan, Walls, and Baggett is incoherent has therefore been demonstrated successfully: my above reasoning by recurrence established by *reductio* that PAP does inevitably entail that for any fallen descendant of Adam, there exists a possible world, directly accessible to him by the sheer use of his free will, wherein he lives a perfectly sinless life, in explicit contradiction of original inclination. Paul Franks, himself a libertarian, potently argues in a similar fashion that if one of these contemplated humans does happen to exploit positively all these alleged possibilities not to sin until his very last possible choice, then it follows that either his last sin is necessitated, or that sinning at all is not necessary after all.[96] Franks's true dilemma is sound, and equally establishes the incompatibility of original inclination with the PAP. Unfortunately, Franks proceeds to reject original inclination in that sense, whereas I take this doctrine to be true (and most biblical) and hence reject PAP instead, but all that matters for the question at hand is that PAP excludes original *inclination*, and hence

94. Ibid., 70–71.

95. This is assuming that there is no such thing as an allergy caused by a combination of items, neither of which is individually sufficient to cause the allergy.

96. Franks, "Original Sin," 358–68.

merely rejecting original guilt does nothing to avoid the force of the present argument: one who maintains the biblical teaching that a fallen descendant of Adam cannot live a perfectly sinless life must reject the PAP.

## TRADING ORIGINAL INCLINATION FOR TRANSWORLD DEPRAVITY

Given that original inclination still excludes the PAP even if one lets go of original guilt, PAP advocates have naturally proceeded to reject original inclination as well. Before I say a word against such a move, let me assess an interesting proposal that doesn't so much *reject* original inclination as it seeks to give a different (and I say problematic) *analysis* of this doctrine, in terms of what Alvin Plantinga called "transworld depravity." Plantinga introduced that interesting concept in the midst of his discussion of the problem of evil, as he tried to show that there is no internal contradiction in the Christian belief that God is perfectly good and all-powerful, while the world contains evil. Plantinga suggested that in virtue of libertarian free will, it may very well be the case that no matter what God did, no matter who God created, humans always *would* act immorally if left free in the libertarian sense: "Every world God can actualize is such that if Curley is significantly free in it, he takes at least one wrong action."[97] And for a man to be such that he *would* go wrong no matter what world God created (wherein the man is free with respect to at least one morally significant action) is to suffer from *transworld depravity*. Plantinga then cashed out the benefits of this hypothetical doctrine as follows: "what is important about the doctrine of transworld depravity is that if a person suffers from it, then it wasn't within God's power to actualize any world in which that person is significantly free but does no wrong."[98] Though I obviously dispute the assumption of libertarianism, it seems to me transworld depravity did the job just fine for Plantinga's immediate purpose vis-à-vis the problem of evil: if that doctrine were true of every possible person, it would indeed follow that God could not actualize worlds with free creatures in the libertarian sense and no evil. But when stating the doctrine, Plantinga added an interesting, parenthetical comment saying: "I leave as homework the problem of comparing transworld depravity with what Calvinists call 'total depravity.'"[99]

That homework assignment (or one closely related) was picked up by Michael Rea, who though he didn't mention total depravity, sought to apply transworld depravity to an analysis of original sin, and particularly of

97. Plantinga, *God, Freedom, and Evil*, 47.
98. Ibid., 48.
99. Ibid.

original inclination.[100] He contemplated the notion of transworld depravity, and made the following suggestion: "one option, then, for those interested in developing a theory of original sin under Molinist assumptions is to identify TWD [transworld depravity] with the sort of corruption that DOS [the doctrine of original sin] takes to be a consequence of the Fall."[101] Indeed, he notes that this condition is something humans would have from birth, that there is no reason to think humans couldn't have it as a consequence (in a sense) of Adam's sin, and if this doctrine were true, he says it would have the consequence that "being free and suffering from transworld depravity guarantees that one will fall into sin."[102] Does this move then properly account for original inclination while preserving the PAP? It does not in fact. On this view, Adam's sin does not guarantee that his fallen descendants will sin. Transworld depravity does guarantee that a given human will sin *if he suffers from the condition*, but his suffering from this malady is itself *not* guaranteed by the fall. Transworld depravity guarantees that humans will sin, *provided that the relevant counterfactuals are true*, namely those affirming that if placed in any possible world containing a free choice, the human *would* sin sooner or later. So transworld depravity guarantees that fallen humans will sin *given the truth of the relevant counterfactuals*, but those counterfactuals are *not* guaranteed by the fall. They are things over which Rea says we fallen humans still have full control, "for any counterfactual of freedom C that is true of [a person] P, P has the power to prevent C from being (or having been) true of her"[103] and hence we perfectly *could* do otherwise than sin. It just so happens that we *wouldn't*, *if* we are transworld-depraved. But that, too, is entirely within our power to avoid, he says: "refraining from sin would keep us from suffering from TWD [transworld depravity]."[104] On the upside, Rea maintains the second contention of my argument to the effect that "refraining from sin is clearly something that we can be blamed for not doing,"[105] but we now see that his proposal, though interesting, doesn't rescue original inclination, the inability of fallen humans to live a perfectly sinless life. Therefore, no matter what other merits transworld depravity may possibly have in discussing the problem of evil with atheists, it is not a successful account of original sin minimally understood as including original inclination; it is instead an inevitable rejection of it.

100. Rea, "Metaphysics of Original Sin," 319–56.
101. Ibid., 350.
102. Ibid.
103. Ibid., 348.
104. Ibid., 350.
105. Ibid.

### Rejecting Original Inclination

Since the PAP still stands refuted by the doctrine of original inclination, PAP advocates have naturally come to reject it as well. What then can be said against such a move? Not only do they do so, but they also bring in some additional, independent considerations to *undermine* original inclination. Let us consider these first.

### What if Adam Could?

A first objection, we can imagine, would point out that sinless perfection is not such an utter impossibility after all, since Adam in his pre-lapsarian nature could have refrained from sin altogether. If Adam could have done it, then there exists a possible world wherein at least one human accomplishes sinless perfection.

The problem with this objection is that it misplaces the strictly post-lapsarian boundaries of Pelagianism and its orthodox rejection. On the orthodox view, it is not just *any* sinless perfection that is said to be impossible—Jesus was a sinless human, after all—rather, it is that of a *fallen* human. What is impossible is for a *fallen* descendant of Adam to work his way to heaven without sinning. There is no possible world wherein a *fallen* person works his way to heaven. But the existence of possible worlds wherein Adam does not sin, or possible worlds wherein not all humans are fallen, or even no fallen human exists, do nothing (if they exist) to undermine the present argument. All the argument affirms is that *fallen* humans are morally responsible for sinning, even though original sin excludes their categorical ability to do otherwise.

As a matter of fact, for him who maintains theological determinism, even Adam did not have that alleged categorical ability to do otherwise than fall. On this view, God's decree ensured that Adam would sin, and he did not have a libertarian ability to do otherwise than sin. Of course Arminians will reject that, but it shows that determinists are not even wedded to seeing Adam's sinless life as a categorical possibility, and this separate contention is no part of the present argument, with respect to which Adam's case is irrelevant. It matters not what they think of Adam, Arminians who reject Pelagianism *are* minimally committed to the fact that *fallen* humans cannot work their way to heaven without sinning, and that is all the argument requires. The PAP does not qualify the kind of person it applies to, so it can and must be applied to all humans, fallen or not. What may or may not follow when applying it to non-fallen ones does nothing to undermine what does follow from applying it to fallen ones. When applied to fallen humans, as was established above, it yields the conclusion of Pelagianism or universalism, and hence is demonstrably false for him who remains orthodox on these two doctrines.

## Death of Infants Before They Get to Sin

Another objection to original inclination might be the fact that some children, at least infants, almost certainly die before they ever get to commit a single personal sin of their own. If that is so, it shows that it is possible after all, at least for some, even fallen humans, to live a life void of personal sins, thereby refuting original inclination. The response of the previous counterargument just above is no longer available, because we are now talking about *fallen* humans. These are fallen descendants of Adam, who still live a life void of personal sins. Couldn't they accordingly be brought forward as positive evidence against original inclination?

I think not. This objection to original inclination is not hard to refute. All it calls for is a very modest, plausible, and most reasonable qualification of one's definition of the doctrine of original inclination. If one states original inclination merely to be the brute impossibility that there be no personal sins in the timespan of any fallen person's life whatsoever, then infant deaths contradict it indeed. But it seems most reasonable and certainly coherent to qualify original inclination as follows: "original inclination guarantees that a fallen descendant of Adam will commit personal sins in this life *as long as his life is not prematurely (in a certain sense) cut short.*"

A few comments are in order. First, this qualification raises the difficult question of what counts as a "premature" death in the relevant sense, and this question promises to be hard to answer with precision, because in some sense, *all* deaths are "unnatural" and "premature."[106] But I think that without a full philosophical treatise on the matter, it can be conceded by all parties that there is an easily grasped difference between an infant killed in a car accident and a ninety year old dying in his bed. Just where the relevant frontier lies between the two I do not always know, but two things are clear: 1. there is such a threshold, and 2. the fallen descendants of Adam who die in infancy and are presently brought forward as a counterexample, belong in the category of the premature deaths.

Secondly, this qualification should not be seen as an afterthought conjured up to conveniently avoid an unforeseen counterargument. It is not

---

106. And in yet another sense, if determinism is true, then *no* death is ever "premature" inasmuch as they occur exactly when God ordained that they should occur. But this is not the sense of "premature" that is in view here.

a case of last minute special pleading in the face of an otherwise potent objection. Why is it not so? Because the very notion of "original inclination" bore from the start the unspoken assumption that an "inclination" requires an *opportunity* in order to express itself. It is rather obvious that our fallen nature, even if it should guarantee that we sin given a single opportunity to do so, just cannot bring this about if absolutely no such opportunity is given. It seems therefore most reasonable to qualify original inclination by demanding the condition that one fallen human's life not be prematurely interrupted before original inclination can kick in and entail that it is impossible for it to be void of sin.

Finally, I shall confirm that with this most reasonable qualification in place, the PAP still fails to uphold original inclination. The PAP cannot be salvaged through the loophole of this modest caveat, because the sort of alternate possibilities demanded by the PAP are ones brought about by the free activity of a human's will; the ability to avoid a sin must be one rooted in the inner character and decision-making faculties of an agent, not in the contingencies of the outside world. Daniel Hill points out that "an incompetent would-be evildoer whose bungled attempts at evil backfire into doing good" is not morally praiseworthy.[107] Indeed, what the PAP demanded for moral responsibility was an ability to "do otherwise," or "choose otherwise," not an opportunity to be struck dead. The PAP, as argued above, entails the ability to live a perfect life because one is *performing* better in the alternate possible world, not because he is killed before dropping the ball. In other words, if the only way to prevent Jones from sinning is to kill Jones, Jones suffers from original inclination indeed. The premature death of sinners (be they infants) who may fail to commit personal sins is thus irrelevant to the truth of original inclination.

Original inclination is therefore seen to resist the charge of the two above objections, but there are still those who might reject it, whether for reasons of their own I was not able to anticipate myself, or simply because they find original inclination less probable than the PAP itself. What then can be said against this move?

*LETTING GO OF ORTHODOXY*

As stated from the onset, the present argument was *premised* on the supposed acceptation of traditional, fairly essential, orthodox doctrines of the Christian faith, namely particularism and original sin. Therefore, the biblical *defense* of the latter—understood as including at least original inclination if

107. Hill, *Maximal Greatness*, 205.

not original guilt—is not a primary goal of this argument, but a few words can still be said for those who may be tempted to reject it. What then is wrong in doing so?

For one, the biblical text strongly supports original inclination. Christians who make the jump and reject this doctrine can no longer properly account for the biblical teaching of fallen humanity's outright inability to do good, and the universality of human sin, condemnation, guilt, and need for atonement which follow from this inability. If it were possible for some to live a life void of personal sin, how would they be included in the universal biblical assertions that "*all* have sinned and fall short of the glory of God" (Rom 3:23), that "one trespass led to condemnation for *all* men" (Rom 5:18), that "death spread to *all* men because *all* sinned" (Rom 5:12), or that "they have *all* turned aside; together they have become corrupt; there is *none* who does good, *not even one*" (Ps 14:3)? "There is no one who does not sin" (1 Kgs 8:46).

It will not do to say that humans *can* avoid sinning but merely *don't*, or just *happen* not to. Certainly, in strict terms of modal logic, the biblical statements above do not affirm explicitly "universal sinfulness is true in this world *and* true in every possible world wherein Adam sins and causes the curse"; they only speak of the current actual world, but are we to understand that even given Adam's sin and its ensuing curse, universal sinfulness is only an accidental, contingent truth of the actual world? Scripture doesn't permit such a reading: we are not told that fallen humans have the categorical ability to be perfectly righteous and simply happen not to be; we are told that they lack the ability altogether. Until the Spirit comes to regenerate a fallen, spiritually dead person, his mind is "set on the flesh," "hostile to God," "does not submit to God's law, indeed it *cannot*. Those who are in the flesh *cannot* please God" (Rom 8:7-8) and they "*cannot* come to the Son" until drawn by the Father (John 6:37, 44). The natural person *cannot* understand the things of the Spirit of God (1 Cor 2:14). Just as the bad tree *cannot* bear good fruit (Matt 7:15-20), so the unregenerate heart cannot produce good works. "Then who can be saved? . . . All things are possible with God," Jesus proclaims, but with man, it is not *difficult* or *improbable*, it is *impossible* (Mark 10:26-27).

And secondly, a full-blown rejection of both original guilt and original inclination must now reasonably be seen as an inevitable embrace of a Pelagian view with a denial of original sin. What sense of original sin remains for one who rejects both original guilt and original inclination? What does original sin do, if it neither declares one guilty nor even prevents one from living a perfectly sinless life? If we suppose that in defiance of original inclination, some succeeded in living a sin-less life, how then would they still need Christ's atonement?

Paul Franks suggests that these possible non-sinning descendants of Adam would still face a gap, a "chasm" in their relationship with God who would "resent" them because of Adam, even though they are not *guilty* of anything.[108] Using Copan's phrase from a similar context, he argues there could still be a sort of "stain" of original sin, a "deformity" of the soul, "that the atonement of Christ can graciously heal."[109] This is becoming hard to refute as it speculates on what would be the case in a situation very unlike ours, but maybe the best one can say is that this falls short of the biblical function of the atonement: Adam's descendants stand condemned and undergo the wrath of God because of *sin* (whether Adam's or theirs), not because of a guiltless "chasm," nor an innocent "deformity." Eschatological judgment is a legal *condemnation* (Rom 5:18; 8:1). It is a righteous *judgment* of a guilty party (2 Cor 5:10). A mere "chasm" or a mere "deformity" does not call for the *forgiveness* of an individual (Col 1:14). It does not demand a wrath-appeasing *propitiation* (Rom 3:25; 1 John 2:2; 4:10); it does not demand a nailing of sins on the cross (Col 2:14).

At this point, one sees an interesting irony arising with the dilemma facing this view: proponents of the PAP who reject original inclination still must (and hence would like to) maintain the universal need for redemption and atonement. But what would those humans who allegedly live a life void of sin, need a sin-atonement for? The only way to maintain their guilty status and need for atonement if they have never committed personal sins is ironically to come back and re-affirm original guilt! One who affirms original guilt could say that an individual who happens to live a life void of personal sins still bears the imputed guilt of Adam's sin in virtue of which atonement and forgiveness are legally necessary. But are incompatibilist PAP advocates prepared to resurrect the doctrine of original guilt that was found so distasteful and jettisoned in the first place? If one comes to reject original inclination, typically, original guilt is already long gone. And yet those most inclined to deny imputation of guilt are those who most need it now to rescue universal sinfulness while rejecting original inclination. But in the war waged between original sin and Arminianism, original guilt is typically the first casualty, long before the credentials of original inclination are even inspected, so it is very doubtful that we would find any incompatibilist advocate of the PAP who strains out the gnat of original inclination while swallowing the camel of original guilt.

108. Franks, "Original Sin," 369–70.
109. Copan, "Original Sin," 530.

For these reasons, and whatever one thinks about original guilt, then, an orthodox account of original sin must include original inclination, and hence allow the present argument to yield its conclusion that PAP is absurd, for entailing either universalism or Pelagianism, neither of which belongs in orthodox Christian theology.

## *"Why then the law?"*

Having argued that humans are morally responsible for sinning while unable to do otherwise, another important objection calls for answers. It is one based on the *purpose* of moral laws, or the lack thereof. David Copp argues that the purpose of a moral command is to bring about obedience to the command; the "hope," or "intent" of the commander is that the command would be followed. He writes: "Any moral theory must somehow account for, or make room for, the intuition that there is a *point* to requiring an action, namely, crudely, to get it done."[110]

But if PAP is false, then we have a set of moral commands on our hands, which are categorically impossible to keep. Consequently, they would be purposeless according to Copp (at least minimally on a divine command theory of ethics), as "There would be no point in God's commanding an agent to do something that the agent could not do."[111] And of course we all presumably agree that God's moral law is in fact *not* purposeless, from which it would follow that PAP is true by *modus tollens*. What then is a compatibilist to respond?

This objection may or may not initially have much of an intuitive pull, but its refutation is surely not difficult. First, because it is not too hard to think of a possible, decent candidate for a moral law's purpose besides its being kept and obeyed; but secondly and remarkably, because compatibilists don't even have to conjure up the answer themselves, as this is yet another objection that the Bible itself anticipates for them: "Why then the law?" Paul anticipated that this objection would be raised against the true preaching of the gospel of grace, and his answer is one of the glorious biblical truths recovered in the protestant Reformation and championed by Martin Luther:

> "By the Law is knowledge of sin," says Paul (Rom 3.20). He does not say: *abolition*, or *avoidance*, of sin. The entire design and power of the law is just to give knowledge, and that of nothing but of sin; not to display or confer any power . . . by the words of the law, man is admonished and taught, not what he can do, but

110. Copp, "'Ought' Implies 'Can,'" 272.
111. Ibid.

> what he ought to do; that is, that he may know his sin, not that
> he may believe that he has any strength.[112]

As Luther quotes above from Romans, "through the law comes knowledge of sin" (Rom 3: 20). Paul testifies, "If it had not been for the law, I would not have known sin" (Rom 7:7). And Galatians provides the final blows to this objection:

> Why then the law? It was added because of transgressions.
> (Gal 3:19)

> If a law had been given that could give life, then righteousness would indeed be by the law. But the scripture imprisoned everything under sin, so that the promise by faith in Jesus Christ might be given to those who believe. (Gal 3:21–22)

> The law was our guardian until Christ came, in order that we might be justified by faith. (Gal 3:24)

Counterintuitive as it may be, God gave us a law that we cannot possibly keep. Not so that we could think that we can, but so that we would know our sin, repent, and be saved by God's grace alone, through faith alone in Christ alone, to God's glory alone.

---

112. Luther, *Bondage of the Will*, 158–59.

# A final few worries and conclusions on moral responsibility

## Conclusion on the principle of alternate possibilities and incompatibilism

In the previous chapters, I have argued that principles of alternate possibilities are not all created equal. Prone to equivocations, they need to be specified with care before they can serve to draw any conclusion about the falsity of compatibilism. I have argued that no such incompatibilist principle has been successfully established, and beyond this failure, I have offered two independent positive arguments to reject the incompatibilist version of the principle. First, this version excludes the coherent coexistence of impeccability and praiseworthiness, a problematic conflict even for atheist moral systems, although the problem is magnified for a Christian according to whom both attributes are exemplified by God himself. And secondly, it entails a true dilemma for orthodox Christians: face the ugly specter of Pelagianism on the one hand, or that of an equally problematic universalism on the other. For the orthodox Christian who maintains God is impeccable and praiseworthy, and who rejects both Pelagianism and universalism, the incompatibilist principle of alternate possibilities must be abandoned. For these reasons, the PAP was found to be not merely unproven, but demonstrably false, and since it was seen that incompatibilism entailed PAP, it established by two different routes that incompatibilism is false for him who remains orthodox on these two doctrines.

## The direct argument for incompatibilism

Before moving on to the second grand argument against Calvinist determinism, a final argument for incompatibilism needs to be addressed. Anticipating that dissenters would likely find fault with the principle of alternate possibilities, van Inwagen separately attempted to reformulate the contention of his consequence argument in a way that would no longer appeal to the PAP. This gave rise to a "direct argument" for incompatibilism.[1] Interestingly, this direct argument exhibits the exact same structure as the third formulation of the consequence argument, with the difference that the operator N is now redefined so as not to involve the concept of alternate choice or alternate possibility. Van Inwagen now defines $Np$ as follows: "$p$, and no one is or ever has been, even partly responsible for the fact that $p$." With N thus defined, the argument's form remains as it was in the third formulation of the consequence argument (with rules $\alpha$ and $\beta$ respectively renamed A and B for the occasion).

A. $\Box p \vdash Np$

B. $N(p \supset q), Np \vdash Nq$

Van Inwagen uses these two rules, similarly to how he did in the consequence argument, to argue that no one is morally responsible about the distant past, and since no one is morally responsible about the fact that the past entails our present actions on determinism, no one is morally responsible for their present actions if determinism is true.

1. $\Box ((P_0 \& L) \supset P)$   (statement of determinism)

2. $\Box (P_0 \supset (L \supset \supset))$   (follows from (1))

3. $N (P_0 \supset (L \supset P))$   (follows from (2) and (A))

4. $N P_0$   (new premise)

5. $N (L \supset P)$   (follows from (3), (4), and (B))

6. $N L$   (new premise)

7. $N P$   (follows from (5), (6), and (B))

The conclusion in (7) is an affirmation that no one is or ever has been even partly responsible for the fact that P, which, since no special assumption was made about P, means that no one is or ever has been even partly responsible for anything. Moreover, in this direct form, there is no longer any possible equivocation in the argument's use of the word "choice," raising (as the consequence argument did) the question of whether it should be understood categorically or conditionally, since it no longer even mentions the concept of choice. The argument thus can't be faulted for that, and compatibilists must deal with its assertions about moral responsibility directly. What then is wrong with this new argument?

First, the principle N is much too strong, because it doesn't exclude God. Stated as it is, $Np$ requires that *no one*—not even God—is or ever has

1. Van Inwagen, *Essay*, 183–85.

been even partly responsible for $p$. But then premise (4) is obviously false on theism: it is not the case that $N\,P_0$. Just because one goes back far enough into the past that one reaches a point in time when humans were not around, it doesn't secure that *no one* was there to be responsible for the state of the world at that time: God was. As the creator and ruler of the universe, it is quite clear that God is at least partially responsible for $P_0$. Therefore premise (4) is false, and this version of the direct argument is a non-starter.

But one may insist that this weakness in the original argument may easily be fixed, by restricting the principle N to humans. I agree. One could (and should) restate principle N so that N$p$ would stand for something like "$p$, and no human is or ever has been, even partly responsible for the fact that $p$." With that version of N, the conclusion of the direct argument in (7), N P, is still inacceptable, and thus calls for a response by compatibilists. So let us assess this move, and ask: if one adopted this modified, more modest definition for principle N, or one very much like it, what then would be wrong with the direct argument?

For one, rule A is false. There is no reason to think that if $p$ is necessary, then no one (or even no human) is or ever has been even partly responsible for the fact that $p$. To support the inference, van Inwagen offers the following considerations:

> The validity of rule (A) seems to me to be beyond dispute. No one is responsible for the fact that $49 \times 18 = 882$, for the fact that arithmetic is essentially incomplete, or, if Kripke is right about necessary truth, for the fact that the atomic number of gold is 79.[2]

And of course compatibilists agree that no one is morally responsible for these three necessary truths, which involve neither moral choices, nor even human actions. But from this it obviously does not follow that agents could not be morally responsible for *other* truths that do exhibit moral choices and actions, be they necessary. Rule A is therefore neither proven, nor, I say, "beyond dispute." Stephen Kearns has offered a number of convincing counter-examples to it,[3] and I add once again that if one doesn't exclude God from principle N as I suggested above, Rule A stands refuted by the above argument I offered, based upon divine praiseworthiness and impeccability. It is necessary that "God never acts unrighteously," and yet it is false that "no one is or ever has been, even partly responsible for the fact that God never acts unrighteously"; God is praiseworthy for his

2. Ibid., 184.
3. Kearns, "Responsibility for Necessities," 307–24.

impeccable righteousness. It is necessary, and God is morally responsible for it. Rule A is false.

This being said, this rejection of rule A, while important, is not all that interesting vis-à-vis the direct argument, since the rule was here again only used to support the inference from (2) to (3), and I happen to think (3) isn't the problem of this argument. With its formulation of operator N that refers directly to human moral responsibility, I think it is rule B that is now false, and must be rejected by compatibilists in response to the direct argument. With B false, the conclusion (7) no longer follows from premises (5) and (6), making the direct argument a *non-sequitur*. So we must ask: is this rejection of rule B permitted? Rule B, assuming we exclude God from the principle as I suggested, states that if no human is responsible for the fact that $p$, and no human is responsible for the fact that $p$ entails $q$, then no human is responsible for the fact that $q$. That rule has no purchase on compatibilists, inasmuch as they maintain that humans are morally responsible for their free actions, which God from eternity past decreed that they would perform freely in a compatibilist sense. Calvinists very much maintain that humans are not responsible for the past fact that God decreed their actions (for indeed, how could they be personally morally responsible for something *God* did?), and that humans are not responsible for the fact that if God decreed their actions, then they would perform these actions; but they do maintain that humans are responsible for their actions. So we have N$p$ and N($p \supset q$), but not N$q$. I thus maintain that Rule B is false, and its use as a premise in this context is question-begging, since no argument is offered as to why these compatibilist beliefs are incoherent.

But as a matter of fact, we no longer even need to leave this response as a mere charge of begging the question; we are now at a point where several positive arguments have been offered to *establish* that Rule B is false. First, if we don't exclude God from principle N, problems arise once again when applying Rule B to God and the uncontroversial fact—determined from eternity past in virtue of the divine nature—that God cannot act unrighteously. God is not morally responsible for having the nature that he has, since this fact ($p$) is not something God himself brought about. But neither is God responsible for the fact that if he has the nature that he has, then he will never act unrighteously; that consequence ($q$) just follows straightforwardly from impeccability being part of God's nature. And yet God *is* morally responsible for never acting unrighteously: he is praiseworthy for the gloriously righteous actions that he performs. So we have N$p$ and N($p \supset q$), but not N$q$. Rule B is false. Similarly, and this time even with the reformulated version of N to only include humans, let's once again try to apply Rule B to fallen human beings and their being born with original inclination

($p$), which entails their inability to live a sinless life ($q$). A fallen human is not morally responsible for the fact that he is born with original inclination; that is a state of affairs he did not personally bring about, a condemnation resulting from the fall which predated his birth. But neither is he morally responsible for the fact that if he suffers from original inclination then he will fail to live a perfectly sinless life. That is what original inclination is. And yet he *is* morally responsible (i.e., blameworthy) for this failure of his, so that we once again have N$p$, N($p \supset q$), and not N$q$. Rule B is false.

Of course these two arguments of mine were seen to presuppose fairly central *Christian* doctrines, and so may not work against just any proponent of the direct argument, but then it will remain that rule B, if not shown false, is at least question-begging, which of course suffices for declaring an argument's failure. In conclusion, the direct argument is unsuccessful to establish incompatibilism, a thesis I have now argued is false on independent Christian grounds.

## The much sought-after sufficient condition for moral responsibility and how it is still missing

On a number of occasions above in the present work, various criteria were encountered, which exclude moral responsibility (coercion, manipulation, mental illness, a conditional inability to do otherwise, etc.). It means that they specify (by their absence) *necessary* conditions for an agent to be morally responsible for a given action. However, none of those conditions was ever declared or admitted to be *sufficient* for moral responsibility. Having encountered a number of them, the question naturally comes to be asked: can we now provide a *sufficient* condition for moral responsibility? Can we offer a nice and tight criterion such that if an agent does satisfy it, then it follows that the agent is morally responsible? At the present time, I sorrowfully confess that I cannot. I suspect that my above criterion of "acting upon one's God-given character and desires" or something like it might come close, but I am not prepared to say it wouldn't admit counterexamples if seen as a sufficient condition for moral responsibility. So at this point, I do not claim to have such a criterion ready at hand, to be used as a rule in all cases to assess the moral responsibility of an agent. Instead, all I can do is comment on the three following questions: 1. "is it disappointing?" 2. "is it surprising?" and 3. "is it bad?"

## Is it disappointing?

The answer to this first question I think has to be yes. It would be a disingenuous impassibility to pretend we didn't wish such a sufficient condition were in our possession. Would it not be wonderful to hold an airtight, simple, logically sufficient condition that serves to declare in any and all cases, that an agent is in fact morally responsible? I think it would. Falling short of this ideal has to be a bit disappointing for knowledge-thirsty philosophers. The struggle is perfectly captured by John Martin Fischer. He comes back to the shortcoming of "conditional analyses," which were discussed in chapter 5. There, we concluded that for an agent to be morally responsible, it was necessary that he have the conditional ability to do otherwise (this principle, we called $PAP_{If}$). While this condition was seen to be *necessary* for moral responsibility, I contended that it is *not sufficient*, nor did it ever try to be. Given this evident shortcoming of the criterion, Fischer reflects on the need to provide additional criteria, which, together with this condition, *would* in fact constitute a sufficient condition for moral responsibility. He writes:

> Some compatibilists about freedom and causal determinism have given up on the conditional analysis in light of such difficulties. Others have sought to give a more refined conditional analysis. So we might distinguish between the generally discredited "simple" conditional analysis, and what might be called the "refined" conditional analysis. Different philosophers have suggested different ways of refining the simple analysis, but the basic idea is somehow to rule out the factors that uncontroversially (that is, without making any assumptions that are contentious within the context of an evaluation of the compatibility of causal determinism and freedom) render an agent unable to choose (and thus unable to act). Along these lines, one might try something like this: An agent S can do X just in case (i) if S were to try to do X, S would do X, and (ii) the agent is not subject to clandestine hypnosis, subliminal advertising, psychological compulsion resulting from past traumatic experiences, direct stimulation of the brain, neurological damage due to a fall or accident, and so forth . . .
>
> An obvious problem with the refined analysis is the "and so forth . . ." It would seem that an indefinitely large number of other conditions (apparently heterogeneous in nature) could in principle be thought to issue in the relevant sort of incapacity. Additionally, there should be a certain discomfort in countenancing as part of the analysis a list of disparate items with no explanation of what ties them together as a class; from a

philosophical point of view, condition (ii) posits an unseemly miscellany. How could one evaluate a proposed addition to the list in a principled way?[4]

Fischer's concerns are heartfelt and probably widely shared. We would love to avoid that "unseemly miscellany," and express a simple condition that ties all of these necessary conditions together into a sufficient one. So our present inability to do so remains a bit frustrating; but is it really surprising?

## Is it surprising?

The desire to put our hands on this golden list of conditions, which together are sufficient to positively entail that an agent is morally responsible, must at present remain frustrated. But was it a reasonable expectation to begin with? It is not clear at all that if such a condition exists we should be able to find and formulate it succinctly. After all, moral responsibility is a rather complex matter. Why should we expect to find a one-size-fits-all, necessary and sufficient condition that encapsulates all moral cases in one fell swoop? A way to appreciate this in the present field of ethics is to contemplate its counterpart in the field of aesthetics. I suggest that the beautiful, like the good, is complex enough to analyze philosophically, that even though we directly apprehend both these realms in human experience, and can identify some principles that appear to govern them, we shouldn't expect to encapsulate any and all such principles into philosophically air-tight, necessary and sufficient conditions. When considering the beauty of a painting, it is much easier (and at times painfully obvious) to point out some features that exclude beauty (a clashing color, blasphemous tones, crassness, etc.) than to specify all the features, which together suffice for the painting to be beautiful.[5] How would one specify that? Rather, we may hold a disparate collection of conditions, which are necessary for beauty, while lacking a fully specified sufficient condition for guaranteeing that a painting is indeed beautiful. In a comparable way, we hold a number of items that exclude moral responsibility if present, but (so far at least I) lack a fully specified sufficient condition for guaranteeing moral responsibility. In that sense,

4. Fischer, "Compatibilism," 51.

5. One might object that the beauty of a painting remains a subjective call. I do assume here a view in which aesthetic judgments no less than moral judgments are true, objective, and anchored in God's nature, but my analogy does not hang or fall on this presupposition. Indeed, even if the conditions for beauty were to be subjective, and vary from an individual to the next, it would remain the case that for any one given individual, such conditions exist, and exhibit the parallel features with moral judgments, which I am pointing out here.

ethical judgments are similar to aesthetic judgments, and we ought not be so surprised that this golden list is still missing from our analysis. But one may still wonder: how problematic is it nonetheless?

# Is it bad?

## Is it bad for compatibilist philosophy?

First, we want to know if this shortcoming is bad for compatibilism. Is the failure to identify this simple sufficient criterion only a problem for compatibilists and thus a possible motivation to reject compatibilism? The answer is no. The difficulties of this philosophical analysis will have to be shared by incompatibilists as well, because the condition "an agent's choice is undetermined" which I argued was not *necessary* for moral responsibility, is neither *sufficient* for it. Remember the possibility of undetermined though coerced choices for example, or undetermined choices made under influencing manipulation, neither of which would be morally responsible, though they are undetermined. Whether one phrases the condition in terms of indeterminism or in terms of a categorical ability to do otherwise, this condition does not seem to suffice for moral responsibility, and we see that incompatibilist philosophers no less than compatibilists must toil to refine their analysis of the attempted sufficient condition; an analysis which is not necessarily simpler than their compatibilist counterparts. Appreciate libertarian Robert Kane's formulation of what he calls "Ultimate Responsibility," and which even he says is merely *necessary*, leaving the door open to yet more conditions being piled on to constitute his sufficient criterion for moral responsibility:

> A willed action is "up to the agent" in the sense required by free will only if the agent is ultimately responsible for it in the following sense.
>
> (UR) An agent is *ultimately responsible* for some (event or state) E's occurring only if (R) the agent is personally responsible for E's occurring in a sense which entails that something the agent voluntarily (or willingly) did or omitted, and for which the agent could have voluntarily done otherwise, either was, or causally contributed to, E's occurrence and made a difference to whether or not E occurred; and (U) for every X and Y (where X and Y represent occurrences of events and/or states) if the agent is personally responsible for X, and if Y is an *arche* (or sufficient

ground or cause or explanation) for X, then the agent must also be personally responsible for Y.[6]

Whether or not Kane's analysis is *true*, it is likely not *simpler* than whatever list compatibilists could produce. The disagreement on the question of whether determinism excludes moral responsibility evidently does not put incompatibilists in a better shape (at least with respect to simplicity) to formulate this golden list of conditions, and hence compatibilism is not (at least at the present moment) worse off than its alternative because of this admitted shortcoming.

## Is it bad for practical life?

Ultimately, one desirable value of holding such criteria would be in their application to real-life cases. In everyday life, we want to be able to assess whether or not a person is morally responsible. So for this purpose, is the absence of a practically assessable sufficient condition for moral responsibility crippling us in the making of proper judgment calls? Admittedly, it would certainly be better to have it, but I do not think our outlook is too grim. On the positive side, what we do have is a number of items, which we do know *exclude* moral responsibility. So philosophically, we can simply go on building up this list of such items whenever we discover them, until maybe one day they cover all the bases and do constitute a sufficient measuring rod for asserting that an agent is in fact morally responsible (whether or not we are aware that they do). For our immediate real-life purposes, however, until that time comes if it ever does, it is not unreasonable to consider that an agent is morally responsible for his choices unless he exhibits one of the criteria that we presently do know figure on that list. In that sense, morally responsible free choices are seen as the default position when agents act; they are the normal use case intended by our creator in granting us the ability to make choices. This is in general what we mean when saying "humans have free will," or "God gave humans free will." Humans "normally" make free choices for which they are responsible, *unless* they find themselves in the unfortunate situation of lacking one of our necessary conditions. That we do not know how to specify philosophically their all-encompassing, exhaustive conjunction no more prevents us from identifying them individually when we encounter them, than our inability to specify philosophically sufficient conditions for beauty prevents us from identifying ugliness when we see it. While it may disappoint us ambitious philosophers, not having a nice and tight sufficient

---

6. Kane, *Significance*, 72.

condition for moral responsibility does not impair practical judgments (and correspondingly judicial decisions) in real life so much.

In conclusion, our failure to identify a simple sufficient condition for moral responsibility should not surprise us, does not count against compatibilism, and does not impede practical life. In short, it is not really a problem.

## Conclusion on determinism and moral responsibility

In conclusion, the following has been argued with respect to determinism and moral responsibility:

Various incompatibilist arguments have been refuted: the "no free will / no choice" argument, the "pets and puppets" argument, the coercion argument, the manipulation argument, the mental illness argument, and the direct argument.

The so-called principle of alternate possibilities was assessed in two different versions. In its version calling for categorical ability ($PAP_{All}$) it was found to be incompatible with determinism but unproven, and in its conditional form ($PAP_{If}$) it was found to be true but compatible with determinism.

Upon securing this conclusion, a few criticisms of the so-called "conditional analysis" of freedom were surveyed, and all were found invalid, for exhibiting misplaced expectations.

Two independent arguments were then offered to refute the PAP in its incompatibilist form ($PAP_{All}$). Frankfurt-style cases were seen to be unsuccessful at doing so, but it was argued first that $PAP_{All}$ stood refuted by the coherence of a God who is both impeccable and praiseworthy and hence entailed that one can be praiseworthy without the categorical ability to do otherwise. And secondly, it was shown by *reductio ad absurdum* that the $PAP_{All}$ entails either Pelagianism if one affirms that it is possible for a fallen human being to live a perfect sinless life, or universalism if one instead maintains this impossibility but still holds to the $PAP_{All}$, which then declares that humans cannot be responsible for this failure of theirs.

On the heels of this refutation of the PAP, a back door argument in favor of compatibilism was offered based upon the falsity of the PAP. It was argued that libertarian free will necessarily entails the ability to do otherwise, from which it followed that incompatibilism entails the truth of the PAP. But since the PAP was shown false, it followed by *modus tollens* that incompatibilism is false, and hence that compatibilism is true.

In sum, with all of these considerations in place, the compatibility of determinism and moral responsibility was not only defended against all its most important critiques, but also positively established by a pair of independently sound arguments on Christian premises. That God determines everything that comes to pass is thus demonstrably no excuse for human immorality; even on Calvinism, God can (and *does*) coherently hold humans morally responsible for their sins. Paul's rhetorical questions "Why does he still find fault? For who can resist his will?" thus accept the following simple answers: "who can resist his will?" On Calvinism, no one. "Why does he still find fault?" Because compatibilism is true.

These are important conclusions, and yet at this point, a word of caution might be called for in the midst of the Calvinist celebration. Since most libertarians are also incompatibilists, and most compatibilists are also determinists, it is not rare to assimilate the debate of "compatibilism vs. incompatibilism" to that of "libertarianism vs. determinism." With the above arguments in hand, which purport to establish the victory of compatibilism in the former debate, it would thus be easy to jump to conclusions and claim victory for determinism in the latter debate as well, but it would be invalid. The above argument establishes that determinism is *compatible with moral responsibility*, not that it is *true*. It establishes compatibilism, not determinism, and hence does not provide everything that Calvinist determinists could wish for. It does nevertheless remain an important first conclusion worth celebrating, because once determinism is demonstrated to peacefully cohabit with moral responsibility, if determinism is later found to be attractive for other considerations (of scripture and/or reason), then moral responsibility will no longer have to be a worry; libertarians have lost one of their two most important motivations for rejecting Calvinist determinism, one of the two anti-Calvinist grand arguments that are the focus of the present work. The next part will tackle the second one, as we now ask along with Arminians and here again with Paul's virtual objector in Romans 9:14, "is there unrighteousness in God?"

# PART II

# Calvinism and Divine Involvement in Evil

"By far the strongest objections to Calvinism are found in the phenomena of sin and moral evil."[1]—William Hasker.

THE SECOND FUNDAMENTAL QUESTION of interest, which arises without fail anytime the scope of God's providence is contemplated on Calvinism, is that of divine evil. If God's providence extends over all things that come to pass, and God's all-encompassing decree brings about all the evil that is obviously witnessed in this world, then is not God unrighteous? This question is a more or less direct corollary of the previous complaint on moral responsibility: it is alleged that if determinism is true, if free will is not libertarian, then humans are not morally responsible for their sin, and therefore, God is—which is presumably unacceptable.

As was the case with the question of human moral responsibility, the question of divine evil is pressed by libertarian controversialists almost universally. Let us hear it from some of its important proponents, in their own (sometimes colorful) formulations.

Richard Rice: "If everything happens just the way God plans it, then God is responsible for everything. This excludes creaturely freedom and it seems to make God responsible for all the evil in the world."[2]

John Sanders: On Calvinism, "there is not enough separation between God and the evil act to alleviate divine responsibility for evil."[3]

Probably owing to the particularly emotional nature and centrality of the question in one's understanding of God, the intensity of the accusation tends to escalate rapidly: for Clark Pinnock, the God of Calvinism is "some kind of terrorist who goes around handing out torture and disaster and even

1. Hasker, "Philosophical Perspective," 153.
2. Rice, "Divine Foreknowledge," 132.
3. Sanders, "Responses to Bruce A. Ware," 145–46.

willing people to do things the Bible says God hates";[4] for Steve Lemke he is "an executioner God who intentionally crushes children and electrocutes fathers";[5] and for William Lane Craig, "The Augustinian-Calvinist view seems, in effect, to turn God into the devil."[6] These strong feelings are shared by Roger Olson who charges Calvinism with making God "at best morally ambiguous and at worst a moral monster hardly distinguishable from the devil,"[7] a thought traced back at least to John Wesley.[8]

Additionally, an important concept to note behind the present charge is that of "authorship" of sin or evil.

Robert Picirilli: "God is not the author of sin."[9]

Roger Olson: "[The] Calvinist doctrine of God makes God arbitrary and the author of sin and evil."[10]

Kenneth Keathley: "God is not the Author, Origin, or Cause of sin (and to say that He is, is not just hyper-Calvinism but blasphemy)."[11]

As is made evident by the statements above, the present argument is specifically directed at the Reformed doctrine of God; it is not directly or primarily concerned with the traditional problem of evil. The problem of evil asks whether it is coherent to believe in the existence of an all-loving, all-powerful, all-knowing God in light of the fact that (so much) evil exists in the world. On the other hand, the present question is asking whether God's moral goodness is compatible with the sort of providence that Calvinists claim he exercises. While they each touch on related concepts, these are two distinct questions, calling for a few remarks on how the anti-Calvinist charge at hand actually relates to the problem of evil, thereby clarifying what the question is *not*.

---

4. Pinnock, "Pinnock's response (to Feinberg)," 58.

5. Lemke, "God's Relation to the World," 212.

6. Craig, "Middle-Knowledge View," 135.

7. Olson, *Against Calvinism*, 84.

8. "[Calvinists] represent God as worse than the devil. More false, more cruel, more unjust." Wesley, *Free Grace*, 17.

9. Picirilli, *Grace, Faith, Free Will*, 47.

10. Olson, "Responses to Paul Helm," 57.

11. Keathley, *Salvation and Sovereignty*, 7.

# 8

# Preliminaries on the problem of evil

## Relationship with the classical problem of evil
## —what the question is not

WITH RESPECT TO THE relationship between the question at hand and the problem of evil, there are two potential red herrings calling for our attention and clarification. First, the question at hand is *not* whether the strictly logical problem of evil pressed by atheists can be refuted—libertarian free will is not *necessary* for that. And second, the question at hand is *not* whether all evil can be explained by human free will gone wrong—libertarian free will is not *sufficient* for that. Let us review each point in turn.

## The logical problem of evil—libertarianism is not necessary to offer the narrow defense

One of the alleged strengths of the libertarian position, and quite possibly the most important reason why so many Christian philosophers are libertarians,[1] is that it offers a very strong answer to the problem of evil: if humans are truly free, it is maintained, God could not determine them to freely refrain from sin, so they freely choose the wrong path, *et voila*, evil turns up everywhere in human affairs and stands outside of God's providential determinations. Jerry Walls and Joseph Dongell declare, "It is clear to us that if God determined all things, including our choices, he *would not* determine the sort of evil and atrocities that we have witnessed in history."[2]

But the Calvinist is not especially exposed to the strictly logical problem of evil. In its logical version, the problem of evil contends that the existence of God is logically incompatible with evil. It is thus stated as follows:

---

1. This judgment is shared by Daniel Johnson who writes "the real reason that Calvinism has not been a live option for most academic philosophers is the central role that libertarian accounts of free will have played in the philosophical responses to the problem of evil over the last half-century." Alexander and Johnson, "Introduction," 2.

2. Walls and Dongell, *Not a Calvinist*, 218.

51. There is no possible world in which both God and evil exist.

52. Evil exists in this world.

*Therefore*

53. God does not exist in this world.

The Christian obviously affirms premise (52) (evil exists!), and denies the conclusion (he maintains that God exists), so he needs to reject premise (51). But to reject the premise that "there is no possible world in which both God and evil exist" is merely to maintain that "there is a possible world in which both evil and God exist." This is a very modest contention, and that is where libertarians have naturally come to respond that there is a possible world in which God grants libertarian free will to his creatures, such that in that possible world, all the moral evil that happens could be blamed on human or demonic libertarian free choices. This can be affirmed even by one who does not believe that that possible world is actually the one we happen to live in. Alvin Plantinga's remarkable contribution to the question of the problem of evil has been to note that a "free-will defense" need not be a theodicy. A *theodicy* would be a detailed account of how one believes that God and evil *actually* coexist in this world,[3] while a free-will defense is merely an envisioned possibility offered to the atheist, and which success-fully gets God off the hook of the logical argument from evil against God's existence. Plantinga explains:

> The free will defence is an effort to show that (1) God is omnipo-tent, omniscient, and wholly good (which I shall take to entail that God exists) is not inconsistent with (2) There is evil in the world. That is, the Free Will Defender aims to show that there is a possible world in which (1) and (2) are both true.[4]

This possible world need not be true and actual. It is an interesting logical fact to remark, and it initially releases Christians from crafting a de-tailed theodicy to the skeptic.

---

3. Or could coexist in this world, given all that we independently believe. W. Paul Franks draws the helpful distinction between a "narrow" free will defense, and a "broad" free will defense. The former is formulated for the sole purpose of answering the problem of evil regardless of one's own beliefs about God, while the latter, short of explaining all evil in the way a theodicy may be thought to require, formulates expla-nations of evil that are consistent with all that one additionally believes about God. "Proponents of a free will defense attempt to give a plausible explanation for why there is evil in this world. Such an explanation must include all that one takes to be true in the actual world, which, of course, includes one's beliefs about God." Franks, "Divine Freedom," 108.

4. Plantinga, *Nature of Necessity*, 165.

Now given this, one might think that even Calvinists could appeal to libertarian free will in that way: they could say there is a possible world in which free will is libertarian and justifies all evil in that world, even though free will *in fact* isn't libertarian in the actual world.[5] This move, however, will not work, because in that envisioned possible world, it is not only indeterminism that must obtain, but also incompatibilism: evil would be explained by libertarian free will in that possible world only if libertarian free will were necessary for moral responsibility, otherwise, God wouldn't be justified in granting this sort of unnecessarily indeterminist free will, resulting in evil for no good reason. But if incompatibilism is true in one possible world, then it is true in every possible world, including the actual world. Conversely, since a Calvinist thinks incompatibilism is false in the actual world, he must think it is false in every possible world, and hence cannot appeal to an alleged possible world in which libertarian free will explains evil.

What then can he say instead? The Christian—Arminian and Calvinist alike—can simply affirm that *it is possible for God to have morally sufficient reasons to allow all the evil that takes place, whether or not God chooses to disclose those reasons.* Of course one cannot always—I would even say that one can rarely—know what reasons any *particular* evil had, but one need not prove that such reasons exist, merely that their existence is possible for all we know, because it successfully refutes the atheist claim of premise (51), that it is impossible for those evils to exist if God exists. If the skeptic wants to use the existence of evil to disprove the existence of an all-loving, all-powerful God, then he needs to carry the heavy burden of proof of showing that it is not possible for God to have morally sufficient reasons to allow evil. But how will he do that? Unless and until that happens, Calvinists and Arminians can maintain that God has morally sufficient reasons for permitting evil, whether or not his desire to preserve human libertarian free will is one such reason.

While libertarianism may be found helpful by Arminians to explain evil, it is therefore not *necessary* to defend the coherence of Christian belief in the face of the problem of evil. Let us then turn to the second red herring I mentioned, and make the important remark that even if Arminians were correct and libertarian free will were a *part* of the explanation for evil, in no way could it be the full picture. Many Arminians who lay evil at the door of the Calvinist God need to realize that they are thereby arguing against their own view of God, because libertarian free will falls far short of explaining all evil in the world, it is simply not *sufficient*.

---

5. Steven Cowan affirms this much as a compatibilist in Cowan, "Sinlessness of the Redeemed," 418.

## Evil occurring under the providence of the Arminian God —libertarianism is not sufficient to explain evil

"No matter how our theodicy tries to exploit creaturely freedom, there is some supplementary work of exoneration to be done"[6]—Hugh J. McCann

The present contention is that libertarian free will, even if it were the true kind of free will that humans possess, would still not be sufficient to account for all evil in the actual world. Very many instances of evil occur every day, which God, even on Arminianism, could fully prevent and yet does not, so that Arminians cannot consistently lay those evils at the door of the Calvinist God for failing to prevent them.

First, there is the problem of so-called "natural evil," which consists in all the devastating pain and suffering that takes place because of natural disasters. When a natural catastrophe occurs (flood, earthquake, hurricane, etc.), it does fall under the providence of an all-loving, all-powerful God who presumably could prevent it, and it needs to be accounted for in one's theodicy. I will postpone further comments on this problem of natural evil until its full discussion to come, in chapter 10.

Secondly, there are a number of disturbing behaviors exhibited by animals, who likely lack self-consciousness, so that it is highly implausible for one to say animals have anything like a libertarian free will that prevents God from fully and meticulously controlling their behaviors. William Hasker blames the Augustinian (and Molinist) conception(s) of God, for such things as a spider trapping and killing a moth, or a pack of wolves starving off the cubs of an opposing pack.[7] If not an outright case of the so-called "pathetic fallacy," to claim these events undermine Augustinianism (which is to say Calvinism) is at least a failure to appreciate that animals are not moral agents, and hence, on any view of providence, do not have free will, much less libertarian free will. These events occur under the full providential control of God, even on libertarianism—not to mention the scriptural testimony to that effect.[8] These animal instances of so-called natural evil have to be accounted for by libertarians apart from any free will postulations.

---

6. McCann, *Creation*, 115.

7. Hasker, "Open Theist Theodicy," 299–300.

8. Alfred Freddoso lists Job 38:25–29, 39–41 and Ps 148:3–10. Freddoso, "Medieval Aristotelianism," 74–75.

Thirdly, there are all the tragic human incidents, which, being involuntary, do not involve free will at all either. Jerry Walls and Joseph Dongell blame the Calvinist God for car accidents:

> Consider the instance of a teenager who is paralyzed in an automobile accident because the brakes in his car failed. Suppose he had done nothing irresponsible but that, unknown to him, there was a defect in the manufacture of his brakes that caused the accident.[9]

They argue against Calvinism, saying that the accident was not sent by God but simply that "the brake failure can be seen as a tragedy resulting from the fact that we live in a world operating by God-ordained natural law and sometimes things designed by human beings fail."[10] But of course who denies that? This car example is irrelevant to the issue at hand, since the Arminian God is just as able as the Calvinist God to prevent the accident without finding any libertarian free will in his way. The car does not have a libertarian free will of its own to break down when it so chooses, thwarting God's providence over the life of the driver. So those cases of evil are also irrelevant to the debate.

Fourthly, there are all the diseases and horrendous sicknesses in this world that an omnipotent God is equally able to cure whether humans have libertarian free will or not. John Sanders's list of charges against the God of the "No-risk" model contains "debilitating illnesses," "birth defects," and "blindness."[11] And Arminian Roger Olson shouts "Amen!" to David Bentley Hart's long list of complaints against a Calvinist God who as "a kind of malevolent or contemptible demiurge" allows such things as "a child dying in agonizing death from diphtheria" or "a young mother ravaged by cancer,"[12] and he makes quite the emotional appeal through the lengthy story of a sick baby screaming in agony at the hospital.[13] Unfortunately, all of this is irrelevant to the debate between Arminians and Calvinists. In effect, what Olson is offering are arguments against theism. Since on Arminianism God is just as able to heal those diseases (cancerous cells and bacteria do not have free will), Olson's complaints are laid at the door of his Arminian view of God as well, and hence do not serve him to uphold libertarianism.

9. Walls and Dongell, *Not a Calvinist*, 208.

10. Ibid.

11. Sanders, *God Who Risks*, 263.

12. Olson, *Against Calvinism*, 86.

13. Ibid., 89.

And finally, even when it comes to human free choices, the truth of libertarianism would only tie God's hands to a certain extent. Given the actual content of this present world, it needs to be conceded that even given libertarianism, God, being omnipotent, is still permitting a great deal of evil and suffering which he could otherwise prevent or at least terminate if he really so wanted. A large amount of wickedness in this world, though occurring through the free agency of human beings, is yet easy enough to prevent that even the Arminian God could pull it off at little cost. God may not be able to "make" criminals "freely" stop their abominations if they have libertarian free will, but he most definitely could righteously strike them dead, or even unconscious. Open theist Gregory Boyd offers a terrifying example to highlight just how wicked God would have to be on Calvinism in light of such evil, which admittedly sometimes occurs in this broken world:

> The innocent, happy world of a charming and witty nine-year-old girl is instantly transformed into an unthinkable nightmare when she is kidnapped by a demented, sadistic pedophile. For years she is imprisoned in a dark cell while being tortured and raped daily. The psychological hell her parents descend into as they for years ponder their beloved daughter's unknown fate is as diabolically dark as the hell experienced by their daughter.[14]

Boyd's conclusion is that God would never decree such horrors, because it is very hard to think of morally sufficient reasons that God may have, and to maintain that God decrees all things "for the good of his children and the glory of his name." Roger Olson, and Jerry Walls and Joseph Dongell offer similar stories of kidnapping and rape.[15] These are admittedly cases of disturbing wickedness, and no Calvinist in his right mind should presume to know for a fact what specific good reason God has for permitting them, but let us not miss the fact that, to a relevantly similar extent, the libertarian view faces much of the same question. Even assuming that the rapist's libertarian free will prevented God from making him *freely* refrain, what prevents God from striking down the monster right before he commits the crime? Or after the first rape? Or the first week? The first year? The first decade? Evidently nothing; and yet on Boyd's view, God did not do so. The Arminian theodicist still needs to account for that fact, and will not find in libertarianism any easier a way out than the Calvinist does. What Boyd would have to say is something like this: "God has morally sufficient reasons to allow this evil, even though we may not understand what those reasons

---

14. Boyd, "Response to Paul Kjoss Helseth," 77.
15. Olson, *Against Calvinism*, 90–91. And Walls and Dongell, *Not a Calvinist*, 208.

are" and all Calvinists shall say "Amen."[16] Arminians, assuming they rightly uphold God's omnipotence, have to agree with Calvinist Gordon Clark's lowest common denominator, that "At the very least, we must say that God was pleased to let history occur as it has occurred."[17]

Two caveats must be added. First, Arminians might say that there is a difference between bringing evil about, and merely allowing it to happen. The point is well taken, and I shall in response discuss the issue of divine "permission" of evil in chapter 10, but the present contention is even more modest than that. It is only the claim that not all evil can be accounted for by God's inability to determine the outcome of libertarian choices. Since Arminians must concede that all these evils (only some of which involve any free will anyway), are at least permitted by God while he could entirely prevent them, the point stands that libertarian free will is not sufficient to account for all this evil.

The second caveat is that in some of these cases, I must grant that libertarian free will may have *some* relevance, if some of that suffering, though fully controlled by God, is seen by Arminians as God's attempt to influence humans to freely make certain good choices. These choices, God could have brought about with less suffering on Calvinism, since God could have controlled the inner workings of the heart more successfully, thereby determining the outcome he wanted without the additional sorrow. But even taking this caveat into account for *some* of these, I think the point remains that not *all* evil can be explained in this way. The many instances of evil listed above make it very likely that libertarianism does not—indeed *cannot*—explain all evil.[18]

Libertarian free will is thus seen to be neither necessary to refute the logical problem of evil, nor sufficient to actually account for all evil. Now that these two side issues are out of the way, the real problem at hand can be properly examined. What is the real argument from evil brought by libertarians against the Calvinist view of God? The actual argument to which we

16. Open theist David Basinger essentially concedes this point when he writes, "In every situation in which a person chooses to buy a car or eat at a given restaurant or rob a bank or abuse a child, the God of FWT [Free Will Theism] possesses the power to keep the individual in question from performing the relevant actions and to keep the actions, once performed, from producing the intended results." Basinger, *Case for Freewill Theism*, 34.

17. Clark, *Predestination*, 42.

18. Hugh McCann reaches the same conclusion and formulates it as follows: "The Free Will Defense does not, as usually formulated, offer a complete solution to the problem of evil. It deals only with moral evil, and while we have seen that this category covers more than might at first be supposed, it does not appear that all of the sorrows and failures of the world can be gathered under it." McCann, "Free Will Defense," 245.

now turn is the charge that Calvinism, because of its underlying determinism, makes God the "author of sin" or something like it, thereby *involving* him in evil improperly. Does Calvinism involve God in evil in such a way that he would himself be evil or blameworthy?

## He is in charge and seems alright with it—a preliminary dose of biblical perspective

"God forbid that we should go one fraction *further* than his Word goes; but may he give us grace to go *as far as* his Word goes."—Arthur W. Pink[19]

An important preliminary point to highlight in this philosophical investigation is that Christians in general and philosophers in particular tend to be very sensitive when it comes to God and evil. It is a legitimate response, because one shouldn't go around affirming that God is evil, but one's struggles need to be put into perspective. The God of the Bible does not shy away from his providence over evil as much as philosophers tend to do on his behalf. God in the Bible is actually quite comfortable affirming his full providence over both good and evil, and his apologists tend to make a bigger deal out of the authorship of evil than the biblical God himself does. In this light, it is important to start by putting the problem in the proper perspective, by first considering the sobering biblical pronouncements that follow:

"I am the LORD and there is no other, besides me there is no god; . . . I form light and I create darkness, I make well-being and I create calamity, I am the LORD who does all these things" (Isa 45:5–7); "I kill and make alive, I wound and I heal" (Deut 32:39); "The LORD kills and brings to life; he brings down to Sheol and raises up" (1 Sam 2:6; "Does disaster come to a city, unless the LORD has done it?" (Amos 3:6); "who has spoken and it came to pass, unless the Lord has commanded it? Is it not from the mouth of the Most High, that good and bad come?" (Lam 3:37–38). And of course, there is Job and "all the evil that the LORD had brought upon him" (Job 42:11).

Not too many Christian philosophers comfortably affirm such things about God. None of them presumably questions that all good comes from God, as James 1:17 clearly enough teaches, but they less readily affirm that God wounds, kills, creates darkness and calamity, brings evil, and that bad comes from his mouth. Yet there it is, in the scriptures, and not just anywhere, but following God's essential affirmation of his very deity: "I am

19. Pink, *The Sovereignty of God*, 80–81.

the LORD and there is no other, besides me there is no god." The prophet is communicating that God's full providence is an important part of what makes him God, so that if one strips God of his providence over good and evil, one tampers with his divinity.

The takeaway from this biblical prelude before proposing compatibilist defenses is that the authorship of evil is a philosophical issue; an important philosophical issue, certainly, but one for which proper Christian expectations ought to be adjusted to the record of scripture, to not attempt to prove more than God reveals, and is comfortable with. So what shall we say, then? A Calvinist determinist account of free will secures that under God's decree humans will in fact sin, and that they shall do so in just the way God determined that they would. Is God then morally blameworthy for sin and evil? Is there a sound argument against Calvinism based on the authorship of sin?

# The "half-baked" argument and three recipes to complete its baking

## Putting the half-baked argument on the table

Just as was the case with the incompatibilist complaint that Calvinism excludes moral responsibility, the claim that Calvinism has God improperly involved in evil is affirmed by virtually every theologian and philosopher who writes against Calvinism—hence the irony I mentioned of finding both complaints anticipated by Paul in Romans 9. However, while they tend to be very vocal in their defense of God against the evil picture painted by Calvinists "giving God a bad name,"[1] they rarely present a solid explanation by way of argumentation. The literature contains abundant assertions along the lines of "God is not the author of sin," "God is not responsible for evil," and "God does not cause sin,"[2] but all these are only gestures toward what Calvinists are right to demand, namely a sound argument. This leads to the central contention of the present section: I contend that all attempts to disqualify Calvinism on the basis of God's involvement in evil are prematurely cut short by their advocates, and thus in culinary terms amount to "half-baked" arguments. Their proponents fall short of demonstrating what they need to defend, and when one unpacks what they actually assert, they, like our prematurely unmolded, "half-baked" cake, quickly collapse. To that effect, I propose to finish the job they often leave unfinished, and proceed to actually offer the logically sound formulation of their argument.

Whether objectors speak of God being "the author of sin," or "the cause of evil," or any similar such claim, the only correct schema into which all the arguments in this family of objections must be fit, is the following:

(Premise 1)—Calvinism entails [Proposition $p$ about divine involvement in evil].

(Premise 2)—But in fact, [Proposition $p$] is false.

1. Hunt, *What Love is This?*, 266.
2. See the brief sample of the literature mentioned earlier in this chapter.

178

(Conclusion)—Therefore Calvinism is false.

In this form, the argument is logically valid so that if its premises are true, its conclusion will logically follow, thereby producing a sound argument that refutes Calvinism. But with this clearer exposition now before one's eyes, it becomes equally clear just how heavy the burden of proof exactly is that objectors must bear. For any of the alleged problems of Calvinism with respect to God's involvement in evil, objectors must provide the exact proposition $p$ expressing the supposed problem, and then establish both premises of the argument: 1. they first must show why Calvinism in fact entails proposition $p$, and then 2. they must show why proposition $p$ in fact cannot be coherently believed. Given that the burden of proof is back once again squarely on the shoulders of the critic of Calvinism making the claim, nothing short of this careful twofold demonstration will do to refute Calvinism. Can one then find the missing link, the "Proposition $p$" that will meet both those criteria and "complete the baking" of the argument against Calvinism?

## Three recipes to complete the baking— the foggy, the ambitious, and the timid

There are three possible ways that objectors can formulate their argument; three possible ways that the "Proposition $p$" can be phrased: a foggy, an ambitious, and a timid. Unfortunately, as I will now proceed to demonstrate, the foggy version is too foggy, the ambitious is too ambitious, and the timid is too timid. None meets the requirement of making both premises of the argument true, let alone convincing.

## Recipe 1—the foggy

The first version of this argument is probably the most commonly found in the literature: it is the so-called "author of sin" problem. Inserted into the acceptable schema above, it becomes:

54. Calvinism entails that God is the author of sin.

55. But in fact God is not the author of sin.

   *Therefore*

3. Calvinism is false.

As noted above, the argument is now logically valid, so that if both premises are true, its conclusion follows, and Calvinism is false. What then happens to be wrong with this formulation? It is simply too ambiguous to even debate. It is uncontroversial that "author of sin" is a metaphor. God is not a human being holding a pen and writing a book. What then does it mean to say that God is the author of sin? Clearly the objection seems to take issue with the fact that—or the way in which—God stands behind evil, but until further explanations are provided, Calvinists are not even sure which premise of the argument they should refuse. Depending on what is meant by "author of sin," Calvinists can reject either of the two premises. If what is meant by the phrase is in fact offensive and problematic, then Calvinists will grant premise (55), reject premise (54), and ask for a reason to believe that Calvinism does entail this problem. But if what is meant by "author of sin" is benign and acceptable (in the way the above scriptures described God's involvement in evil, for example), then Calvinists will grant premise (54), reject premise (55), and ask why on this acceptable understanding it would be a problem for God to be the so-called "author of sin."[3] If it's not a problem, Calvinists have nothing to answer for—although I would in any case discourage the use of the expression "author of sin" altogether, because it is not biblical, and it is hardly neutral in its connotations. In either case, then, the Calvinist is off the hook. As long as it is not clear what is meant by "author of sin," objectors cannot corner Calvinists and press them to accept any of the two premises. They need to go one step further, and explain what they mean by "author of sin," by giving a clearer expression of what they find to be wrong with Calvinism. That is what recipes 2 and 3 attempt to do. When one digs deeper into the possible meaning of "author of sin," what emerges is that objectors take issue with the Calvinist God for standing behind evil; for "causing" in some way or "bringing about" in some way all the evil in the world. There are accordingly two ways one can protest about this. One can complain *that* the Calvinist God brings about evil, or one can complain about *how* he does so. The ambitious recipe does the former, and the timid does the latter.

## Recipe 2—the ambitious

The ambitious recipe complains *that* God brings about evil in some way. It is properly described as "ambitious," because in order to be a sound argument,

3. Hugh McCann puts it this way: "There is no denying that the relation in question makes God the author of sin in one sense: namely, that he is the First Cause of those acts of will in which we sin. . . . The question is only whether this leads to the unacceptable consequence that God himself incurs *guilt* in the process." McCann, *Creation*, 116.

it must in turn claim that God does not bring about evil in *any* way. Indeed, let us once again insert the proposition into the acceptable schema:

56. On Calvinism, God brings about evil in *some* way.

57. But in fact God does not bring about evil in *any* way.

*Therefore*

3. Calvinism is false.

Immediately, it appears that Premise (57) is unreasonably hard to believe, let alone prove; yet it is the only way that this ambitious argument can be valid. Without specifying in premise (56) *how* the Calvinist God brings about evil, in order to reject Calvinism, objectors are left to argue in premise (57) that God does not bring about evil in *any* way. So will that work out? Hardly so. The ambitious is too ambitious: it proves too much. If it is successful, it refutes not only Calvinism, but along with it both the Bible, and all brands of Arminianism. Indeed, as surveyed above, the Bible is explicit that God stands behind evil *in some way*. He kills, wounds, creates darkness, creates calamity, and bad comes from his mouth (Deut 32:39; Isa 45:5–7; Lam 3:37–38). And as to Arminianism, in *some* way, all brands of Arminianism, although they are libertarian, likewise maintain that God more or less stands behind evil *in some fashion*, no matter how remote. Whether one is a Molinist or a classical (simple foreknowledge) Arminian or an open theist, every libertarian must affirm this much: God gave a libertarian free will to human beings while knowing that a libertarian free will could (and on some views *would*) be used for evil; minimally, God took the risk, and evil occurred as a result. So, all of these views, in one way or another, will need to maintain that in *some fashion* God is involved in evil. They cannot outright claim that God is not involved in any way, without thereby destroying whatever amount of providence was left for God in their own model, thereby stepping far outside of orthodoxy. The ambitious recipe therefore will not work. It is much too blunt a tool, and objectors will need to refine the argument, to pinpoint more specifically what is wrong with the *way* in which the Calvinist God uniquely stands behind evil. This is what the final recipe attempts to do.

## Recipe 3—the timid

Once objectors realize that the previous ambitious recipe proves too much, they must pinpoint exactly the *way* in which the Calvinist God brings about evil, and criticize *that*. The substantial difference between Calvinism and all brands of Arminianism is in the specific *way* in which God stands behind evil, namely a way that involves *determinism*. On Calvinism, God brings about evil and sin in a way that does not involve creaturely libertarian free will, which means that God unilaterally decrees that sin and evil shall come to be by way of theological determinism. No indeterminist, libertarian, human free will can thwart those decreed purposes involving all evil. This and this alone is the proper identification of what may be uniquely wrong with Calvinism. Unfortunately, a new problem now appears when this version of the complaint is inserted into the correct argument schema above. It produces the following syllogism:

58. Calvinism entails that God stands behind evil in such a way that evil is divinely determined.

59. But in fact God does not stand behind evil in such a way that evil is divinely determined.

*Therefore*

3. Calvinism is false.

The argument is still logically valid, and finally features a first premise (58) that Calvinists are forced to accept, but as a result, its second premise (59) has become question-begging. The argument now presupposes in premise (59) that determinism is false; but this is precisely what is at stake in this debate. It is circular reasoning to assert that Calvinism is false because determinism is false. Since determinism is the Calvinist view, it is arguing "Calvinism is false because Calvinism is false." This timid version of the argument, then, falls flat again, because it begs the question against determinism.

This, at bottom, is the fundamental problem at hand for the libertarian objector, stuck between recipe 2 and recipe 3, between the ambitious and the timid. Any proposed contention that is not specific enough to refute Calvinism alone will end up refuting the Bible and Arminianism, but any proposed contention that is specific enough that it uniquely refutes Calvinism will find itself to be question-begging, because on some level, it rejects Calvinism on the basis that it is Calvinism. I therefore contend that by inevitably falling in one or other of these categories, arguments against Calvinism based on divine involvement in evil are unsound. When objectors offer such an argument, Calvinists are invited to ask the question: which recipe is it? Foggy, ambitious, or timid? Does it fail to define its terms, does it prove too much, or does it beg the question? Without fail, it will be one of those three. By way of illustration (and justification), let us now turn to a more specific review of such arguments that have been offered in the literature (or could be offered) against Calvinism on the basis of its divine involvement in evil.

# IO

## The specific arguments from evil against determinism

### The foggy recipe unfolded

Is God authoring sin?

LET US BEGIN WITH an assessment of the claims that fall broadly under the umbrella of what I have called "the foggy recipe," namely the under-specified complaint that God is the "author of sin or evil," and the failure to explain in what sense God is thus, or more importantly in what sense that would be a problem. Of course, since my present claim is precisely that we are not told enough, there isn't much by way of refutation that needs to (or could) be added here. Still, what *can* be done is, on the one hand, to point out the important Calvinist voices acknowledging the issue, making it known that they are fully aware that God is in *some sense* "authoring" the evil which he determines shall occur, and demanding that critics of Calvinism tell us why (in that sense) that would be a problem; and on the other hand, to point out that those critics fail to meet the demand, and ultimately fall short of clearing up the "fog" in question. Here, then, are those representative samples for each side.

On the Calvinist side, some (almost all, says John Frame[1]) take the phrase to mean God is guilty of sin, and hence univocally reject it. This is what John Calvin does, arguing instead that God is the "remote cause" and we are the "proximate cause," so God is not the author of sin.[2] The Westminster Confession's classic statement also denies this much, contending God "neither is nor can be the author or approver of sin."[3] That is of course the

1. "The term *authors* is almost universally condemned in the theological literature. It is rarely defined, but it seems to mean both that God is the efficient cause of evil and that by causing evil he actually does something wrong." Frame, *Doctrine of God*, 174.

2. Calvin, *Eternal Predestination of God*, 179–81 quoted in Sanders, *God Who Risks*, 264.

3. Westminster Confession of Faith, 3.1 quoted in Frame, *Doctrine of God*, 174.

proper response to this understanding of the phrase, but as other Calvinists note, there are different ways of understanding the "authorship" in question. Paul Helm[4] and James Anderson[5] clearly enough describe this equivocation, as does Edwards, who, as is often the case, voices my sentiment on the matter so precisely that he is worth quoting exhaustively:

> They who object, that this doctrine makes God the author of sin, ought distinctly to explain what they mean by that phrase, *the author of sin*. I know the phrase, as it is commonly used, signifies something very ill. If, by *the author of sin*, be meant the sinner, the agent, or actor of sin, or the doer of a wicked thing; so it would be a reproach and blasphemy to suppose God to be the author of sin. In this sense, I utterly deny God to be the author of sin; rejecting such an imputation on the Most High, as what is infinitely to be abhorred; and deny any such thing to be the consequence of what I have laid down. But if, by *the author of sin*, is meant the permitter, or not a hinderer of sin, and, at the same time, a disposer of the state of events, in such a manner, for wise, holy, and most excellent ends and purposes, that sin, if it be permitted, or not hindered, will most certainly and infallibly follow; —I say, if this be all that is meant by being the author of sin, I do not deny that God is the author of sin, (though I dislike and reject the phrase, as that which by use and custom is apt to carry another sense), it is not reproach for the Most High to be thus the author of sin.[6]

For such objectors to Calvinism on the basis of God's "authorship" of sin and evil, the challenge is hereby extended. Unfortunately, the objector's

4. "It is certainly the case that the conclusion that God is the author of sin is an unwelcome one even to those theologians and philosophers who are explicitly predestinarian in their theology. . . . Others, equally predestinarian, have wished to distinguish between different senses of the words 'the author of sin,' regarding some of these senses at least as acceptable. They have not been ready to allow that 'the author of sin' is synonymous with 'is morally culpable for every sinful action' or with 'is sinful.' And they have not been prepared to allow the inference 'If God is the author of A and ordains B, which is sinful, to follow as a consequence of A, then God is the author of B.'" Helm, *Eternal God*, 160.

5. "There are morally unobjectionable senses in which someone can be 'the author of sin.' . . . The real question is whether Calvinism implies that God is 'the author of sin' in any *morally objectionable* sense." Anderson, "First Sin," 211.

And "In sum, what is widely regarded as a grave problem for Calvinism—that it makes God the author of sin—only appears so while the term 'author' is left ambiguous and unanalyzed. The critics have much more work to do if this commonplace objection is to have any real bite." Ibid., 213.

6. Edwards, *Freedom of the Will*, 287–88.

resultant shortcoming is not just that this challenge has never been met, but that few have even tried to do so. John Sanders quotes David Hume, who thinks it is impossible to reconcile God as the mediate "cause of all the actions of men without being the author of sin and moral turpitude,"[7] but does not independently support the assertion any further than Hume did. Roger Olson presses the objection multiple times as well[8] without additional argumentation. William Hasker in his treatment of providence[9] gives conflicting voices on the matter: on the one hand he says that he is not arguing that "given Calvinism, God is morally guilty for the world's sins,"[10] but later on he does press the question of sin's authorship, only not quite arguing it, but rather merely asking the rhetorical question "Given the assumptions of the no-risk view . . . how does God escape being responsible for moral evil—from being, as some have said, the 'author of sin'?"[11] So he does not supply arguments one could assess, let alone refute. When Alfred Freddoso's introduction to Luis De Molina's *Concordia* finally comes to deal with the fully determinist view on God's control of evil (as opposed to the hybrid view of the "Bañezians"[12] Molina most interacts with), all we are told is that it is the erroneous view of the Protestant reformers,[13] or as Molina puts it, "Lutherans and other heretics."[14] This Calvinist enjoys a bit of name calling if well done and when appropriate, but straightforwardly enough, this is not much of a reason to doubt the Reformed view. Kevin Timpe voices the sentiment that "to say that God is not the author of some evil act even though He is the ultimate cause of that act appears to many to be doublespeak,"[15] but it is not

---

7. Hume, *Inquiry Concerning Human Understanding*, 111 quoted in Sanders, *God Who Risks*, 266.

8. "The real reason Arminians reject divine control of every human choice and action is that this would make God the author of sin and evil." Olson, *Arminian Theology*, 65; "[The] Calvinist doctrine of God makes God arbitrary and the author of sin and evil" Olson, "Responses to Paul Helm," 57.

9. Hasker, *Providence*.

10. Ibid., 111.

11. Ibid., 129.

12. Freddoso explains the salient point of the Bañezian view: "So on the Bañezian scheme God foreknows the *good* contingent effects of created agents just because He causally predetermines those effects. The *evil* effects He knows by the very fact that He has *not* efficaciously concurred with their causes to produce the corresponding good effects." Freddoso, introduction to Molina, *On Divine Foreknowledge*, 37.

13. "This is just the error that Catholics accuse the reformers of making, as Molina is only too happy to point out." Ibid., 40.

14. Ibid., 218.

15. Timpe, "Christians Might be Libertarians," 284.

doublespeak, it is simply pointing out an equivocation on the word "author," beyond which arguments against determinism fail to take us.

Finally, Anthony Kenny presses the charge in these terms: "If determinism is true, it is comparatively easy to explain how he can infallibly foresee free action, but impossibly difficult to show how he is not the author of sin"[16] and yet he doesn't say much about this authorship. He does have more to say about God's "responsibility," which will be properly reviewed in the very next section of the present chapter, dealing with this separate (though related) contention.

Nothing else is offered with respect to unpacking the "authorship" problem. Of course, the reader must trust that nothing more of substance is added by these authors, because one cannot quite quote silence, nor can one footnote what an author does not say, but if I am wrong about this, if I have missed a substantial response to Edwards's challenge, then let this be the occasion of further conversation: let the alleged argument be brought forward, and its proponent tell us what it means for God to "author" sin and evil, and why *in that sense* that would be morally wrong. Unless and until that happens, Edwards's challenge can be seen as provisionally settling the matter of sin and evil's divine "authorship."

## Is God responsible for sin?

The same sort of equivocation as that I pointed out above on "authorship" is present with respect to another word that critics sometimes employ to object to Calvinism: that God is "responsible" for what he determines. Allegedly, "there is not enough separation between God and the evil act to alleviate divine responsibility for evil."[17] Here is how the objection is pressed by Anthony Kenny:

> If an agent freely and knowingly sets in motion a deterministic process with a certain upshot, it seems that he must be responsible for that upshot. Calvin argued rightly that the truth of determinism would not make everything that happens in the world happen by God's intention: only some of the events of history would be chosen by God as ends or means, others could be merely consequences of his choices. But that would not suffice to acquit God of responsibility for sin. For moral agents are responsible not only for their intentional actions, but also for

16. Kenny, *God of the Philosophers*, 87.
17. Sanders, "Responses to Bruce A. Ware," 145–46.

the consequences of their actions: for states of affairs which they bring about voluntarily but not intentionally.[18]

We are here offered a bit more of a case for why that would be a problem for God to providentially determine that humans perform evil. Unfortunately, it is still trading on an equivocation, one that Reformed thinkers have also highlighted in their own writings. There is a sense of "responsibility" that is of course moral (namely moral guilt and moral praiseworthiness, as was discussed thoroughly in the earlier part of the present work), and yet there is also another one that is purely mechanistic, having to do with explanations of origins, or causes, without necessarily moral implications. We might call the former "moral responsibility" and the latter "causal responsibility."[19] This intuitive distinction is well explained by Paul Helm who points out that in the latter sense, that of causal responsibility, we might say that "too many strawberries are responsible for my stomach ache," "my genetic structure is responsible for my maleness,"[20] "the termites were responsible for the collapse of the chair," or "the rain was responsible for my bumper potato crop."[21] In that causal sense, Helm is happy to say God is "responsible" for the evil he providentially decrees,[22] but God is not *guilty* for it. Susan Wolf remarks that "when we hold an individual morally responsible for some event, we are doing more than identifying her particular role in the causal series that brings about the event in question. We are regarding her as a fit subject for credit or discredit on the basis of the role she plays."[23] Accordingly, Calvinists maintain[24] (and even critics admit[25]) that moral re-

18. Kenny, *God of the Philosophers*, 86.

19. This terminology seems to be usual, as it is also adopted in Fischer and Ravizza, *Responsibility and Control*, 1–2; as well as Vicens, "Critical Consideration," 147; and Campbell, *Free Will*, 31.

20. Helm, "Authorship of Sin," 119.

21. Examples offered in personal correspondence.

22. See Helm, *Eternal God*, 158 and 164.

23. Wolf, *Freedom Within Reason*, 40–41.

24. James N. Anderson: "If S causes some evil E it may well follow that S is responsible for E (at least in part) but it doesn't necessarily follow that S is culpable for E." Anderson, "First Sin." And Steven Cowan concedes God's "causal responsibility" for evil in Cowan, "Sinlessness of the Redeemed," 418.

25. Leigh Vicens: "But, of course, causal responsibility does not necessarily make one *morally* responsible." Vicens, "Critical Consideration," 147. And William Rowe: "I shall be very brief concerning whether God must be morally evil, or the author of sin, if he decides that I shall make a sinful or morally evil decision. McCann is right: the answer is no. It does follow, I believe, that God is responsible for the existence of a morally evil decision, but the morally evil decision is mine, not God's, as McCann points out." Rowe, "Problem of Divine Sovereignty," 99.

sponsibility does not necessarily follow from causal responsibility. So when Katherin Rogers argues that theological determinism "seems to make God responsible for sin and hence to make God do and be evil,"[26] we need support for that "hence."

Now here is why the equivocal claim is nevertheless appealing: in very many of the cases we care about most in this world, moral responsibility does follow from causal responsibility. We *are* morally responsible for much of what we causally bring about. But the two responsibilities are not in fact equivalent, and the connection does not hold necessarily, even within this world, let alone for its transcendent creator. In this world, instances of causal responsibility without moral responsibility were found in all sorts of situations reviewed above in this work: coercion, manipulation, mental illness, ignorance of the relevant facts, all these conditions were seen to entail (when the proper caveats I delineated above are met) that a person, though causally responsible for his actions, is not morally responsible. At the time, that was precisely the point of the objector! Now one could very well object that none of these conditions is available to God, and that would be quite true: God indeed couldn't be coerced, or manipulated, or mentally ill, etc. The point at hand, though, is not to say that *these* peculiarities would apply to God; rather, it is to note that *some* peculiarities of certain moral agents break the usual connection between causal responsibility and moral responsibility within this world, so that in the case of God, who is a *most* peculiar moral agent as he transcends all other reality, we can reasonably expect him also to be excluded from the norm, in virtue of this peculiarity of his, that God is the transcendent creator of all other things. So the exact claim at hand is an *a fortiori* as follows: if causal responsibility in this world does not necessarily entail moral responsibility, how much more in the case of God who is the prime candidate for such an exclusion from the norm, are we owed an argument for why his being causally responsible for sin (which Calvinists are quite open to concede) should entail his being morally responsible (guilty) for it?

I here note also that this issue is one of *guilt* more than one of *responsibility* proper. Calvinists maintain that God's moral *guilt* doesn't follow from his causal responsibility for evil, but if these evils have morally sufficient reasons for why their occurrence would be overall preferable (which is exactly the claim being made here), then it could well be that God is even *praiseworthy* for bringing about these preferable states of affairs that include evil. So in that sense, God *would* be morally responsible, just not morally *guilty*. In any case, the more modest claim made by Calvinists is that God's moral

26. Rogers, "Does God Cause Sin?" 372.

guilt just doesn't follow from his providentially determining the occurrence of sin and evil—and further explanations will even be offered below as to why that is. Now, if they are wrong about this, further argumentation to show this is welcome, but the equivocal claim that a deterministic causal relation entails "responsibility" left unqualified will not suffice to dissipate the ambiguity of this still foggy recipe.

## The ambitious and timid recipes— starting out timid, ending up ambitious

The so-called foggy recipe was shown above to be unsuccessful as its wording remains too foggy, whether one speaks of God as "author" of sin, or "responsible" for it. We now turn to the other two recipes—the ambitious and the timid. These strategies were explained to exhibit the following failures: the ambitious recipe is self-defeating for it finds fault with Calvinism on the basis of a property that it shares with the objector's very own view; and the timid recipe is properly identifying a unique feature of Calvinism but begs the question by its failure to establish that this property is in fact problematic. Though this made for a nice theoretical classification of the two faults at hand, the distinction is not always so clear in the literature, and any given argument or series of contentions is more likely to fall somewhere in the middle, alternately treading on both faults at one point or another. We now turn to the assessment of these remaining arguments from evil against Calvinism.

## Natural evil

Arguments from evil against Calvinism rarely start out with ambitious claims that are outright incompatible with the objector's own view, but as it turns out, one of them likely does, depending on how it is pressed. It is the contention (briefly mentioned earlier) that natural evil makes God evil on Calvinism. As was mentioned then, natural evil consists in all the pain and suffering that is caused by natural phenomena or disasters such as earthquakes, hurricanes, floods, fires, sicknesses, etc. All these events occur by way of natural causes, and therefore plausibly do so deterministically. Storms, earthquakes, and viruses do not have a libertarian free will to freely cause human suffering in an indeterminist fashion that God cannot prevent without stepping on anyone's free will. Yet a number of critics have pressed them as a reason to reject Calvinism. Aiming to do so, open theist John Sanders ends up finding indeterminism even in sicknesses[27] and in natural disasters, attributing to the natural elements "a degree of autonomy."[28] Roger Olson similarly criticizes Calvinist John Piper for saying that God causes natural disasters,[29] and William Hasker argues for what he calls a "general purpose" theodicy, even for the natural order: he says that God's providential activity accounts for the fact that there are hurricanes and earthquakes *in general*, but not for why this or that hurricane or earthquake occurs there and then.[30]

But these non-Calvinist views face the same challenge of natural evil, and would likely find themselves equally refuted if the present arguments were sound. On these views, what is supposed to limit divine providence in this fashion? Where does this alleged "degree of autonomy" come from? If these events unfold according to determinist laws of nature, the argument straightforwardly exhibits the problem of the ambitious recipe I described above, as it also applies to the objector's own view, refuting it equally. Instead, for the argument not to be self-refuting, it would require natural evil somehow not to be determined by God. Indeed, the only way to exclude these natural events from the scope of what God providentially determines is straightforwardly to reintroduce some degree of indeterminism at some time and in some place in their natural unfolding. But the candidates for an explanation to such indeterminacy are few: either it stems from the exercise of indeterminist libertarian free will, or it is a physical indeterminacy of the natural order, and neither option delivers a plausible argument against determinism.

Let us consider the latter option first. On certain possible interpretations of quantum physics, the observed indeterminacy of certain particles at the quantum level is not just epistemic, but is actually ontic. I am personally inclined (for theological reasons I need not defend here) to adopt instead the equally scientifically possible view that this indeterminacy is merely epistemic rather than ontic, but let us suppose I am wrong about this: what if there is real indeterminacy in the natural order? Even then, it will not work to remove natural evil from being under God's providential control. Even if God does not causally bring about certain physical events, on any orthodox understanding of omnipotence, God does retain the ability to intervene in the unfolding of this initially indeterminist chain

27. "The people Jesus healed were not made ill by God in order to identify Jesus as the Messiah. Jesus is not going around 'cleaning up' the diseases God has spread (as is the case if one affirms divine pancausality)." Sanders, *God Who Risks*, 100–101.

28. Ibid., 90.

29. Olson, *Against Calvinism*, 22.

30. Hasker, "Open Theist Theodicy," 288.

of events, and prevent in a determinist fashion what would have otherwise occurred, had God not intervened. Even if a storm was caused at sea by some indeterminist quantum events that God did not cause (a rather implausible scenario one must say), when the storm starts to threaten the safety of a boat we shall suppose God wants to spare, God full well retains the ability to causally stop the storm, refraining it from causing any natural evil. "Even wind and sea obey him" (Mark 4:41). So if God, motivated by morally sufficient reasons, decides instead *not* to shelter the boat, as the storm comes and sinks it, it remains that the occurring of this natural evil *is* fully controlled by God, even if we suppose that there might have been some quantum indeterminacy at some point in the process of the storm formation. So merely physical (quantum) indeterminism will not do to exclude natural evil from the realm of divine providence: the argument is too ambitious, it refutes the objector's own view.

Let us then consider the former supposition, that natural evil would be indeterminist because rooted not in natural and physical indeterminacy, but rather in the indeterminist libertarian free will of moral agents. Clearly enough, on a Christian understanding, it would not be the free will of "mother nature." The elements being impersonal do not have a libertarian free will that limits God's providence. So only two kinds of personal agents might be said to possess a libertarian free will that accounts for these phenomena: human creatures, or non-human creatures. If one were to pin natural evil on *human* libertarian free will, there aren't too many possible logical connections this evil could have with human free will: humans don't typically *cause* earthquakes and hurricanes with their own free will, so it would have to be explained instead in one of two ways: either 1. God is determining the behavior of the natural elements, but as humans have libertarian free will, he cannot guarantee that they do not geographically "run into" the cataclysms, thereby making them disasters, or 2. the suffering that takes place by way of natural causes is instead divine judgment against human moral evil, the proper deserving of which is brought about by the wrongful exercise of human libertarian free will.

Option 1 is hardly credible. On the one hand, it is true that the natural events of a hurricane or an earthquake are neither good nor bad in themselves; they only become "natural evil" when humans "run into them," and suffer loss because of them. But on the other hand, it seems equally clear that God fully controls how they (the natural events) behave, and so even if we suppose that God neither determines nor even foreknows the outcome of human free decisions, at the very least God knows in the present what humans are doing, and hence he knows exactly the kind of natural evil that would result if he were to launch (or refrain from preventing) a quake or a hurricane. So one cannot seriously maintain that natural evil occurs because God couldn't avoid hurting us moving targets, after a tornado slipped out of his hands: God remains fully in control of the natural order and its resulting natural evil. At any rate, such an anthropocentric natural evil theodicy wouldn't work well for things like human sicknesses, which God controls and are often independent from the libertarian free moves of the human will.

Option 2, the idea that natural evil should be read as divine judgment on human free will gone wrong doesn't fare much better as an argument against Calvinist determinism. First, it is no longer compatible with the claims made by our initial objectors. Remember that Sanders, Olson, and Hasker, quoted above, were maintaining that the natural elements had "some degree of autonomy," that God "wasn't causing" natural disasters, and that God wasn't responsible for why this or that hurricane happened there and then. All of this is false if God is sending this natural evil as a means of judgment rather than uncontrollably letting it happen because of a natural indeterminism. Secondly, one has to ask: what sort of judgment is in view? Is this a judgment for sin in general, or a special judgment for the sins of some individuals? The hypothesis of a special judgment fails on several counts. Besides the fact that it is intuitively very implausible (the victims of natural disasters are rarely if ever more wicked than survivors), scripture settles the matter and refutes this view explicitly. Jesus himself provides the two relevant counterexamples, wherein both natural disaster and sickness are said *not* to be special judgment on sin: the tower which fell and killed eighteen people at Siloam did not target especially evil men (Luke 13:4), nor were a man born blind or his parents especially sinful, but "that the works of God might be displayed in him" (John 9:3). Natural evil therefore should not be read (at least not always) as special divine judgment on human moral evil. If, on the other hand, the objector presses evil as divine judgment for sin in general, say, if disasters and sicknesses are part of a judicial infliction on the world consequent on Adam's sin, then they could just claim Adam's sin was undetermined, and that would provide a consistent story for how natural evil could result from human libertarian free will. When phrased in this way, I no longer have an argument that *refutes* this thesis, it is no longer too ambitious, but neither is there a good argument in favor of it, which means it's back to being timid: if meant as an argument against Calvinism, it begs the question. In conclusion, no matter which way they are pressed, we see that attempts to hang natural evil on human libertarian free will fail to provide a successful argument against Calvinist determinism.

All that remains, then, is to consider that natural evil might be brought about by *non-human* libertarian free will. Whose? That of demons. It might seem fanciful at first to see a "demon behind every bush" more literally than was ever thought, but the hypothesis does boast the support of no less than Augustine,[31] and Alvin Plantinga points out that if not *true*, it is at least metaphysically possible.[32] So what follows if one espouses this view? What follows is that the category of truly "natural evil" becomes empty.[33] All evil on this view must be seen as moral evil, mostly demonic, and indeterminist. From this, it follows that the objection at hand based on natural evil against determinism probably no longer commits the fault of being too ambitious;[34] it no longer blames Calvinism for a determinist view of natural evil that the objector himself happens to affirm equally. But taken as an argument against Calvinism, if no longer self-defeating, it nevertheless remains question-begging and thus too timid, in that it still fails to say why God would be evil to determine the occurrence of natural evil. In any case, it is improbable that a great number of critics of Calvinism are prepared to take these wholly quantum or demonic understandings of natural evil, so they most likely remain committed to there being natural evil occurring deterministically under God's providence. Calvinists can accordingly press the point that if God can determine natural evil and there be nothing wrong with that, then he can determine moral evil, and it doesn't incriminate him any more—or any less—than natural evil. If natural evil is determinist and unobjectionable, moral evil shouldn't be relevantly any different, or, minimally, has not been shown to be relevantly different.

Still, a relevant difference might be thought to hold, in that natural evil has in fact more to do with pain and suffering than with "evil" *per se*; there isn't any *vice* or *wickedness* involved in natural evil, as there is in moral evil,

31. Augustine's view on the matter is mentioned in Plantinga, *God, Freedom, and Evil*, 58.

32. Ibid.

33. This is how the consequence is phrased in endnote 15 of McCann, *Creation*, 246.

34. Calvinists might still want to maintain that just as natural evil occasioned by quantum indeterminacy remained fully within God's providential control posterior to its indeterminist origins, natural evil occasioned by libertarian demonic activity might remain fully within God's providential control, in that God could still prevent any demonic activity, albeit libertarian, from actually producing its evil consequences, by intervening before the indeterminist event produces its evil effect. This response might be less available however in the case of demonically caused natural evil than it was in the case of "quantum caused" natural evil, since one might otherwise press that God may be committed not to annul the outcome of demonic free choices, for the sake of preserving the meaningfulness of their free will. I find it unlikely that God would be out seeking not to frustrate demons, but it is coherent to think God cares about the meaningfulness of demons' free will, while clearly incoherent to think he would care about a quantum particle's free "will."

which might be just the problem. We shall thus continue our investigation of divine involvement in moral evil, by reviewing further attempts to find fault with God on determinism. These are strategies that would seek to navigate between the aforementioned timid and ambitious recipes, attempting to fall on neither side of the horse.

## Is God sinning?

One way in which the problem of moral evil is pressed against God on determinism is by claiming that if moral evil is determined by God's decree, God is the one sinning. If that contention is true, it successfully takes the objector beyond the timid recipe, and refutes Calvinism without making ambitious claims that also refute his own view. The problem however, is that the contention at hand is a non sequitur, so that the affirmation of the inference is still begging the question. That God sins does not follow from his determining that we humans sin under his decree, nor are we told why it would; Roger Olson only tells us *that* it would: "For Arminians, this [divine control of every choice and action] makes God at least morally ambiguous and at worst the *only* sinner."[35] In more formal terms, the claim rests on the truth of the following principle: "whenever a person X causes another person Y to do moral evil, X must also do the moral evil."[36] It seems clear to me that Calvinists must reject this principle, but this is not a very high price to pay, since this principle also seems to me to be obviously false. If this principle seems at all plausible to non-Calvinist objectors, it must I think come from a different objection located in its neighborhood the plausibility of which it illicitly borrows from, but this one specific claim, worded as it is, cannot possibly be true. If God in his providence determines that a certain human being commit a certain sin, it obviously doesn't follow that God himself *performed* that very sin, whatever other fault one might want to find with God for having done so. It seems to me entirely coherent to maintain with Paul Helm and James Anderson respectively, that "in ordaining a murder God cannot Himself be murderous,"[37] and that "creatures commit evil acts, but God never commits evil acts, even though he foreordains the evil acts of creatures—which is not the same thing at all."[38]

35. Olson, *Arminian Theology*, 99.

36. This is Paul Helm's reconstruction of Peter Byrne's argument resting on a principle attributed to Anthony Kenny. Helm, "Authorship of Sin," 119.

37. Ibid.

38. Anderson, "First Sin."

This much shouldn't be controversial.[39] Rather, what I think motivates the objector toward this sort of claim is a slightly different and more plausible objection, one based on analogy: it is thought that in ordaining sin, God must be morally responsible for (because improperly involved in) the sin, as when, for example, we humans do such things, we thereby contract moral guilt. Let us then turn to this more promising objection, raising the question of whether God's involvement in evil on Calvinism is relevantly analogous to human manipulation in that way.

## Is God's involvement in evil analogous to human manipulation?

As mentioned above, the present objection probably lies *implicitly* behind a number of other objections offered by critics of Calvinism, but it is at times very *explicitly* phrased by these objectors. William Lane Craig helpfully presses it in the form of the following principle:

> The deterministic view holds that even the movement of the human will is caused by God. God moves people to choose evil, and they cannot do otherwise. God determines their choices and makes them do wrong. *If it is evil to make another person do wrong, then in this view God not only is the cause of sin and evil, but he becomes evil himself,* which is absurd.[40]

Roger Olson offers the analogy of a father manipulating his son to rob money, and concludes:

> I cannot think of a single example in human experience where one person who renders it certain that another person will do something evil is considered innocent—even if he meant it for good. In my analogy, the manipulative father intended to use the money his son stole to help the poor, which would not lessen his legal liability for the robbery.[41]

The case is I think rather compelling that such a father would be morally guilty and legally liable indeed. The difficulty to make this relevant to theological determinism, however, lies in establishing that there is no relevant difference between the manipulating father, and God the creator and

---

39. It is ultimately granted to Hugh McCann by William Rowe already quoted above: "It does follow, I believe, that God is responsible for the existence of a morally evil decision, but the morally evil decision is mine, not God's, as McCann points out." Rowe, "Problem of Divine Sovereignty," 99.

40. Craig, "Response to Paul Kjoss Helseth," 60–61.

41. Olson, *Against Calvinism*, 183.

ruler of the universe. The objector can once again present his argument by analogy in the form of either the weaker claim, that there is some relevant similarity between God and the human manipulator, or the stronger claim, that there is no relevant difference between them. Since the weaker claim is question-begging (inasmuch as the alleged relevant similarity isn't given us), the objector is left arguing the stronger claim, that if God has a certain property that allows him to exercise such control over sin without himself sinning, then the manipulating human father must necessarily have that property as well. It must be shown that there is no property that: 1. is featured in cases of human manipulation, 2. entails that the manipulator is evil, and 3. is not featured in normal cases of divine providential determination of human choices. This burden is unbearable. On the contrary, it is not hard to think of a number of such properties; such differences between God and the manipulating father, that matter a great deal in how we judge whether it is morally adequate for each of them to do what they do. For one, God is the legitimate creator and ruler of all human beings, and the human manipulator is not. This illegitimate exercise of authority over another is uncontroversially featured in the case of human manipulation, entails the manipulator does something wrong, and is not committed by God who does have the proper authority. So this property already refutes the present argument from analogy, but another one could be added: omniscience. Omniscience is very likely to be a relevant factor in assessing the rightness of one's determining a human's evil choices for right purposes. God in his omniscience has the luxury of knowing perfectly well the justifying, righteous outcomes of our unrighteous choices, and a human manipulator does not. To do so without omniscience would be unrighteously playing with fire. Interestingly, such a manipulator would be accused of "playing God"; a phrase that fittingly highlights that such providential activity is the prerogative of God, and not of human fathers.

I should point out that theological determinism was already shown in chapter 3 to be dis-analogous to manipulation in that way. Let me thus not repeat the claims: what was said there in the context of assessing the moral responsibility of the controlled agent is applicable here in assessing the moral righteousness of the controller: God and human manipulators are not analogous in that way, and the charge must fail if left in those general terms. Let us then focus instead on giving a brief response to more specific formulations of this charge pressed by objectors to Calvinism: Jerry Walls and William Hasker.

Jerry Walls, who calls theological determinism "the most metaphysically majestic account of manipulation ever devised,"[42] concludes that God would be evil on theological determinism, based on a universal principle about manipulation, the "evil manipulator principle":

> A being who determines (manipulates) another being to perform evil actions is himself evil. It is even more perverse if a being determines a being to perform evil actions and then holds him accountable, and punishes him for those actions.[43]

First, the second part of his claim, the one about the impropriety of holding those beings accountable and punishing them for those evil actions is irrelevant to the present question of divine evil on determinism. Indeed, if in spite of determinism such human evil actions are still morally responsible (the demonstration of which was the main burden of much of the present work above), then it is perfectly appropriate for any properly credentialed judge to hold them accountable for these morally responsible actions, whether or not the one judging them is also the one determining their actions. It just so happens that God is both the providential ruler and the righteous judge, but his being the former doesn't provide reason to find him unrighteous in light of his also being the latter. Leigh Vicens offers a similar complaint, proposing that "a judge who punishes people for sins for which he himself is morally responsible is blameworthy."[44] This seems confused. If the judge is presupposed to be "morally responsible" for those sins, then he is blameworthy wholly apart from whether or not he additionally judges them: blameworthiness just is what is meant here by "moral responsibility" for those sins. But on the contrary, if God the ruler in fact doesn't contract guilt in providentially bringing about human sin, then of course God the judge doesn't contract any more guilt when righteously standing in judgment of it.

In any case, regardless of the propriety of this divine "dual mandate," the problem with Walls's argument in the first place is that he leaves the "evil manipulator principle" wholly unjustified. At no point are we given a reason to think God is thus analogous to human manipulators; it is just taken to be true. But that is precisely what is disputed, so the argument still falls short of establishing the adequacy of the analogy, by supporting the relevant principle.

42. Walls, "No Classical Theist," 84.

43. Ibid., 88.

44. Vicens, "Critical Consideration," 148.

William Hasker also uses a principle along these lines, the *transfer-of-responsibility principle*:

> TR If agent A deliberately and knowingly places agent B in a situation where B unavoidably performs some morally wrong act, the moral responsibility for that act is transferred from B to A, *provided that* the morally wrong act results exclusively from A's actions and is not the result of an evil disposition in B which preceded A's action.[45]

Hasker does not himself establish the truth of TR, but he rightly notes that theological determinists must reject it (at least as applicable to God), and hold the following principle instead that pertains to God; the *no-transfer-of-responsibility principle*:

> NTR If God deliberately and knowingly places a human agent in a situation where that agent unavoidably performs some morally wrong act, the moral responsibility for that act is *not* transferred from the agent to God but remains solely with the human agent, even though the morally wrong act results exclusively from God's actions and is not the result of an evil disposition in the human agent which preceded God's actions.[46]

This characterization is probably acceptable by theological determinists. He then asks: "is there any morally credible reason why (NTR) should be accepted?"[47] But that is improperly shifting the burden of proof. It is not up to theological determinists to give reasons why Hasker should accept NTR; rather, it is his burden to show that they cannot coherently do so. Hasker continues:

> Does it not have every appearance of being a desperate expedient—an arbitrary exception to an apparently compelling principle, adopted only because its denial is fatal to theological determinism?[48]

This objection now alleges that a theological determinist's endorsement of NTR is a case of special pleading, that of arbitrarily excluding God from a principle that ought to be universal. This accusation or one very much like it was anticipated in the previous discussion on manipulation and moral responsibility: it is not arbitrary to think God is a very special

45. Hasker, *Providence*, 131.
46. Ibid., 132.
47. Ibid.
48. Ibid.

case and relevantly dissimilar to humans, given that God is the creator and rightful ruler, not just another human manipulator. Given that God is the divine creator of the universe, who has the essential properties of perfect knowledge, wisdom, justice, holiness, and all divine perfections, he is as good a candidate as there could be for a non-arbitrary exception to that otherwise universal (human) principle, and no reason is given why he shouldn't be. These objections notwithstanding, it thus remains secured that God's involvement in evil *is* relevantly dis-analogous to human manipulation, and that even if my above account had failed to convince of that, it would remain, at the very least, that God's involvement in evil and human manipulation have not been shown to be analogous.

## Is God causing sin?

Beyond the question of whether God "commits" the sin, or "manipulates" the sin (in a way that is relevantly analogous to human manipulation), a more basic objection is pressed in the literature through the complaint that God shouldn't be said to "cause" sin. The charge is so straightforward that it makes for a very simple syllogism:

60. If determinism is true, then God causes sin.

61. God does not cause sin.

    *Therefore*

3a Determinism is false.

The deductive argument is expressed in almost exactly these words by Leigh Vicens: "if God *causes* humans to commit sin—that is, to act in ways that *deserve* condemnation—then he is morally blameworthy, *even if he does not actually condemn human sin*,"[49] and Kenneth Keathley:

> If 10,000 dominoes are in a row with each one falling one after the other, then the main question is about who tipped over the first one. So it is with determinism and the existence of evil. If determinism is true, then God is the first cause of sin. . . . However, since God is not the cause of sin, then causal determinism cannot be true.[50]

---

49. Vicens, "Critical Consideration," 150–51.
50. Ibid., 150–51.

As we come to assess the argument, it must be noted that it likely falls within one of two of the so-called "recipes" I mentioned above: the foggy, or the timid.

First, it very well might be the foggy recipe for its ambiguity and failure to explicate the deceptively common word "cause." Though much about the concept of "cause" is intuitive and successfully employed in every day life, when it comes to using it in a philosophical argument, it is notoriously difficult to analyze "causality" without facing a flood of controversy. To quote Peter van Inwagen again, causation is "a morass in which I for one refuse to set foot. Or not unless I am pushed."[51]

But one may easily reply as follows: if the notion is found too difficult by philosophers in the ivory towers of academia, maybe it just means that we ought not to press the philosophical analysis *ad nauseam* in that way, and instead stay content with our everyday notion of causality. Using the intuitive concept of our everyday use, we could simply take "Agent A *causes* event E" to mean "Agent A engages in an activity that necessarily results in the occurrence of event E" or something very much like that. In that case, the objection probably leaves the realm of the foggy, and it does produce an acceptably clarified equivalence between "God causes sin" and "God determines sin." This means that Calvinists must concede and affirm the first premise in light of their theological determinism. But once there, the argument becomes timid, for its failure to support the second premise. "Since God is not the cause of sin," said Keathley above, but no support is offered for that "since." The short claim that God does not cause (determine) sin becomes plainly enough question-begging, and we would need a decent argument to the effect that God does not cause sin in that sense.

Another proponent of the objection, Katherin Rogers, takes on that burden, in an article entitled "Does God Cause Sin?"[52] She states her main thesis as follows: "God does not cause sin. Were He, per impossibile, to do so, He would be blameworthy, Edwards' arguments notwithstanding."[53] The projected conclusion is promising; the only problem is that Rogers's article goes on to argue a significantly different point instead. She (inspired by Anselm) contends that sin is defined as what God does not will, and if God causes all things, then God wills all things, so that on determinism, nothing is actually sinful. This is an interesting argument against determinism, but not one that supports her announced thesis. The actual thesis that follows from her argument, if successful, is this: "if God caused human sin,

51. Van Inwagen, *Essay*, 60.

52. Rogers, "Does God Cause Sin?"

53. Ibid., 371.

then it wouldn't be sin after all"; but remember that what was promised instead was a case for the view that "if God caused human sin, he would be blameworthy." Each of these theses does entail that "God cannot cause sin," but that initial allegation of *blameworthiness* remains unsupported,[54] and thus leaves determinism unchallenged in our present discussion of God's *righteousness* in the face of his involvement in sin and evil.

This being said, Rogers's different argument is challenging determinism nonetheless, and hence needs a proper response in its own right, to which we now turn through an important discussion of God's "will" with respect to sin and evil.

## Is God willing sin?

> "Do not be foolish, but understand what the will
> of the Lord is"—Paul, Ephesians 5:17.

Katherin Rogers's argument to the effect that God cannot "will" sin because sin is defined as "what God does not will" is a good starting point to discuss a key issue in the present debate, that of God's "will," and whether or not it is coherent to maintain that he "wills" sin. She starts out with Anselm's (fine) definition of sin, and presents her argument as inspired by his:

> Anselm holds that to sin is to will what God wills that you
> should not will. But in that case, he goes on, it is logically impos-
> sible that God could make you sin, since that would entail that
> God wills that you should will what God wills that you should
> not will.[55]

Once again, this argument makes for a rather straightforward syllogism:

62. If determinism is true, then God wills all things.

63. Sin is (by definition) something that God does not will.

---

54. The closest she comes to discussing her announced thesis, short of arguing it, is by stating her following difficulty: "But it is very difficult to see how, if God causes the molester complete with his choice to abuse, He is not to blame for the choice and the ensuing act." Ibid., 372–73. Her finding this question "difficult" is not something one can really refute, but I'm inclined to think my coming discussion of God's "wills" and the contrast between God's righteous intentions and the sinners unrighteous motives will go a long way in defusing that "difficulty" for those who may find the question difficult indeed.

55. Rogers, "Does God Cause Sin?" 372.

*Therefore*

3b Determinism is false.[56]

In response, one must point out that this argument falls prey to the charge of equivocation. The word "will"—or "want"—is here used in two different premises with two different meanings. There are (at least) two different things that theologians have properly referred to as "God's will." The above argument equivocates between two of them, sometimes called the "preceptive" will of God, and the "decretive" will of God. The "preceptive" will of God is what God, on some level, desires (or wills) that we do, in virtue of his moral commands to us: "God wants us to tell the truth," "God wants us to love our neighbors as ourselves," "God wants us to forgive one another," "God does not want us to murder," etc. This is the sense in which Rogers and Anselm above properly affirmed that sin is willing "what God does not will." On any Christian view of providence and free will, this preceptive will of God can be—and often is—upset by our poor sinful choices. God prescribes that humans should act morally, and yet they sin. This much is uncontroversial.

The "decretive" will of God, however, is that which God decrees will inevitably happen. It may be thought of as God's "ultimate" will, because, on theological determinism, it is indeed in all cases what God ensures ultimately occurs. On determinism, God's ultimate will is providentially satisfied all the time, and yields a successful decree in all things: what God most desires that humans do, God decrees that they do, and they always actually do. The question is then raised: is it coherent to think, as Calvinists must, that one and the same item can be the object of God's preceptive will but not his decretive will? Could it be that God both wills something in the preceptive sense and doesn't will that same thing in the decretive sense? Could God's decree come into conflict with what he prescribes? The answer ought to be "of course it can." Keep in mind at this point the question isn't whether for a fact God decrees all things, sin included; this much is understandably contested by non-Calvinists. The question at hand, rather, is whether "it is possible for any individual in general (and God in particular), to desire something on some level and at the same time decide against it for overriding reasons?" This much shouldn't be controversial. It is

---

56. The syllogism is laid out in just about those terms by William Lane Craig: "Since Highfield thinks that God's will is invariably done and nothing escapes his will, it follows that God wills moral evil and even causes it to occur. Given that that is impossible, there must be no moral evil. Here is an argument to that effect: 1-Nothing that God unconditionally wills is evil 2-God wills unconditionally everything that happens 3-Therefore, nothing that happens is evil." Craig, "Response to Ron Highfield," 173.

a universally experienced fact of life, and all it takes is a constellation of desires that are mutually exclusive. God obviously could and indeed does have those whether or not determinism is true. God does not will that Joseph be sold into slavery, and yet it is God who "sends" him thus, and hence willed it so to occur, intending it for good, that many lives may be saved (Gen 45:7). God does not will that Jesus be murdered, and yet "it was the will of the LORD to crush him" (Isa 53:10). So the present argument pressed by Rogers and attributed to Anselm is invalid inasmuch as it equivocates between God's preceptive and decretive wills: the "will" of premise (62) is decretive, and that of premise (63) is preceptive. There *can* be such a thing as sin on determinism: only, sin is willing and doing what God *preceptively* wills that we should not will, even as determinism entails that this same item, God often *decretively* wills that we shall will.

Rogers acknowledges this response, but presses on:

> If one allows that God is responsible for the choice and the act, but justified because He is aiming at some greater good, then it is hard to see that the choice and the act are not themselves justified as necessary means to the divinely desired ends.[57]

The acts *are* necessary means to the divinely desired ends, from which it does not follow that it is morally justified for the human sinners to perform them. The decreeing of them is justified *for God* in light of his righteous purposes, but the humans involved are still breaking God's precepts, performing the sinful acts with only their wicked ends in view. She adds: "In that case God would be the cause of all choices, but all choices are justified and so should have happened."[58] The equivocation is thereby transferred to the word "should." It should have happened in the sense that its occurring is what God most wanted to happen: God decreed that it should happen; but it remains coherent to maintain that the act was contrary to the human's duty, and hence in that sense the sinner morally *should not* have done it. This exact equivocation on "should" is pressed by Leigh Vicens:

> The divine determinist must reason that if some horrific evil was divinely determined, then it was necessary for some greater good. But then, it must have been good, all things considered, that such an evil occurred. And so it would have been bad, all things considered, if someone had prevented its occurrence. So, no one should have prevented its occurrence.[59]

57. Rogers, "Does God Cause Sin?" 373.
58. Ibid.
59. Vicens, "Critical Consideration," 240–41.

No one should have prevented it in the sense that God decreed the evil for the greater good, but with respect to human duty, it remains that humans *should* fight evil wherever it is found. The paradoxical use of the same word for two different notions in two propositions—one true and one false—should not obscure the fact that the concepts are perfectly coherent. Contra Rogers, determinism does not entail that "There is no sin in Anselm's sense,"[60] unless one equivocates on the meaning of "God's will."

This being the case, let us move on to examining similar formulations of this argument by other objectors. Roger Olson makes virtually the same point with respect to evil:

> If divine determinism is true, nothing is really evil. Think about it. If the good and all-powerful God has specifically willed and rendered certain every single event in history, how can anything really be evil? Must this not be the best of all possible worlds?[61]

It has now been made clear that God can "will and render certain" various events, which he otherwise does not "will" in the sense that they involve human sinners breaking his commands. Olson here assumes that "real evil" must be "categorically purposeless evil." But why think so? Why can't the best possible world (which, though I'm tentatively prepared to, not even all determinists might grant is actual[62]) contain moral evil for the sake of the greater good it (the evil) entails? No inconsistency has been shown in this.

Along the same lines, John Sanders says that on determinism, everything is what ought to be; everything is "right," even sin and evil: "it is, nonetheless, 'right' in the sense of being precisely what God intended to happen."[63] Yes, given determinism, it is "right" in *that* sense, but it doesn't follow that it is right in the preceptive sense, as being morally righteous for the human sinner.

Some further objectors do not make this an issue of there being no sin, but still contend that God cannot be said to decree things that he does not will. The equivocation should by now be rather apparent in the following sample of such objections:

Clark Pinnock: "Contrary to Calvin and Augustine, God's will is *not* always done."[64]

60. Rogers, "Does God Cause Sin?" 373.

61. Olson, *Against Calvinism*, 176.

62. As mentioned earlier, the question of whether there is a single best possible world is fascinating, but irrelevant to the controversial questions examined in this work.

63. Sanders, *God Who Risks*, 267.

64. Pinnock, "Pinnock's response (to Feinberg)," 58.

William Hasker: "[On Calvinism] all the evil that is done in the world—from the murder of Abel to ethnic cleansing in Bosnia—is precisely what God wanted to happen."[65]

Randall Basinger: "Things can occur that God does not will or want."[66]

I. Howard Marshall: "It is not true that everything that happens is what God desires."[67]

Once the two meanings of the phrase "God's will" are clarified, the shortcoming of the objection takes the form of a true dilemma: if these writers are talking about the preceptive will of God, then their claim is a triviality, no one disagrees, and it proves nothing of interest; but if they are talking about the decretive will of God, then it is plainly begging the question.

Now some yet further advocates of this "divine will" objection press it with an alternative angle, and make it more about the *intensity* of God's complaint or lament against sin. This would seem to perhaps concede God could coherently have some degree of desire toward what he does not decree, but then argue that the *level* to which God complains about certain events in scripture is incompatible with his decreeing those. William Hasker contends that "given Calvinism, it is unintelligible to suppose God to be so utterly, implacably opposed to evil as the scriptures represent him as being,"[68] and John Sanders argues the so-called "O Felix Culpa" strategy of the Calvinist to explain sin "undermines the idea that God is opposed to evil . . . it cannot be claimed that God is *fundamentally* opposed to sin."[69] Both authors go on to develop the contention; Hasker explains:

> Does not Calvinism attribute to God an attitude toward evil that is logically incoherent? God, the Calvinists say, is wholly good; everything that occurs God has willed to occur in preference to any other logically possible state of affairs God might have chosen. And then a just and loving God assumes toward part of what he himself has chosen to create and bring about—namely sin and moral evil—an attitude of utter, implacable hostility. So the Calvinist must believe—but is this even coherent let alone plausible?[70]

65. Hasker, "Philosophical Perspective," 143.

66. Basinger, "Exhaustive Divine Sovereignty," 196.

67. Marshall, "Predestination," 139.

68. Hasker, *Providence*, 111.

69. Sanders, *God Who Risks*, 266.

70. Hasker, "Philosophical Perspective," 143.

And similarly, Sanders argues that on determinism, there is no place for the biblical texts of divine "lament" wherein God vividly deplores the sins of his creatures:

> it does not make sense in the no-risk model for the biblical writers to say that God was genuinely grieved (Gen 6:6) or angered (Is 1:10–15) by sin. . . . If God gets precisely what he intends in each and every specific situation (since his secret will is never thwarted), then it is incoherent to also claim that God gets upset at certain of these situations. Does God get upset with himself?[71]

This alternate strategy of argumentation is interesting, but there is no reason to think it is more successful than the standard complaint against the two wills of God. If there indeed is a possible discrepancy between God's precept and what occurs (in God's decree), then the intensity of God's complaint or lament will be a function of just how far apart the decree is from the precept. If, as has been shown, it is coherent to maintain that God does not will sin, and can consistently complain about it, then it will follow that extreme sin calls for extreme complaint, without having to posit that God's ultimate (decretive) will was thwarted. As a matter of fact, this heightened "distance" or "spread" between the precept and the decree is an excellent candidate for a Calvinist explanation of various texts normally used by open theists. When God, through the mouth of the prophet Jeremiah, repeatedly declares of the wicked sin of the sons of Judah who burnt their sons and daughters "I did not command them, nor did it enter into my mind" (Jer 7:31; 19:5; 32:35), open theists who take literally the teaching of divine ignorance often argue that it is *incoherent* for Calvinists to hold these texts (as they certainly do) to be figurative language, because even figurative speech needs to convey *some* literal reality behind the imagery; and allegedly, no possible reality can be conveyed here that is consistent with Calvinism.[72] The present concept of a large distance between precept and decree accomplishes exactly that: it explains what lies behind the figurative language of divine "ignorance" of such sin. It tells us that even though God's providence is never thwarted, his preceptive will was deeply violated—such wickedness, he "never commanded"; as a precept, it "never entered his mind." Hence, there is no reason to think the breach of God's precept involves the thwarting of God's decree, even as God's anger toward sin follows in magnitude the size of the spread between the two wills.

Yet further objections are offered against the "two wills" response. Jerry Walls repeatedly refers to the Calvinist view on the matter as

71. Sanders, *God Who Risks*, 267.
72. See Boyd, *God of the Possible*, 119–20.

"consequentialism," because the "consequences" of the evil actions that God decrees seem to justify the rightness of his decreeing them.[73] But that is not consequentialism. Consequentialism is the view that the moral rightness of any action is determined only by its consequences. That is not what Calvinists are asserting, nor does it follow from what they say. Rather, they claim that God, having good purposes and the proper authority to rule over creation, decrees that moral wrongs would be committed by human sinners. God himself thereby commits no wrong, as he has proper motives (Gen 50:20) and proper authority (Rom 9:21). But as to the moral rightness or wrongness *of these human acts*, it is not determined by their consequences, otherwise the humans committing them would be said not to have done anything wrong either, which of course Calvinists do not for a moment concede. Rather, the rightness of the human actions is determined by God's preceptive will, his commands to humans. The ugly specter of consequentialism raised by Walls is therefore a red herring, and does not impugn the "two wills" response.

Finally, Katherin Rogers objects to the "two wills" under other names they're known by: "the revealed will" (for God's precepts), and the "secret will" (for God's decree), on the basis that it makes God deceptive or untruthful to "secretly" want something to happen that he doesn't reveal.[74] But this is a misreading of the labels. God's having a so-called "secret" will doesn't make him improperly "secretive" or unworthy of trust. As a matter of fact, those who use the "secret vs. revealed" conceptuality (which I personally don't have much use for), do not maintain that all God's decrees are "secret," but that those that are secret are so for a good reason. Ultimately, our concern is to be with God's revealed will, and our efforts ought to be in following his revealed precepts. Given his knowledge and desire of preferable outcomes, his decretive will might not ultimately align with the revealed precepts, but this is none of our concern, nor should it be. Rogers then argues that if God has such a decretive will at times going against his revealed precepts, then it is the decretive will that we should seek to uncover and bring about:

> It is the secret will which really embodies what God wants to have happen in the universe. If one knew that God's revealed will conflicted with His secret will, wouldn't it be better to obey the more fundamental will which actually expresses the divine sovereignty?[75]

73. Walls, "No Classical Theist."
74. Rogers, "Does God Cause Sin?" 375.
75. Ibid.

Here again, it is hard to see how that follows. The decretive will of God is judged (by him) to be "better" indeed, in the sense that it will involve a state of affairs that is overall preferable in the grand scheme of things, but in no way is it "better" *for the individual* to breach God's moral precepts. Human duty lies squarely with God's revealed precepts, and it possibly still would even if humans knew all about the compensating goods behind their potential sins, which they don't anyway. Actualizing moral wrongs for the sake of maximizing the goodness of larger states of affairs is the prerogative of God, and he neither needs nor accepts human help in the matter.

Having addressed a constellation of objections to the idea that God has two wills, one of which may properly be described as willing that sin occur, let me close with two final remarks that should help dispel any remaining apprehensions about this "two wills" response: 1. it is nothing new, and 2. it is nothing exclusively Calvinist.

First, then, I should note that those concepts involving two wills in God are nothing new. They are not a recent retreat of Calvinist theologians trying to make excuses for a God who decrees what he does not prescribe. John Piper's helpful essay on the matter points out the impeccable historical credentials of such concepts:

> Theologians have spoken of sovereign will and moral will, efficient will and permissive will, secret will and revealed will, will of decree and will of command, decretive will and prescriptive will, *voluntas signi* (will of sign) and *voluntas beneplaciti* (will of good pleasure).[76]

These concepts have long been recognized to hold for God, and it makes good sense, since, as I argued above, they are perfectly intuitive and universally experienced in everyday life, as soon as one's alarm goes off, and he "wills" to stay in bed, and yet also "wills" to get up and go to work. It is hard to see why objectors would have such difficulty with this, and would even hold the concept to be outright incoherent. Roger Olson says that these explanations "make God double-minded,"[77] Clark Pinnock speaks of the "exceedingly paradoxical notion of two divine wills,"[78] Norman Geisler asks "How can God desire contrary to His own eternal and unchangeable

---

76. Piper, "Two Wills in God?," 109.
77. Olson, *Against Calvinism*, 99.
78. Pinnock, *Grace Unlimited*, 13.

decree?"[79] And Steve Lemke says "obviously, portraying God as having a divided mind and will is not the way we want to go."[80]

These strong contentions are the occasion for my second and final point. It is the place to point out that the above objectors have crossed the line into the territory of the "ambitious recipe." They are arguing against a concept, which their very own view rationally commits them to. The objection proves too much, because the notion of two divine wills *must* be affirmed by libertarians also. Even libertarians must affirm that God "wills" some events in one sense (a preceptive sense very much like the Calvinist affirms), and yet does not bring it about because he "wills" something else more, namely the free expression of libertarian free will! God wills that certain righteous acts be performed, but he "wills" more that these acts be performed freely in the libertarian sense, and therefore he gives up on bringing about the event even though he willed it. The concept is employed very explicitly in the writings of libertarians such as Thomas Flint,[81] I. Howard Marshall,[82] William Mann,[83] and Peter van Inwagen,[84] who realize it is precisely what all Christians claim about *evil*: God does not want evil for the sake of it, but he has morally sufficient reasons to permit it. Only libertarians believe that one such morally sufficient reason is the giving of libertarian free will to humans, but in this, they agree with Calvinists that God has two wills. Since libertarians say that God *prefers* to have evil in his world rather than to take away libertarian free will, they affirm concerning evil that God wills it, although he does not will it. It thus remains perfectly coherent—and necessary for all Christians—to affirm that God "wills" that sin be, even as he opposes it morally, thereby "willing" that it not be.

79. Geisler, *Chosen But Free*, 88–89.

80. Lemke, "Critique of Irresistible Grace," 147.

81. This is secured by his Molinist contention that God *willingly* picked this feasible world (and all its evil) over other possible worlds: "God knowingly and lovingly willed to create this very world." Flint, "Two Accounts," 151.

82. "We must certainly distinguish between what God would like to see happen and what he actually does will to happen, and both of these things can be spoken of as God's will." Marshall, "Universal Grace and Atonement," 56.

83. "It would seem that the only thing that could frustrate one of God's desires would be another of God's desires of equal or greater strength, and the frustration would have to be at the level of incompatibility; otherwise both desires could be satisfied." Mann "God's Freedom, Human Freedom," 193.

84. "Granted, in some sense of the word, the non-existence of evil must be what a morally perfect being wants. But we often don't bring about states of affairs we can bring about and want. . . . So it may be that someone has a very strong desire for something and is able to obtain this thing, but does not act on this desire—because he has reasons for not doing so that seem to him to outweigh the desirability of the thing." Van Inwagen, "Argument from Evil," 60–61.

# Is God "permitting" sin?

A final significant worry for determinists with respect to God's involvement in evil needs to be addressed: it is the question of whether a language of "permission" is called for to describe God's providence over evil. Wouldn't we want to say that God merely "permits" sin? And if determinism is true, in which case God determines all things, can we sensibly affirm his mere "permission" of sin? These are not innocent questions; they're the occasion of a straightforward *argument* against theological determinism, one that takes the following form:

64. If determinism is true, then it cannot properly be said that God "permits" sin.

65. It must properly be said that God "permits" sin.

    *Therefore*

3a Determinism is false.

Some Calvinists might be inclined to protest about premise (65), but I for one think it is fine. There is a perfectly appropriate sense in which I want to say that God "permits" evil, and so the big question resides on premise (64), and whether that language is coherent given Calvinist determinism.

Let us read the charge directly from the pen of some of its libertarian proponents.

Thomas Flint:

> If God is perfectly good, then we cannot have him directly caus-
> ing evil, especially the morally evil actions which his free beings
> all too often perform. Evil is *permitted* but not *intended* by God;
> hence, we cannot have him predetermining it via intrinsically
> efficacious concurrent activity.[85]

Roger Olson: "If it is logical for Calvinists to say God permits or allows evil, they can only mean that in a highly attenuated and unusual sense of 'permits' and 'allows'—one that falls outside the ordinary language of most people."[86] Olson's formulation of the argument puts into focus the word "properly" I employed in premises (64) and (65) of the above syllogism. This controversy is really about the meaning of the word "permission"; it is a debate about semantics, but it does not mean it is a vain debate: if the word "permission" is indeed called for, then we would

---

85. Flint, *Divine Providence*, 87–88.
86. Olson, *Against Calvinism*, 88.

rather not abuse language to make it fit in artificially with determinism; we would like to use the word properly.

The issue at hand is also one of *asymmetry* between good and evil. It is the question of whether determinists can maintain a difference in "kind" between God's providence over the good and his providence over evil. Can it properly be said that God "intends" the good (or something of the sort), but "permits" evil, *in distinction to* what he does in the case of the good? Anthony Kenny presses that charge as follows: "An indeterminist can make a distinction between those states of affairs which God causes, and those which he merely permits: but in a deterministic created universe the distinction between causing and permitting would have no application to God."[87]

So the gauntlet is thrown down: how can theists maintain an asymmetry in God's providence over good and evil, and can determinists properly use "permission" language for God's control of human sin?

### Ambitious still—asymmetry is everyone's problem

I will aim to show in a moment that libertarianism is not necessary for asymmetry and divine permission, but I shall first argue that libertarianism is not *sufficient* for such, so that whether or not libertarianism is true, it is not the right anchor for the language of divine permission. The objection is too ambitious; it proves too much. The reason for this is that the sort of divine permission we are interested in must feature a divine *asymmetry* with respect to good and evil, which, if it is a problem, is a problem for both sides of the debate—not uniquely for Calvinists. Why so? Because libertarianism, just like determinism, is affirmed by its proponents of *all* directly free, morally responsible choices; *both* good *and* evil, *both* praiseworthy *and* blameworthy. So the libertarian who takes issue with the idea that God would determine evil will not solve the problem of asymmetry by merely making free will indeterminist; it will result in God no longer determining the good either, thereby failing to introduce any asymmetry. If indeterminism suffices for "permission" language, then libertarians will find themselves having to say in that sense that God merely "permits" the good as well. Like a bump in the carpet that reappears elsewhere when depressed, the issue of asymmetry will not be solved by simply bringing in libertarianism to avoid a divine authorship of evil: it will equally jettison any divine authorship of the good. William Lane Craig argues that "if God foreordains and brings about evil thoughts and deeds, it seems impossible to give an adequate account of

87. Kenny, *God of Philosophers*, 87.

this biblical asymmetry."[88] But if Craig's libertarianism relieves God from "foreordaining and bringing about" human thoughts and deeds, then it does away with the *good* thoughts and deeds just as much as the *evil* thoughts and deeds. Similarly, when John Wesley says "Whatsoever good is in man, or is done by man, God is the author and doer of it,"[89] or when Kenneth Keathley says "God is the cause of whatever I do that is right; I am the cause of all my sins,"[90] they clearly owe us just as much an explanation of how that is possible given their libertarianism. So this issue of asymmetry is admittedly a difficult question, but it is one that all camps need to wrestle with, and a mere libertarianism cannot be the answer to our present question.

To this, libertarians may retort that indeterminism isn't sufficient indeed, but remains necessary. Maybe the proper use of permission language doesn't follow from mere indeterminism, but it perhaps requires it, and only follows from indeterminism *plus* something else (like an asymmetry in God's commands, or his promptings, or something of that sort), a "something else" that is either not available to determinists, or available to them but not sufficient by itself to justify permission language apart from indeterminism. Perhaps it is so. The problem is that libertarian writers never give us that "something else" in their own model, let alone explain why it wouldn't be equally available to justify the asymmetry on determinism also. Rather, when libertarians raise the issue of "permission" language on determinism, they just take indeterminism to be the adequate solution, which I have just explained it isn't. Hence, it remains plausible that no libertarian can (or at least none does) offer the present objection consistently given his own view on the matter.

This being said, it might refute the objector, but it does not defuse his objection, and if left at that, the present answer would be a case of the *tu quoque* fallacy: pointing out that libertarians face the same problem doesn't solve the problem. So let us deal positively with the issue, and see how Christians in general and Calvinists in particular should in fact properly account for permission and asymmetry.

*Asymmetry of divine will is not sufficient*

Some Calvinists have suggested that divine asymmetry may be found in the fact that God's "attitude" toward the good he brings about differs from that which he holds toward evil (all of which God equally brings about). They

88. Craig, *Only Wise God*, 47.
89. Wesley, *Free Grace*, 5.
90. Keathley, *Salvation and Sovereignty*, 91.

use the thesis of the so-called "two-wills" of God, described and defended above in this chapter. While determinism entails that both good and evil in this world are "willed" by God in the decretive sense, an asymmetry remains in his "preceptive" will, in that the good is in agreement with God's precepts, while evil goes against them. There is in that sense an asymmetry in God's will with respect to good and evil, and John Frame describes a move in this direction by Reformed theologians:

> If God's permission is efficacious, how does it differ from other exercises of his will? Evidently, the Reformed use permit mainly as a more delicate term than cause, suggesting that God brings sin about with a kind of reluctance born of his holy hatred of it.[91]

I will concede that this "reluctance" of his when bringing about evil, as opposed to his presumed endorsement of the good, does amount to a certain asymmetry, but I think this cannot plausibly be the full answer. A language of "permission" of evil seems to demand more than this, because it doesn't merely describe an asymmetry in God's "feelings" or "attitude"; rather, it requires an asymmetry in God's *activity*; an asymmetry in God's providential *dealings*. It is plausibly an asymmetry in what God *does*, not merely in what God *thinks* about what he does. So let us press on, and unpack what "permission" calls for in terms of divine activity.

### Permission language and "active/passive counterfactual pairs"

Since the debate at bottom lies over the proper use of an English word, the dictionary is a good place to start. *The Oxford English Dictionary* defines permission as "The action of permitting, allowing, or giving consent; consent, leave, or liberty to do something," and "A licence or freedom to do something; the granting of such freedom."[92] Contemplating such dictionary entries, there are two definitions or common uses that need to be acknowledged, and rejected for our present purposes.

First, there is a *purely moral* understanding that says nothing about providence. It is the idea of permission as giving moral consent, or legal right to do something, as in "it is permitted to run around the swimming pool," or "it is not permitted to sell alcohol to children." It is a fine use of the word, perhaps even its most common use, but in our case, we are talking about God's permission *of evil*, which by definition is *not* legally permitted

---

91. Frame, *Doctrine of God*, 178.

92. "permission, n." OED Online. December 2013. Oxford University Press. 11 February 2014 <http://www.oed.com/view/Entry/141214?redirectedFrom=permission>.

in that way. Evil is a breach of God's moral law, and hence, whatever is meant by God's "permission" of evil, it isn't the giving of a moral license; it involves instead a sense of *providence*, wherein God is "making room for," or "refraining to prevent" a certain action, which, being evil, is still not legally, morally permitted.

And on the other hand, there is a use of "permission" that is *purely providential* and has no moral component whatsoever. It is also a perfectly acceptable sense of the word, whereby God is said to "permit" an outcome and "not permit" another, neither of which is morally good or evil. Verse 7 of Acts 16 is probably one such instance: "And when they [Paul and Silas] had come up to Mysia, they attempted to go into Bithynia, but the Spirit of Jesus *did not allow them*." In the absence of divine command, there was presumably nothing moral or immoral about going into Bithynia or going down to Troas instead—the option God permitted. This type of permission, purely providential in nature, is still not the sense intended by our present objector, who very much presses Calvinists to justify divine permission *of evil*. So the sense of divine permission Calvinism is said to exclude is one that is both *providential* and *moral* (or rather *immoral*, really: a permission of evil). One's use of the word should capture a certain kind of "passivity" in the one permitting. The action of "permitting" is supposed to feature a "hands-off" attitude, almost a passive disengagement on the part of God. It must be a "refraining" from some sort of intervention, thereby letting, or allowing, the evil action to unfold without stepping in. These concepts are the reason why determinism is thought to be problematic here, because if God determines all things, how can he be "hands-off" anything in the requisite sense?

To answer that question and unpack these notions of passivity, permission, and asymmetry, it is helpful to start with a simple, intuitive, and uncontroversial example, which captures well the sense of permission we are looking for. Suppose that a burglar is climbing up a ladder to break into the window of a 3$^{rd}$ floor apartment, when a passer-by approaches the foot of the ladder and sees him up there, halfway to the top, climbing to break in. At this point, the passer-by has a decision to make. Among the numerous possibilities open to him, two of them are of special interest for us: on the one hand, he could decide to prevent the burglary, say by pushing down the ladder and tripping the burglar. If he were to do so, the burglary would be prevented. Otherwise, if for whatever reason the passer-by thinks it preferable not to do so (he might find it wrong to send the burglar to a likely hospital bed, or he might be scared by the prospect of a future vengeance, or any good reason one could imagine), he then might decide to refrain from intervening, passively allowing the burglary to occur. This sort of situation captures very well the intuitions at play when we think of "permission" of evil in the sense relevant for our present purposes. The asymmetry in the passer-by's *action* is easy to appreciate here: whether or not the burglary occurs is at this point fully under his control; it is providentially up to him, *but* depending on which option he chooses, his *action* will vary in kind: if he decides against the burglary, he will need to actively, intently, perform the positive action of pushing the ladder, thereby preventing the evil at hand. But if he finds it preferable for the burglary to occur, then his control will be a purely passive refraining from any intervention, thereby *permitting* this evil, knowing that if he were to not intervene, the burglary would occur. This situation exhibits the sense of asymmetry we are looking for, and I suggest that if theologians are to properly apply permission language to God, it will involve something very much like that. But of course, some differences between the passer-by and God (especially on Calvinism) immediately come to mind. For one, the passer-by is not involved at all in the burglar's prior character formation, nor does he actively draw on the burglar's heart and mind to influence his decision at the moment of choice, whereas on Calvinism, God providentially determines the character and choice of the burglar in the first place, and when it comes to "intervening" or not, though external interventions of the same type as "kicking a ladder" are certainly available to God, the type of intervention Christians typically have in view is an *internal* intervention, providentially influencing the hearts and minds of persons directly. These points are well taken and I shall discuss what can and cannot carry over when applying these concepts to God. Nevertheless, there is *something* that the ladder-kicking passer-by and the burglar tell us about permission and asymmetry in divine providence, and I suggest that it is this: they tell us that proper use of permission language to rescue asymmetry in one's providential activity rests upon the truth of two important conditional, counterfactual statements that were casually stated above in the discussion of the passer-by. These two statements were as follows:

1. If the passer-by *were* to actively intervene (by kicking the ladder), the burglar *would not* commit the crime.

And,

2. If the passer-by *were* to passively refrain from intervening, the burglar *would* commit the crime.

Let us name the first one the "active counterfactual," and the second one the "passive counterfactual," giving us an "active/passive counterfactual pair." I contend that permission language and asymmetry in providential activity are premised upon exactly this kind of "active/passive counterfactual pairs." I will explain in a moment how these can be applied to divine providence, but interestingly enough, Jonathan Edwards himself offered an analogy that is not unlike mine to analyze the asymmetry at play in divine providence. He spoke of the relationship between the sun's presence and the production of light and warmth or darkness and coldness:

> There is a vast difference between the sun's being the cause of the lightsomeness and warmth of the atmosphere, and brightness of gold and diamonds, by its presence and positive influence; and its being the occasion of darkness and frost in the night, by its motion, whereby it descends below the horizon. The motion of the sun is the occasion of the latter kind of events; but it is not the proper cause efficient, or producer of them: though they are necessarily consequent on that motion, under such circumstances: no more is any action of the Divine Being the cause of the evil of men's wills.[93]

And then he unpacked the asymmetry in terms that come very close to my aforementioned "active/passive counterfactual pair":

> It would be strange arguing, indeed, because men never commit sin, but only when God leaves them to themselves, and necessarily sin when he does so, that therefore their sin is not from themselves, but from God; and so, that God must be a sinful being: as strange as it would be to argue, because it is always dark when the sun is gone, and never dark when the sun is present, that therefore all darkness is from the sun, and that his disc and beams must needs be black.[94]

Edwards rests the asymmetry upon the facts that if the sun *were* to approach and actively shine upon the location, there *would* be light, and if it *were* to passively withdraw from the location, there *would* be darkness instead. Such active/passive counterfactuals secure the asymmetry.

For good measure and before seeking to apply this material to divine providence, let me offer one final such illustration. Think of a bobsled, or a luge, sliding down the track under the control of its pilot, and consider the events of its acceleration and deceleration. For the pilot to bring about the one or the other, very different actions are required: to accelerate, all the pilot needs to do is let the sled slide, whereas a deceleration requires an active triggering of the brakes. This asymmetry of active and passive behaviors is

---

93. Edwards, *Freedom of the Will*, 293.
94. Ibid., 294.

secured by the fact that the sled is on a slippery downward track, guarantee-ing that: 1. if the sled was left to its own device, it *would* accelerate, and 2. if the brakes were actively triggered, the sled *would* decelerate. This makes it very appropriate to describe the pilot's action as either actively stopping the sled, or passively "permitting" it to slide, albeit under his full control. Asymmetry and permission language are secured by the truth of active/passive counterfactuals.

Let us then seek to apply this material to God and his divine providence over good and evil. Can anything like that be affirmed of God's control of human choices if Calvinism is true? For this to be done, the two so-called "active/passive counterfactuals" would now have to be counterfactuals *of free-dom*. They would have to be counterfactual statements about what humans *would* or *would not* freely do in various sets of circumstances, under various influences, divine and otherwise. This sort of language might begin to sound like Molinism,[95] but it need not be: as long as determinism is affirmed and libertarian free will denied, there is nothing un-Calvinist about the truth of counterfactuals. The choices to which these counterfactual statements pertain are free in the compatibilist sense, the notion of free will that is affirmed by Calvinists and denied by Molinists and all other libertarians.

Let us then examine these active/passive counterfactuals of determin-ist free will. For any given sinner and sin about which one wants to maintain a language of divine permission in the sense under discussion, Calvinists would have to affirm:

1. If God *were* to actively intervene, the sinner *would not* commit the sin

    And,

2. If God *were* to passively refrain from intervening, the sinner *would* commit the sin.

To establish the coherence of the model at hand, the question to ad-dress is this: how can Calvinists affirm those propositions, and more specifi-cally, how could God be said to "passively refrain" from anything, if he is determining even the very choice to sin? To answer this question, let me begin by drawing an important distinction between two different sorts of causal factors that are at play in determining whether or not the sinner will sin. That human decision is influenced by two sorts of such factors: on the one hand are this person's nature, nurture, life events, and character-forma-tion history, all the way from his conception up until the moment of choice,

---

95. See my discussion of Molinism and so-called Calvinist middle-knowledge later in this chapter.

and on the other hand are all the immediate influencers *at that moment of choice*: which circumstances he is placed in, and which forces—internal and external, natural and supernatural—are, on that moment, drawing him in different directions to make his choice one way or the other. Note that this conceptual distinction is uncontroversial: these two types of influences are affirmed by all libertarians as well. Only they maintain that all these influences do not collectively *determine* the choice one way or the other, but they do influence it.[96] This uncontroversial distinction, then, allows Calvinists to affirm this: God is in full providential control of both sorts of influences, but his so-called "passivity" or "refraining from intervention" can be expressed legitimately with respect to his supernatural influence *on the moment of choice*. That is a point at which Calvinists can find a very legitimate asymmetry of divine action. If God were to refrain *from that active drawing on the moment of choice*, then the sinner *would* sin, because all that would be left within him to express itself in decision-making would be his nature and prior character, which of course Calvinists affirm are corrupted by original sin. Apart from God actively extending his grace to them, fallen sinners sin. "Man without grace can will nothing but evil," says Martin Luther.[97] The doctrine of original sin, understood very minimally as entailing that humans have a fallen nature that inclines them uniformly toward sin (no need here for anything stronger like total depravity, original guilt or anything remotely controversial for Christians), explains the truth of one of our two counterfactuals: "If God were to refrain from divine intervention (namely an inner intervention in the form of a positive drawing of grace on the heart of the fallen sinner), the sinner *would* sin."

This conclusion is secured for every choice made by persons affected by original sin. Of course, one may raise the question of Adam's sin, but I shall come back to it later. For now, let us turn to the second counterfactual in the pair, namely "If God were to actively intervene, the sinner would refrain from sinning." It is all the more easily affirmed by Calvinists in light of their doctrine of so-called "irresistible grace."[98] There is according to Calvinists no amount of sinful inclination that divine grace cannot overcome. Philosophically, this comes from their upholding determinism,

96. "Of course this should not be taken to mean that freedom is the absence of influences, either external or internal. For someone to act, certain causal conditions are necessary. Rather, it means that these do not determine or necessitate our choices or actions." Reichenbach, "Reformed View of God," 69. See also Walls and Dongell, *Not a Calvinist*, 107.

97. Luther, *Bondage of the Will*, 318.

98. It might even be that no one *but* Calvinists can affirm such strong counterfactuals.

and it yields exactly the desired theological result: there always exists a type of supernatural drawing available to God, such that if he were to apply it, the sinner would refrain from sinning and would do the right thing instead. This secures the counterfactual at hand, and with it the truth of the active/passive counterfactual pair, thereby justifying the asymmetry at the moment of choice in this specific type of situation, and hence an appropriate language of divine permission in the face of determinism.

I have yet to discuss whether this rescues a true asymmetry in God's providence between *all* good and *all* evil, but before I do, let me address a possible objection to this specific situation. I suppose that one could object that focusing in this way on God's action at the moment of sin in relative disregard to his prior involvement in the person's character-building is inappropriate (maybe even disingenuous) for Calvinists as they must maintain that God determined *both*, but this would be missing the point of the maneuver. The point was not to relieve God from his control of evil, whether in creating sinners or in providentially controlling their sins. On Calvinism, God clearly determines all these things. Whether or not that involves God improperly in evil as the "author of sin" or something like it is no longer the question (that objection was already answered above). Rather, the aim of the present model is to explain why *in determining human actions*, there can be an asymmetry of divine action in God's actualizing the evil and the good. This much is secured by the present model. Coming back to the above illustration of the bobsled, one can similarly appreciate that the sled was initially placed on the track by the very same persons who subsequently piloted it down the track. They are thoroughly causally responsible for its present sliding down the track, but it remains that their controlling action during the race exhibits the proper asymmetry and justifies permission language: when they refrain from hitting the brakes, they properly "permit" the sled to slide. The same goes for God on Calvinism who as a result of the fall ordained that humans would have corrupted natures, but regulates their evil, particularly on the moment of choice, by a justifiably asymmetrical control. He actively extends grace to prevent sin, or passively refrains to do so, allowing naturally sinful people to sin when his good purposes require it.

Now someone else might complain that my model rescues asymmetry in this specific case, but fails to apply to *all* cases of good and evil. Couldn't we imagine a case where the situation is reversed, replacing our burglar on the ladder by a fire fighter, this time climbing to risk his life and rescue a baby from the flames? In that case, a passer-by who refrains from kicking the ladder would be "permitting the good." Is it not a failure of my model to rescue the proper asymmetry between good and evil? Let me make two responses.

First, I don't know that I necessarily need to refute the charge. Maybe my model applies here too, and *sometimes* justifies also a use of permission language for the good. Even so, it successfully refutes our initial Arminian objection, which was that the language of divine permission of evil was *never* justified on determinism. I need not show that *all* evil is only permitted in that way and that this understanding of permission is *never* applicable to the good. All I need to do is show that *some* situations feature a providential control of evil justifying a language of permission in a way that would not apply to the good *in that situation*. This much I have done.

But secondly, I think we could fine-tune my account to actually satisfy the objection. We could say that a language of permission is excluded if God needs to actively intervene *on the moment of choice* to produce a righteous choice, *or at any point in his past life, to produce the righteous character that would naturally lead to his choosing the good*. Since original sin has humans beginning life with a disposition toward evil, any subsequent sin is just an expression of this original inclination that needs no divine intervention. But conversely, any righteous deed is the result of a character that has been actively improved by God's direct, active intervention, whether at the moment of choice, or at any point before it. This qualification nicely rescues a full asymmetry for every single good action and every single evil one after the fall. In that sense, all evil is permitted, and all good is actively extended. I think this conceptual analysis nicely unfolds a philosophically loaded statement by John Calvin: "simply to will is the part of man, to will ill the part of corrupt nature, to will well the part of grace."[99]

All that is left to explain, now, is the first sin of Adam. Since he had not yet fallen, one cannot use original sin to explain *his* first inclination toward evil. Does this reveal a failure of my model? I think not. Without original sin, what I fail to provide is an entirely uncontroversial *explanation* for Adam's first inclination toward evil, but the *fact* that he had such an inclination should not be controversial: how could he have sinned if he lacked even an inclination? Phrasing it in terms of counterfactuals (supposing with Molinists that there are such truths), it is either the case that Adam *would* sin in the biblical circumstances, or he *wouldn't* sin in those. And since he *did* sin, then it's obviously the case that he *would* sin if God didn't actively extend additional grace to prevent the fall. So I may not have an uncontroversial explanation for *how* that counterfactual came to be true, but given the uncontroversial *truth* of this counterfactual, my model can just assume it, and with it, successfully explain the asymmetry in Adam's

99. Calvin, *Institutes*, Book Second, Chapter 3, Section 5, 181.

choice: he *would* sin if left to his own device, and God passively permitted it—whether or not it was determined.

## A few more libertarian complaints

With these concepts in place, a couple of statements and objections by libertarians can now be assessed. In his critique of determinism, William Lane Craig equates God's causal determination of sin with his "moving" the will of the sinner to do evil:

> By contrast, in the Thomist/Reformed view, God causes the agent to sin by *moving his will to choose evil,* which makes the allegation that God is the author of sin difficult to deny.[100]

In the relevant sense, this description of divine providential activity is inappropriate given the model offered above. On that view God determines all that comes to pass, yet given the truth of the active/passive counterfactual pair, God could be said to "move" the will toward the *good* only, working against the tide of sinful nature, but on the moment of sin cannot in that sense be said to "move the will of the sinner to do evil." To *sin,* a fallen human will needs no special "moving" by God; it is what it *would* do naturally apart from a particular divine intervention with special grace.

Another criticism is offered by John Sanders, contending that "permission" requires the leaving open of *multiple options.*

> the use of the word *permission* is problematic in the no-risk model. According to specific sovereignty, everything that occurs is precisely what God meticulously controls to occur. In this case, the term *permission* seems to mean the following. Suppose God had a rat that he wanted to run through a maze. Suppose further that every time the rat began to go down a path that God did not intend it to go, God placed a gate in its way that did not "permit" him to go that way. Eventually, the rat goes in the direction in which God "permits," since other paths were closed. This, however, would be a tendentious use of the word *permission.*[101]

Of course I am less than cheerful about comparing humans to rats, and we are not told what the relevantly shared property would be between the rat in the maze and the human being whose free will is determined—see my treatment of the "pets and puppets" argument in chapter 1 (provided rats

100. Craig, "Response to Paul Kjoss Helseth," 57.
101. Sanders, *God Who Risks,* 265.

qualify as pets)—but more importantly, we are not told what is wrong with the use of the word "permission" in that sense. It seems perfectly appropriate to say that by blocking roads God is "not permitting" the rat to escape and by opening one he is "permitting" the rat to escape. Sanders thinks that for permission to be meaningful, God *must* leave several roads categorically open (which he presumably takes to entail indeterminism). But why think that? While the concept of leaving multiple options is certainly allowed by the word, it is not an essential part of the concept of permission, or in any case it is not shown to be so. Furthermore, as I have already pointed out a few times by now, if permission is thus rescued merely by asserting that God leaves the choice open between good and evil, then God thereby "permits" evil in the same sense as he "permits" the good, and providential asymmetry is unacceptably sacrificed.

A final difficulty is pressed by Jerry Walls, who takes permission to mean that the one permitting should "prefer" that an alternate choice be made. He explains:

> The problem is that permission language does not make much sense on compatibilist premises. Typically, to say an action is permitted is imply [sic] that one is not controlling that action. For instance, parents may permit their children to make bad decisions that they would prefer them not to make.[102]

And because determinism entails that God specifically chooses and providentially actualizes every contingent state of affairs in the world, it would seem that God wouldn't prefer things to be any different. But the sense of "preferring" that is relevant for permission language is in fact compatible with determinism. Logically, when God brings about a state of affairs that contains evil, on Calvinism, it is because in the grand scheme of things, this state of affairs will produce a compensating, greater good—whatever that good is, Christians are rarely told, though sometimes they are. God simply assessed that it was preferable to actualize this state of affairs containing evil, for the sake of the compensating greater good that it entails. In that sense, it is perfectly appropriate to say that God "would prefer" this evil not occur, *if only that greater good could be obtained without the necessary evil leading to it*. But on Calvinist premises, it cannot. Therefore, God, preferring the overall greater state of affairs, actualizes one he would "other things being the same" prefer not to obtain, but which "all things considered" he *permits* for good reasons.

In the end, William Hasker concedes that the concepts are coherent, and he only insists on the boundaries that determinists must keep in mind:

> No doubt, in this view, God "permits" evil actions without actively assisting them in the way that he assists good actions through his gracious influence. Nevertheless, *the evil actions are the necessary consequences of causes that were deliberately created by God with full knowledge of what their results would be.* God's involvement may be less direct than in the case of good actions, but it is no less decisive.[103]

That is exactly the correct distinction that Calvinists must maintain: permission of evil is less active, but no less decisive. Of course Hasker finds it too weak, but he grants that it is coherent, which concedes the present point: Calvinists can (and I shall) coherently maintain an asymmetry between God's control of the good and his control of evil; more than merely in his attitude, it is an asymmetry in his very providence, whereby he actively brings about the good, and more passively "permits" evil, both of which still occur under his meticulous control.

### Is permission language indeed called for and for what purpose?

The argument against determinism under discussion contends that permission language is: 1. required for Christians, and 2. unavailable to determinists. The above analysis has established that permission language was in fact compatible with determinism, but the first question remains: is it in fact called for? Calvinists might be tempted to dismiss this language altogether and for all they care, might not miss it much. Who says we should affirm divine permission? My above description justifies its coherent use, but is it something Calvinists *should* embrace? While not obviously so, I think it is, if for no other reason because the Bible at times seems to employ such permission language to describe divine providence,[104] and some of

---

103. Hasker, *Providence*, 130.

104. Bruce Ware surveys the biblical language of divine permission and lists the following: "Your father [Laban] has cheated me [Jacob] and changed my wages ten times. But *God did not permit him to harm me*" (Gen 31:7); "Whoever strikes a man so that he dies shall be put to death. But if he did not lie in wait for him, but *God let him fall into his hand*, then I will appoint for you a place to which he may flee" (Exod 21:12–13); ". . . and they [the demons in the Gerasene demoniac] begged him, saying, 'Send us to the pigs; let us enter them.' *So he gave them permission.* And the unclean spirits came out, and entered the pigs" (Mark 5:12–13); "In past generations *he allowed all the nations to walk in their own ways*" (Acts 14:16); "And when they [Paul and Silas] had come up to Mysia, they attempted to go into Bithynia, but *the Spirit of Jesus did not allow them*"

the most important Reformed theologians and Reformed confessions of faith seem to do so as well.[105]

So if it is coherent and found in the Bible and the Reformed tradition, Calvinists should want to make good use of it, but let me say a word about the proper place of such language. It ought not be a strict, universal requirement in how one ought to speak of all divine providence over evil. The Bible sometimes uses permission language, but at other times, it also does not shy away from using very direct, active language in describing divine involvement in evil.[106] That means that the one isn't supposed to exclude the other; rather, both are meant to describe true aspects of God's control of evil, namely on the one hand that God is in full control of it, and yet on the other hand, that God does not endorse it for its own sake and that his mode of action in bringing it about differs from that of his bringing about the good. That is all. Permission language is not a device to diminish divine control of evil or excuse God for his involvement in it. John Sanders mentions "permission" as an attempted way out of making God the author of evil on Calvinism.[107] I agree it is not a good strategy, and should not be employed in that way. In that sense, I fully concur with Leigh Vicens when she objects that "the appeal to divine permission will not help the divine determinist in absolving God of causal responsibility for sin."[108] It will not, because it cannot, and indeed need not do that for Calvinists. Permission language is not necessary for maintaining divine sinlessness, as long as one maintains God neither does evil nor is evil—as I have properly defended earlier in this chapter. These misplaced concerns are the reason why John Calvin himself was critical of the language (as non-Calvinists are keen to point out[109]). But as John Frame explains, Calvin's concern was with the

---

(Acts 16:7); "For I do not want to see you now just in passing. I hope to spend some time with you, *If the Lord permits*" (1 Cor 16:7); "And this we will do *if God permits*" (Heb 6:3). Ware, *God's Greater Glory*, 106–7.

105. R. C. Sproul mentions Augustine, Aquinas, Luther, Calvin, Zanchius, Turrettini, Edwards, Hodge, Warfield, Bavinck, and Berkouwer, and offers the samples of the following confessions, exhibiting the asymmetry in view, which he calls "positive/negative": The Reformed Confession: 1536, French Confession of Faith: 1559, The Belgic Confession of Faith: 1561, The Second Helvetic Confession: 1566, The Westminster Confession of Faith: 1643. Sproul, "Double Predestination."

106. In making that very same point, Daniel Johnson lists Gen 50:20; Exod 4:21; Deut 2:30; and Josh 11:19–20. Johnson, "Map of the Territory," 31.

107. Sanders, *God Who Risks*, 264.

108. Vicens, "Critical Consideration," 179.

109. "The notion of permission loses all significant meaning in a Calvinist framework. Therefore, it's not surprising that Calvin himself was suspicious of the idea and warned against using it." Walls and Dongell, *Not a Calvinist*, 132.

idea of "*mere* permission" as an attempt to reduce the scope of divine providence.[110] With a different intent, Calvin saw a proper place for permission language, if used only presumably to describe the asymmetrical realities I explained above. He quotes Augustine approvingly: "For it [sin] would not be done if He did not permit it, and permission is given not without but by His will."[111] This is indeed probably how Calvinists should relate to divine permission language: warn against its possible misuse, but use it coherently to express the proper notions of divine disapproval of sin and asymmetry in divine action, while maintaining meticulous divine providence in light of their Calvinist determinism.

## Calvinists and middle knowledge

Finally, I should note that a handful of Calvinists before me have sought to employ God's knowledge of counterfactuals of free will (as understood in a compatibilist, determinist fashion) to explain (among other things) this asymmetry in divine providence over good and evil. My present model is very much indebted to their endeavor. Most notable among them are Bruce Ware[112] and Terrence Tiessen.[113] (Bruce Ware also lists John Frame as using the concept if not the same terminology.[114]) This Calvinist endeavor has been occasioned by a recent renewal of Christian interest in *Molinism*, the view of providence put forward by the counter-Reformer Jesuit Luis de Molina. Put very briefly,[115] the Molinist view posited that human free will is libertarian, but sought to maintain a high view of divine providence by claiming that God has knowledge (and makes good use) of all counterfactuals of freedom (understood as libertarian freedom). He posited that this divine knowledge of counterfactuals, being both *contingent* and yet *pre-volitional for God*, was logically "located" between God's so-called "natural knowledge" of all possibilities (truths that are necessary and pre-volitional for God), and God's so-called "free knowledge" of actualities (truths that

110. "Reformed theologians have also used the term, but they have insisted that God's permission of sin is no less efficacious than his ordination of good. Calvin denies that there is any 'mere permission' in God." Frame, *Doctrine of God*, 177.

111. St Augustine, *Enchiridion*, chapter 100, quoted in Calvin, *Eternal Predestination*, 68.

112. See Ware, *God's Greater Glory*.

113. See Tiessen, "Why Calvinists Should Believe," 345–66 and Tiessen, *Providence and Prayer*.

114. Ware, "Robots, Royalty and Relationships?," 200.

115. For full expositions of the view, see Molina, *Divine Foreknowledge*; and Flint, *Divine Providence*.

are contingent and post-volitional for God), and hence would be appropriately named "middle knowledge." Accordingly, the Calvinists in question
have labeled their view "Calvinist middle knowledge." Their proposal has
been met with opposition from both Calvinists[116] and Molinists,[117] who
have questioned the coherence of affirming "middle knowledge" while rejecting the libertarian nature of free will that was essential to Molinism.
John Laing has argued that if free will is not libertarian, God's knowledge of
counterfactuals is no longer pre-volitional, and hence is not in the middle
of anything,[118] and will collapse into either God's natural knowledge or his
free knowledge. Both Ware and Tiessen have come to affirm it as a subset
of natural knowledge indeed,[119] Ware maintaining that the label "middle"
knowledge remains useful and justified,[120] while Tiessen gave it up to avoid
confusion with Molinism.[121] In the end, John Laing invited these theologians (short of adopting his own Molinist view) to see these counterfactuals as part of God's free knowledge instead.[122]

For our present purposes, it is not necessary to arbitrate these debates.
None of what I have argued above commits me to any controversial view on
these questions. Should my view be called "Calvinist middle knowledge"?
Should the counterfactuals of compatibilist free will I focused on be seen
as a subset of God's natural knowledge or his free knowledge?[123] None of
these questions matters for the proposal at hand. All I care to affirm is that
God has knowledge of such counterfactuals—however one wants to call this
body of knowledge—the truths of which justify an asymmetry in divine
providence over good and evil, affording a proper use of "divine permission"
language in the way I explained above. However one ultimately resolves the

116. See Helm, "Classical Calvinist," 47.

117. Laing, "Calvinism and Middle Knowledge," 455–67.

118. Ibid., 467.

119. "Although it is a subset of God's natural knowledge, it is a useful subset!" Ware,
"Responses to Paul Helm," 74; "God's knowledge of counterfactuals is not different
from his knowledge of possibilities; it is therefore part of his necessary knowledge."
Tiessen in Helm and Tiessen, "Room for Middle Knowledge," 448.

120. Ware, "Responses to Paul Helm," 74.

121. Tiessen comments on his change of opinion in Helm and Tiessen, "Room for
Middle Knowledge," 452.

122. Laing, "Assumption of Libertarian Freedom."

123. On that matter, following Thomas Flint and Luke Van Horn, I am personally
convinced that it is mainly a matter of whether or not one includes God's concurrent
activity in the "circumstances" of a counterfactual's antecedent. If one does, such counterfactuals will count as natural knowledge, and if one does not, they will count as free
knowledge. See Flint, "Two Accounts," 166–67 and Van Horn, "Incorporating Middle
Knowledge," 818–19.

interesting debates sparked by "middle knowledge Calvinists," my proposal stands and justifies asymmetry and divine permission, thereby refuting the argument at hand against Calvinism based upon the necessity of affirming divine permission of sin.

This final argument's rebuttal concludes the present refutation of the grand argument that determinism improperly involves God in evil. "What shall we say then? Is there injustice on God's part? By no means!" (Rom 9:14)

# Conclusion

## *Determinism, purpose in evil, and humility*

THE PRESENT WORK HAS offered detailed defenses of the views that theological determinism is compatible with human moral responsibility and with divine righteousness. Of course, this alone does not serve as an argument *for* determinism. It could be that determinism is perfectly compatible with these important Christian doctrines and yet fails to obtain, even given the truth of said doctrines. Nevertheless, it remains a significant victory to see that the two most serious objections to determinism are unsuccessful, because it means that they leave the door wide open to affirming determinism if good reasons are independently found to motivate the move: Calvinist theologians and philosophers can marshal all sorts of good reasons to affirm Calvinism, knowing that plausibly no good reason exists not to. This positive Calvinist case typically rests on biblical exegesis and philosophical arguments. On the biblical front, Calvinists find that a number of texts are best interpreted to teach or entail Calvinist soteriology and Calvinist determinism, to the exclusion of libertarianism.[1] On the philosophical front, Calvinists may contend that libertarian free will unacceptably makes free choices arbitrary and random,[2] or that libertarian free will unacceptably excludes divine foreknowledge of the future[3] or of counterfactuals of freedom,[4] or that libertarian free will unacceptably compromises meticulous divine providence over

1. For such excellent exegetical cases in contemporary works, see White, *Potter's Freedom*, and Part I ("Biblical Analyses") of Schreiner and Ware, *Still Sovereign*.

2. The classic defense of this argument is found in Edwards, *Freedom of the Will*. For a contemporary articulation, see Haji, "Indeterminism, Explanation, and Luck," 211–35.

3. This argument is also offered by Edwards. For a contemporary articulation, see Helm, *Eternal God*. I for one don't find the argument compelling at this point.

4. The so-called "grounding objection" to middle knowledge.

human affairs, or again that libertarian free will unacceptably entails truly purposeless evil without any justifying goods.[5]

If any of these traditional arguments is found convincing, Christians are now free to accept their conclusion and affirm Calvinist determinism, without worrying that moral responsibility and divine righteousness hang in the balance.

Having established this much, it might be helpful to close this study with a few words on the application of these truth claims to the Christian life. On one level, just knowing the truth about God and his ways is a fine end in itself (Jer 9:24), but if and when controversial doctrines also have practical implications for the Christian life, they are worth noting. As it turns out, a significant application follows from the determinist model developed above, around each of the two topics that have been discussed: divine involvement in evil, and human moral responsibility. These are as follows: 1. While God is not guilty for the presence of evil in the world, theological determinism ensures that there is purpose in all of it, and 2. while humans are morally responsible for their actions, theological determinism ensures that there is no room for boasting in human righteousness in general and in salvation in particular. Let me say a word about each.

The direct practical consequence of theological determinism on the issue of evil stems from the fact that free will, if libertarian, very likely forces God to include some otherwise purposeless evil in his plan. If God leaves human choices undetermined, it is overwhelmingly probable that at least some of these will bring about instances of evil that God must just accommodate if he is to preserve libertarian free will, and hence the world will contain some evil whose sole purpose is to avoid determinism. This unfortunate state of affairs is avoided on theological determinism, wherein every instance of suffering is specifically intended to play a part in God's good plan. This affords the believer a stronger sense of purpose in suffering. When tribulation comes his way, the Christian rarely knows what good purposes lie behind his suffering (though sometimes he is told), but he can rest assured that all of it is occurring under the meticulous providence of God who works all things for his glory and the good of his children. Therefore, while the person suffering may not obtain an answer to his probing "why Lord?" he can at least find comfort in the knowledge that an answer actually exists. This is particularly important, because when tragic suffering occurs to us and we ask "why?" it is usually not so much out of a desire to know the specific meaning or purpose of that instance of suffering, but to know whether it has any meaning at all. Calvinism doesn't give the specifics any more than Arminianism does, but it gives what matters most: a "yes" answer to the question of purpose.

5. See discussion of Calvinism and purpose in evil, in the conclusion below.

This being said, it is important to remark that technically, "an answer" also exists on libertarianism; even on libertarian views, as long as God exists, there is no such thing as a *truly* purposeless evil; rather, what libertarianism entails is that the "answer" to the "why?" question would likely be (for at least some evil) as follows: the evil and suffering occurred *only* because those sinning had libertarian free will. Hence, the evil in question is not truly purposeless, but its sole purpose was to make room for libertarian free will (either because libertarian free will is an intrinsic good, or because it is a means to other good ends such as genuine love, moral responsibility, etc.). This of course is not very satisfying—especially when it is doubtful that libertarian free will is necessary for moral responsibility and love, or for safeguarding divine righteousness, and hence for anything worth this evil—and it therefore constitutes the first practical consequence of determinism: all our wounds serve a specific purpose in the providential plan of a good God who works all things according to the council of his will (Eph 1:11).

The second issue at hand is that of moral responsibility. The present work has defended the consistency of the Calvinist contention that even though humans are morally responsible for their choices, it is God who ultimately determines all their outcomes. This feature of Calvinism raises the question of human merit, particularly with respect to salvation, as it permits Calvinists to say that ultimately, the difference between the redeemed in heaven and the reprobate in hell will not be found in the fact that the former were intrinsically "better" than the latter; they were not more "righteous" of themselves. Certainly, they are not saved because of their good works given that salvation is affirmed by Calvinists and Arminians alike to be by grace alone through faith alone, but beyond this common affirmation, on Calvinism alone, even their repentance and faith were freely *granted* to them, as a result of their election unto eternal life, seen by Calvinists as truly unconditional. This is rightly said to provide particularly strong grounds for humility, as the regenerate Christian must affirm that his salvation and, more generally, all his righteous actions are fully the work of God in him, thereby leaving no room for boasting. "What do you have that you did not receive? If then you received it, why do you boast as if you did not receive it?" (1 Cor 4:7).

This line of reasoning is sound, but here again a word of caution is called for. In an attempt to exclude boasting, theologians (Calvinists in particular) might be tempted to say that there is no *praiseworthiness* in any righteous deed in general, and in the decision to repent and believe in particular. This move is commendable in its intent, but unviable in its realization. Praiseworthiness and blameworthiness are the two sides of the one same coin of moral responsibility. If one goes, the other one goes with it, and denying praiseworthiness would, I'm afraid, come at the cost of denying blameworthiness also, which is unacceptable given orthodox views of divine judgment. The burden of much of the present work has been to defend the compatibility of moral responsibility with determinism, in the obvious hope of maintaining the *truth* of both of them. So determinists ought not deny any moral praiseworthiness for righteous deeds, as there is no asymmetry at that level between praiseworthiness for the good and blameworthiness for evil: both are entailed by human moral responsibility. There is, however, another level of discourse at which an asymmetry can be affirmed, and that asymmetry stems directly from that which was affirmed in our above discussion of divine permission of evil, an asymmetry in divine providence. The human impossibility of boasting (while remaining praiseworthy) comes from the truth of the aforementioned "active/passive counterfactual pair." The sinner who under the active intervention of God refrains from sinning *is* morally responsible (praiseworthy) for his righteous choice, but he should not boast precisely because he *would* have sinned if it had not been for God's special intervention. Given this, if one considers another person who in the same (or similar) circumstances actually sinned instead, we are in a position to say the one who sinned was not better, in and of himself, than the one who didn't. The two are equally fallen, *would* have equally committed the sin if left to their own nature, and are only made to differ by God's providential choice, for good reasons of his own, to permit the one to sin while graciously preserving the other in righteousness. Applied to salvation and election, it justifies the above claim that the saved can hardly boast of their being saved, given that they would have rejected the gospel if not for God's electing love and providential extension of effectual grace. As John Calvin sees it, "Jacob, therefore, is chosen, while Esau is rejected; the predestination of God makes a distinction where none existed in respect of merit."[6] This makes for genuine humility in human righteousness, and calls for compassion in the face of moral failure. Calvinism thereby provides a particularly solid foundation for these Christian virtues. As J. I. Packer puts it, "Arminianism gives Christians much to thank God for, but Calvinism gives them more."[7]

In the end, Calvinism best explains why all the glory in human righteousness belongs to God in the way Jesus described: "In the same way, let your light shine before others, so that they may see your good works and give glory *to your Father* who is in heaven" (Matt 5:16). This has always been and remains the most attractive feature of Calvinism: *Soli Deo Gloria*. In human righteousness and salvation, it gives *all* of the glory to God: "*To him who sits on the throne and to the Lamb* be blessing and honor and glory and might forever and ever" (Rev 5:13).

6. Calvin, *Institutes*, Book Third, Chapter 22, Section 6, 618.
7. Packer, "Love of God," 286.

# Bibliography

Adams, Robert M. *The Virtue of Faith and Other Essays in Philosophical Theology*. New York: Oxford University Press, 1987.

Alexander, David E., and Daniel M. Johnson, "Introduction." In *Calvinism and the Problem of Evil*, edited by David E. Alexander and Daniel M. Johnson, 1–18. Eugene, OR: Pickwick, 2016.

Allen, David L., and Steve W. Lemke, eds. *Whosoever Will: A Biblical-Theological Critique of Five-Point Calvinism*. Nashville, TN: B&H, 2010.

Anderson, James N. "Calvinism and the First Sin." In *Calvinism and the Problem of Evil*, edited by David E. Alexander and Daniel M. Johnson, 200–232. Eugene, OR: Pickwick, 2016.

Arminius, James. "Friendly Conference with Mr. Francis Junius." Quoted in Alan P. F. Sell, *The Great Debate: Calvinism, Arminianism and Salvation*. Grand Rapids: Baker, 1982, 13.

Baggett, David, and Jerry L. Walls. *Good God: The Theistic Foundations of Morality*. New York: Oxford University Press, 2011.

Bailey, Andrew M. "Incompatibilism and the Past." *Philosophy and Phenomenological Research* 85.2 (2012) 351–75.

Basinger, David. "Biblical Paradox: Does Revelation Challenge Logic?" *Journal of the Evangelical Theological Society* 30.2 (1987) 205–13.

———. *The Case for Freewill Theism: A Philosophical Assessment*. Downers Grove, IL: InterVarsity, 1996.

Basinger, David, and Randall Basinger, eds. *Predestination & Free Will: Four Views of Divine Sovereignty & Human Freedom*. Downers Grove, IL: InterVarsity, 1986.

Basinger, Randall G. "Exhaustive Divine Sovereignty: A Practical Critique." In *The Grace of God and the Will of Man*, edited by Clark H. Pinnock, 191–206. Bloomington, MN: Bethany House, 1995.

Bergmann, Michael, and J. A. Cover, "Divine Responsibility without Divine Freedom." *Faith and Philosophy* 23.4 (2006) 381–408.

Boettner, Loraine. *The Reformed Doctrine of Predestination*. Phillipsburg, NJ: P&R, 1932.

Boyd, Gregory A. *God of the Possible: A Biblical Introduction to the Open View of God*. Grand Rapids: Baker, 2000.

———. "Response to Paul Kjoss Helseth." In *Four Views on Divine Providence*, edited by Stanley N. Gundry and Dennis W. Jowers, 69–77. Grand Rapids: Zondervan, 2011.

Calvin, John. *Concerning the Eternal Predestination of God*. Louisville, KY: Westminster John Knox, 1997.

————. *Institutes of the Christian Religion*. Translated by Henry Beveridge. Peabody, MA: Hendrickson, 2008.

Campbell, Joseph Keim. *Free Will*. Malden, MA: Polity, 2011.

————. "Free Will and the Necessity of the Past." *Analysis* 67.2 (2007) 105–11.

Campbell, Travis James. "Middle Knowledge: A Reformed Critique." *Westminster Theological Journal* 68.1 (2006) 22.

Ciocchi, David M. "Reconciling Divine Sovereignty and Human Freedom." *Journal of the Evangelical Theological Society* 37.3 (1994) 395–412.

Clark, Gordon H. *Predestination*. Unicoi, TN: The Trinity Foundation, 1987.

Copan, Paul. "Original Sin and Christian Philosophy." *Philosophia Christi* 5.2 (2003) 519–41.

Copp, David. "'Ought' Implies 'Can,' Blameworthiness, and the Principle of Alternate Possibilities." In *Moral Responsibility and Alternative Possibilities: Essays on the Importance of Alternative Possibilities*, edited by David Widerker and Michael McKenna, 265–99. Burlington, VT: Ashgate, 2006.

Cottrell, Jack W. "The Nature of the Divine Sovereignty." In *The Grace of God and the Will of Man*, edited by Clark H. Pinnock, 97–119. Bloomington, MN: Bethany House, 1995.

Cowan, Steven B. "Compatibilism and the Sinlessness of the Redeemed in Heaven." *Faith and Philosophy* 28.4 (2011) 416–31.

Crabtree, J. A. *The Most Real Being: A Biblical and Philosophical Defense of Divine Determinism*. Eugene, OR: Gutenberg College Press, 2004.

Craig, William Lane. *Divine Foreknowledge and Human Freedom: The Coherence of Theism: Omniscience*. New York: Brill, 1991.

————. "The Middle-Knowledge View." In *Divine Foreknowledge: Four Views*, edited by James K. Beilby and Paul R. Eddy, 119–43. Downers Grove, IL: InterVarsity, 2001.

————. *The Only Wise God: The Compatibility of Divine Foreknowledge and Human Freedom*. Reprint. Eugene, OR: Wipf and Stock, 2000.

————. "Response to Gregory A. Boyd." In *Four Views on Divine Providence*, edited by Stanley N. Gundry and Dennis W. Jowers, 224–30. Grand Rapids: Zondervan, 2011.

————. "Response to Paul Kjoss Helseth." In *Four Views on Divine Providence*, edited by Stanley N. Gundry and Dennis W. Jowers, 53–62. Grand Rapids: Zondervan, 2011.

————. "Response to Ron Highfield." In *Four Views on Divine Providence*, edited by Stanley N. Gundry and Dennis W. Jowers, 170–75. Grand Rapids: Zondervan, 2011.

————. "This Most Gruesome of Guests." In *Is Goodness Without God Good Enough? A Debate on Faith, Secularism, and Ethics*, edited by Robert K. Garcia and Nathan L. King, 167–88. Lanham, MD: Rowan & Littlefield, 2009.

Crisp, Oliver. *Deviant Calvinism: Broadening Reformed Theology*. Minneapolis, MN: Fortress, 2014.

Dennett, Daniel C. *Elbow Room: The Varieties of Free Will Worth Wanting*. Cambridge, MA: Bradford, 1984.

Edwards, Jonathan. *Freedom of the Will*. New York: Cosimo Classics, 2007.

Ekstrom, Laura Waddell. *Free Will: A Philosophical Study*. Boulder, CO: Westview, 2000.

First, Michael B. "Harmonization of ICD-11 and DSM-V: Opportunities and Challenges." *The British Journal of Psychiatry* 195.5 (2009) 382–90.

Fischer, John Martin. "Introduction: A Framework for Moral Responsibility." In *My Way: Essays on Moral Responsibility*, 1–37. New York: Oxford University Press, 2006.

———. "Responsibility and Agent-Causation." In *My Way: Essays on Moral Responsibility*, 143–58. New York: Oxford University Press, 2006.

———. "Responsibility and Alternative Possibilities." In *My Way: Essays on Moral Responsibility*, 38–62. New York: Oxford University Press, 2006.

Fischer, John Martin, and Mark Ravizza. *Responsibility and Control: A Theory of Moral Responsibility*. New York: Cambridge University Press, 1998.

Fischer, John Martin, Robert Kane, Derk Pereboom, and Manuel Vargas. *Four Views on Free Will*. Malden, MA: Blackwell, 2007.

Flint, Thomas P. "Compatibilism and the Argument from Unavoidability." *The Journal of Philosophy* 84.8 (1987) 423–40.

———. *Divine Providence: The Molinist Account*. Ithaca, NY: Cornell University Press, 2006.

———. "The Problem of Divine Freedom." *American Philosophical Quarterly* 20.3 (1983) 255–64.

———. "Two Accounts of Providence." In *Divine & Human Action: Essays in the Metaphysics of Theism*, edited by Thomas V. Morris, 147–81. Ithaca, NY: Cornell University Press, 1988.

Forlines, F. Leroy. *Classical Arminianism: A Theology of Salvation*. Edited by J. Matthew Pinson. Nashville, TN: Randall House, 2011.

Frame, John M. *The Doctrine of God*. Phillipsburg, NJ: P&R, 2002.

Frances, Allen. *Saving Normal: An Insider's Revolt Against Out-Of-Control Diagnosis, DSM-5, Big Pharma, and the Medicalization of Ordinary Life*. New York: William Morrow, 2013.

Frankfurt, Harry G. "Alternate Possibilities and Moral Responsibility." In *The Importance of What We Care About*, 1–10. New York: Cambridge University Press, 1998.

———. "Coercion and Moral Responsibility." In *The Importance of What We Care About*, 26–46. New York: Cambridge University Press, 1998.

———. "What We Are Morally Responsible For." In *The Importance of What We Care About*, 95–103. New York: Cambridge University Press, 1998.

Fischer, John Martin, and Garrett Pendergraft. "Does the Consequence Argument Beg the Question." *Philosophical Studies* 166.3 (2013) 575–95.

Franks, W. Paul. "Divine Freedom and Free Will Defenses." *The Heythrop Journal* 56.1 (2015) 108–19.

———. "Original Sin and Broad Free-Will Defense." *Philosophia Christi* 14.2 (2012) 353–71.

———. "A Rational Problem of Evil: The Coherence of Christian Doctrine with a Broad Free Will Defense." PhD diss., University of Oklahoma, 2012.

Freddoso, Afred J. Introduction to Luis De Molina, *On Divine Foreknowledge: Part IV of the Concordia*. Ithaca, NY: Cornell University Press, 2004.

———. "Medieval Aristotelianism and the Case against Secondary Causation in Nature." In *Divine & Human Action: Essays in the Metaphysics of Theism*, edited by Thomas V. Morris, 74–118. Ithaca, NY: Cornell University Press, 1988.

Garcia, Robert K., and Nathan L. King, eds. *Is Goodness Without God Good Enough? A Debate on Faith, Secularism, and Ethics*. Lanham, MD: Rowan & Littlefield, 2009.

Geisler, Norman. *Chosen But Free: A Balanced View of God's Sovereignty and Free Will*. 3rd ed. Minneapolis, MN: Bethany House, 2010.

———. "Norman Geisler's response (to Bruce Reichenbach)." In *Predestination & Free Will: Four Views of Divine Sovereignty & Human Freedom*, edited by David Basinger and Randall Basinger, 131–35. Downers Grove, IL: InterVarsity, 1986.

Ginet, Carl. "In Defense of the Principle of Alternative Possibilities: Why I Don't Find Frankfurt's Argument Convincing." In *Moral Responsibility and Alternative Possibilities: Essays on the Importance of Alternative Possibilities*, edited by David Widerker and Michael McKenna, 75–90. Burlington, VT: Ashgate, 2006.

Grudem, Wayne. *Systematic Theology: An Introduction to Biblical Doctrine*. Grand Rapids: Zondervan, 1994.

Guleserian, Theodore. "Divine Freedom and the Problem of Evil." *Faith and Philosophy* 17.3 (2000) 348–66.

Gundry, Stanley N., and Dennis W. Jowers, eds. *Four Views on Divine Providence*. Grand Rapids: Zondervan, 2011.

Haji, Ishtiyaque. *Incompatibilism's Allure: Principal Arguments for Incompatibilism*. Peterborough, Ontario: Broadview, 2009.

———. "Indeterminism, Explanation, and Luck." *The Journal of Ethics* 4.3 (2000) 211–35.

Hasker, William. *Metaphysics: Constructing a World View*. Edited by C. Stephen Evans. Downers Grove, IL: InterVarsity, 1983.

———. "An Open Theist Theodicy of Natural Evil." In *Molinism: The Contemporary Debate*, edited by Ken Perszyk, 281–302. New York: Oxford University Press, 2011.

———. "A Philosophical Perspective." In *The Openness of God: A Biblical Challenge to the Traditional Understanding of God*, 126–54. Downers Grove, IL: InterVarsity, 1994.

———. *Providence, Evil and the Openness of God*. New York: Routledge, 2004.

Helm, Paul. "Classical Calvinist Doctrine of God." In *Perspectives on the Doctrine of God: 4 Views*, edited by Bruce A. Ware, 5–52. Nashville, TN: B&H Academic, 2008.

———. *Eternal God: A Study of God Without Time*. 2nd ed. New York: Oxford University Press, 2010.

———. "God, Compatibilism, and the Authorship of Sin." *Religious Studies* 46.1 (2010) 115–24.

———. *The Providence of God*. Downers Grove, IL: InterVarsity, 1993.

Helm, Paul, and Terrance L. Tiessen. "Does Calvinism Have Room for Middle Knowledge? A Conversation." *Westminster Theological Journal* 71.2 (2009) 437–54.

Hill, Christopher S. "Van Inwagen on the Consequence Argument." *Analysis* 52.2 (1992) 49–55.

Hill, Daniel J. *Divinity and Maximal Greatness*. New York: Routledge, 2005.

Howard-Snyder, Daniel and Frances. "How an Unsurpassable Being Can Create a Surpassable World." *Faith and Philosophy* 11.2 (1994) 260–68.

Howard-Snyder, Frances and Daniel. "The Real Problem of No Best World." *Faith and Philosophy* 13.3 (1996) 422–25.

Hunt, Dave. *What Love Is This? Calvinism's Misrepresentation of God*. 3rd ed. Bend, OR: The Berean Call, 2006.

Hume, David. *An Inquiry Concerning Human Understanding.* Edited by Charles W. Hendel. New York: Bobbs-Merrill, 1955.

Johnson, Daniel M. "Calvinism and the Problem of Evil: A Map of the Territory." In *Calvinism and the Problem of Evil,* edited by David E. Alexander and Daniel M. Johnson, 19–55. Eugene, OR: Pickwick, 2016.

Jordan, Jeff, and Daniel Howard-Snyder, eds. *Faith, Freedom, and Rationality.* Boston: Roman & Littlefield, 1996.

Kane, Robert, ed. *The Oxford Handbook of Free Will.* 2nd ed. New York: Oxford University Press, 2011.

———. *The Significance of Free Will.* New York: Oxford University Press, 1998.

Kearns, Stephen. "Responsibility for Necessities." *Philosophical Studies* 155.2 (2011) 307–24.

Keathley, Kenneth. *Salvation and Sovereignty: A Molinist Approach.* Nashville, TN: B&H, 2010.

Kenny, Anthony. *The God of the Philosophers.* Oxford: Clarendon, 1979.

Laing, John D. "The Compatibility of Calvinism and Middle Knowledge." *Journal of the Evangelical Theological Society* 47.3 (2004) 455–67.

———. "Middle Knowledge and the Assumption of Libertarian Freedom: A Response to Ware." Paper presented at the annual meeting of the Evangelical Theological Society in Baltimore, MD, November 2013.

Langtry, Bruce. "God and the Best." *Faith and Philosophy* 13.3 (1996) 311–28.

Leftow, Brian. "Tempting God." *Faith and Philosophy* 31.1 (2014) 3–23.

Lehrer, Keith. "'Can' in Theory and Practice." In *Action Theory,* edited by Myles Brand and Douglas Walton, 241–70. Dordrecht: Reidel, 1976.

Lemke, Steve W. "A Biblical and Theological Critique of Irresistible Grace." In *Whosoever Will: A Biblical-Theological Critique of Five-Point Calvinism,* edited by David L. Allen and Steve W. Lemke, 109–62. Nashville, TN: B&H, 2010.

———. "God's Relation to the World: Terrance Tiessen's Proposal on Providence and Prayer." *Criswell Theological Review* 1.2 (2004) 205–13.

Lewis, David. "Are We Free to Break the Laws?" In *Free Will,* 2nd ed., edited by Gary Watson, 122–29. New York: Oxford University Press, 2003.

Luther, Martin. *The Bondage of the Will.* Translated by J. I. Packer and O. R. Johnston. Grand Rapids: Revell, 2009.

MacArthur, John. *Body Dynamics.* Wheaton, IL: Victor, 1982.

MacDonald, Scott, ed. *Being and Goodness.* Ithaca, NY: Cornell University Press, 1990.

MacDonald, William G. "The Spirit of Grace." In *Grace Unlimited,* edited by Clark H. Pinnock, 74–94. Reprint. Eugene, OR: Wipf and Stock, 1999.

Mann, William E. "God's Freedom, Human Freedom, and God's Responsibility for Sin." In *Divine & Human Action: Essays in the Metaphysics of Theism,* edited by Thomas V. Morris, 182–210. Ithaca, NY: Cornell University Press, 1988.

Marshall, I. Howard. "Predestination in the New Testament." In *Grace Unlimited,* edited by Clark H. Pinnock, 127–43. Reprint. Eugene, OR: Wipf and Stock, 1999.

———. "Universal Grace and Atonement in the Pastoral Epistles." In *The Grace of God and the Will of Man,* edited by Clark H. Pinnock, 51–69. Bloomington, MN: Bethany House, 1995.

McCann, Hugh J. *Creation and the Sovereignty of God.* Bloomington, IN: Indiana University Press, 2012.

————. "The Free Will Defense." In *Molinism: The Contemporary Debate*, edited by Ken Perszyk, 240–61. New York: Oxford University Press, 2011.

————. *The Works of Agency: On Human Action, Will, and Freedom*. Ithaca, NY: Cornell University Press, 1998.

Mele, Alfred R. *Free Will and Luck*. New York: Oxford University Press, 2006.

————. "Manipulation, Compatibilism, and Moral Responsibility." *Journal of Ethics* 12.3 (2008) 263–86.

Menssen, Sandra L., and Thomas D. Sullivan. "Must God Create?" *Faith and Philosophy* 12.3 (1995) 321–41.

De Molina, Luis. *On Divine Foreknowledge: Part IV of the Concordia*. Translated by Alfred J. Freddoso. Ithaca, NY: Cornell University Press, 2004.

Moore, G. E. *Ethics*. New York: Oxford University Press, 1912.

Moreland, J. P., and William Lane Craig. *Philosophical Foundations for a Christian Worldview*. Downers Grove, IL: InterVarsity, 2003.

Morris, Thomas V. ed. *Divine & Human Action: Essays in the Metaphysics of Theism*. Ithaca, NY: Cornell University Press, 1988.

Morriston, Wesley. "Is God 'Significantly' Free?" *Faith and Philosophy* 2.3 (1985) 257–64.

————. "What Is So Good about Moral Freedom?" *The Philosophical Quarterly* 50.200 (2000) 344–58.

Olson, Roger E. *Against Calvinism*. Grand Rapids: Zondervan, 2011.

————. *Arminian Theology: Myths and Realities*. Downers Grove, IL: InterVarsity, 2006.

————. "Responses to Bruce A. Ware." In *Perspectives on the Doctrine of God: 4 Views*, edited by Bruce A. Ware, 129–36. Nashville, TN: B&H Academic, 2008.

————. "Responses to Paul Helm." In *Perspectives on the Doctrine of God: 4 Views*, edited by Bruce A. Ware, 53–58. Nashville, TN: B&H Academic, 2008.

Packer, J. I. "The Love of God: Universal and Particular." In *Still Sovereign: Contemporary Perspectives on Election, Foreknowledge, and Grace*, edited by Thomas R. Schreiner and Bruce A. Ware, 277–91. Grand Rapids: Baker, 2000.

Palmer, Edwin H. *The Five Points of Calvinism: A Study Guide*. 3rd ed. Grand Rapids: Baker, 2010.

Parry, Robin A. "A Universalist View." In *Four Views on Hell*, edited by Stanley N. Gundry and Preston M. Sprinkle, 101–27. Grand Rapids: Zondervan, 2016.

Pawl, Timothy, and Kevin Timpe. "Incompatibilism, Sin, and Free Will in Heaven." *Faith and Philosophy* 26.4 (2009) 396–417.

Pereboom, Derk. "Free Will, Evil, and Divine Providence." In *Arguing about Religion*, edited by Kevin Timpe, 317–32. New York: Routledge, 2009.

————. *Living Without Free Will*. New York: Cambridge University Press, 2001.

Perszyk, Ken. "Introduction." In *Molinism: The Contemporary Debate*, edited by Ken Perszyk, 1–24. New York: Oxford University Press, 2011.

Picirilli, Robert E. *Grace, Faith, Free Will: Contrasting Views of Salvation: Calvinism and Arminianism*. Nashville, TN: Randall House, 2002.

Pink, Arthur W. *The Sovereignty of God*. Reset ed. Edinburgh: Banner of Truth, 2009.

Pinnock, Clark. "Clark Pinnock's Response (to John Feinberg)." In *Predestination & Free Will: Four Views of Divine Sovereignty & Human Freedom*, edited by David Basinger and Randall Basinger, 57–60. Downers Grove, IL: InterVarsity, 1986.

————, ed. *Grace Unlimited*. Reprint. Eugene, OR: Wipf and Stock, 1999.

——. "There is Room For Us: A Reply to Bruce Ware." *Journal of the Evangelical Theological Society* 45.2 (2002) 213–19.

Pinnock, Clark H., Richard Rice, John Sanders, William Hasker, and David Basinger. *The Openness of God: A Biblical Challenge to the Traditional Understanding of God.* Downers Grove, IL: IVP Academic, 1994.

Piper, John. "Are There Two Wills in God?" In *Still Sovereign: Contemporary Perspectives on Election, Foreknowledge, and Grace*, edited by Thomas R. Schreiner and Bruce A. Ware, 107–31. Grand Rapids: Baker, 2000.

Plantinga, Alvin. "Advice to Christian Philosophers." *Faith and Philosophy* 1.3 (1984) 253–71.

——. *Does God Have a Nature?* 5th printing. Milwaukee, WI: Marquette University Press, 2007.

——. *God, Freedom, and Evil.* Grand Rapids: Eerdmans, 1977.

——. *The Nature of Necessity.* Oxford: Oxford University Press, 1974.

——. *Warranted Christian Belief.* New York: Oxford University Press, 2000.

Pruss, Alexander R. "The Essential Divine-Perfection Objection to the Free-Will Defence." *Religious Studies* 44.4 (2008) 433–44.

Rasmussen, Joshua. "On the Value of Freedom to Do Evil." *Faith and Philosophy* 30.4 (2013) 418–28.

Rea, Michael C. "The Metaphysics of Original Sin." In *Persons: Divine and Human*, edited by Peter van Inwagen and Dean Zimmerman, 319–56. New York: Oxford University Press, 2007.

Reichenbach, Bruce R. "Evil and a Reformed View of God." *International Journal for Philosophy of Religion* 24.1/2 (1988) 67–85.

——. "Freedom, Justice and Moral Responsibility." In *The Grace of God and the Will of Man*, edited by Clark H. Pinnock, 277–303. Bloomington, MN: Bethany House, 1995.

Rice, Richard. "Divine Foreknowledge and Free-Will Theism." In *The Grace of God and the Will of Man*, edited by Clark H. Pinnock, 121–39. Bloomington, MN: Bethany House, 1995.

Rogers, Katherin A. "The Divine Controller Argument for Incompatibilism." *Faith and Philosophy* 29.3 (2012) 275–94.

——. "Does God Cause Sin? Anselm of Canterbury Versus Jonathan Edwards on Human Freedom and Divine Sovereignty." *Faith and Philosophy* 20.3 (2003) 371–78.

Rowe, William L. *Can God Be Free?* New York: Oxford University Press, 2004.

——. "The Problem of Divine Sovereignty and Human Freedom." *Faith and Philosophy* 16.1 (1999) 98–101.

——. "The Problem of No Best World." *Faith and Philosophy* 11.2 (1994) 269–71.

Sanders, John. *The God Who Risks: A Theology of Divine Providence.* 2nd ed. Downers Grove, IL: InterVarsity, 2007.

——. "Responses to Bruce A. Ware." In *Perspectives on the Doctrine of God: 4 Views*, edited by Bruce A. Ware, 137–47. Nashville, TN: B&H Academic, 2008.

Schreiner, Thomas R., and Bruce A. Ware, eds. *Still Sovereign: Contemporary Perspectives on Election, Foreknowledge, and Grace.* Grand Rapids: Baker Books, 2000.

Sontag, Frederick, and M. Darrol Bryant, eds. *God: The Contemporary Discussion.* New York: Rose of Sharon, 1982.

Speak, Daniel. "The Consequence Argument Revisited." In *The Oxford Handbook of Free Will*, 2nd ed., edited by Robert Kane, 115–30. New York: Oxford University Press, 2011.

Sproul, R. C. "Double Predestination." Online: http://www.ligonier.org/learn/articles/double-predestination. (Accessed February 2015.)

Stump, Eleonore. "Moral Responsibility Without Alternative Possibilities." In *Moral Responsibility and Alternative Possibilities: Essays on the Importance of Alternative Possibilities*, edited by David Widerker and Michael McKenna, 139–58. Burlington, VT: Ashgate, 2006.

———, ed. *Reasoned Faith*. Ithaca, NY: Cornell University Press, 1993.

Talbott, Thomas B. "On the Divine Nature and The Nature of Divine Freedom." *Faith and Philosophy* 5.1 (1988) 3–24.

———. "Universal Reconciliation and the Inclusive Nature of Election." In *Perspectives on Election: Five Views*, edited by Chad Owen Brand, 206–61. Nashville, TN: B&H Academic, 2006.

Tiessen, Terrance L. *Providence and Prayer: How Does God Work in the World?* Downers Grove, IL: IVP Academics, 2000.

———. "Why Calvinists Should Believe in Divine Middle Knowledge, Although They Reject Molinism." *Westminster Theological Journal* 69.2 (2007) 345–66.

Timpe, Kevin. *Free Will in Philosophical Theology*. New York: Bloomsbury Academic, 2015.

———. *Free Will: Sourcehood and its Alternatives*. 2nd ed. New York: Bloomsbury, 2013.

———. "Why Christians Might be Libertarians: A Response to Lynne Rudder Baker." *Philosophia Christi* 6.2 (2004) 279–88.

Van Horn, Luke. "On Incorporating Middle Knowledge Into Calvinism: A Theological/Metaphysical Muddle?" *Journal of the Evangelical Theological Society* 55.4 (2012) 807–27.

Van Inwagen, Peter. "The Argument from Evil." In *Christian Faith and the Problem of Evil*, edited by Peter van Inwagen, 55–73. Grand Rapids: Eerdmans, 2004.

———, ed. *Christian Faith and the Problem of Evil*. Grand Rapids: Eerdmans, 2004.

———. *An Essay on Free Will*. Oxford: Clarendon, 1983.

Vicens, Leigh C. "Divine Determinism: A Critical Consideration." PhD diss., University of Wisconsin-Madison, 2012.

———. "Divine Determinism, Human Freedom, and the Consequence Argument." *International Journal for Philosophy of Religion* 71.2 (2012) 145–55.

Vines, Jerry. "Sermon on John 3:16." In *Whosoever Will: A Biblical-Theological Critique of Five-Point Calvinism*, edited by David L. Allen and Steve W. Lemke, 13–28. Nashville, TN: B&H, 2010.

Walls, Jerry L. "Why No Classical Theist, Let Alone Orthodox Christian, Should Ever Be a Compatibilist." *Philosophia Christi* 13.1 (2011) 75–104.

Walls, Jerry L., and Joseph R. Dongell. *Why I Am Not a Calvinist*. Downers Grove, IL: InterVarsity, 2004.

Ware, Bruce A. *God's Greater Glory: The Exalted God of Scripture and the Christian Faith*. Wheaton, IL: Crossway, 2004.

———, ed. *Perspectives on the Doctrine of God: 4 Views*. Nashville, TN: B&H Academic, 2008.

———. "Robots, Royalty and Relationships? Toward a Clarified Understanding of Real Human Relations with the God Who Knows and Decrees All That Is." *Criswell Theological Review* 1.2 (2004) 191–203.

Watson, Gary, ed. *Free Will*, 2nd ed. New York: Oxford University Press, 2003.

Wesley, John. *Free Grace: A Sermon Preach'd at Bristol*. London: W. Strahan, 1740.

White, James R. *The Potter's Freedom: A Defense of the Reformation and a Rebuttal to Norman Geisler's Chosen But Free*. 2nd ed. Lincroft, NJ: Calvary, 2009.

Widerker, David, and Michael McKenna, eds. *Moral Responsibility and Alternative Possibilities: Essays on the Importance of Alternative Possibilities*. Burlington, VT: Ashgate, 2006.

Wierenga, Edward. "The Freedom of God." *Faith and Philosophy* 19.4 (2002) 425–36.

Wolf, Susan. *Freedom Within Reason*. New York: Oxford University Press, 1990.

Wood, Allen W. "Coercion, Manipulation, Exploitation." In *Manipulation: Theory and Practice*, edited by Christian Coons and Michael Weber, 17–50. New York: Oxford University Press, 2014.

Wyma, Keith. "Innocent Sinfulness, Guilty Sin: Original Sin and Divine Justice." In *Christian Faith and the Problem of Evil*, edited by Peter van Inwagen, 263–76. Grand Rapids: Eerdmans, 2004.

Zagzebski, Linda. "Does Libertarian Freedom Require Alternate Possibilities?" *Philosophical Perspectives* 14 (2000) 231–48.